To Paul

Love MA
Claire.

DONEGAL
& THE CIVIL WAR

LIAM Ó DUIBHIR

DONEGAL
& THE CIVIL WAR

THE UNTOLD STORY

MERCIER PRESS
IRISH PUBLISHER – IRISH STORY

MERCIER PRESS
Cork
www.mercierpress.ie

© Liam Ó Duibhir, 2011

ISBN: 978 1 85635 720 3

10 9 8 7 6 5 4 3 2 1

A CIP record for this title is available from the British Library

This book is sold subject to the condition that it shall not, by way of trade or otherwise, be lent, resold, hired out or otherwise circulated without the publisher's prior consent in any form of binding or cover other than that in which it is published and without a similar condition including this condition being imposed on the subsequent purchaser.

No part of this publication may be reproduced or transmitted in any form or by any means, electronic or mechanical, including photocopying, recording or any information or retrieval system, without the prior permission of the publisher in writing.

Printed and bound in the EU.

Contents

Acknowledgements	11
Introduction	15
A Brief Review of the War of Independence in Donegal	20
1921 – The Truce and Breathing Space	27
Eithne Coyle and the Mountjoy Escape	32
The IRA Civic Police	37
The Treaty Signed, but not Sealed	41
Donegal Debates the Treaty	48
1922 – The Treaty Debates and Vote	51
1922 – The Released Prisoners and the Condemned Prisoners	58
The Special Powers Bill and the Six-County Policy	72
The IRA Convention and Split	83
Changing of the Guard and the Belfast Boycott	86
The Northern Offensive and the Newtowncunningham Tragedy	100
The Battles at Pettigo and Belleek	119
The Constitution of Saorstát Éireann and the 1922 Election	132
The Wilson Assassination – A Catalyst for Civil War	139
An Cogadh na gCarad – The War between Friends	144
Another Effort to Avert Civil War in Donegal	156

The Battles at Skeog	163
The Drumkeen Ambush	166
The Fall of Inch Fort	170
Republican Column 'On the Run'	173
Raids, Arrests and Escapes	184
Eithne Coyle's War Ends	198
Emergency Powers	200
Newbridge Internment Camp and the Escape	206
Arrests and Executions	210
1923 – Pettigo Reclaimed	216
Courts Martial and Executions in Donegal	222
Peadar O'Donnell – Held to Ransom	233
Conclusion	240
Internment Records of Donegal Internees	245
Glossary	253
Notes	255
Bibliography	272
Index	275

Map of Donegal with the main towns and villages and the areas of the different IRA brigades marked

THIS BOOK IS DEDICATED
TO MY MOTHER MARY
AND MY LATE FATHER LIAM DIVER

Acknowledgements

I would like to take this opportunity to thank so many people for assisting and helping in different ways in the writing of this book. I would like to thank the staff at the Bureau of Military Archives and in particular Victor Laing, Lisa Dolan, Noelle Grothier and other members of staff for assistance when researching. The staff of the Archives Department at UCD, Belfield, Dublin, were also very helpful during the research for this book and I would like to thank Seamus Helferty and the staff for their assistance and generosity.

I am again indebted and owe a special thanks to Liam MacElhinney, Lifford, County Donegal, for all the invaluable assistance, direction and original photographs and documents. Liam gave me many original resources and he is a great authority on the history of this period generally and more importantly at a local level. Liam was also one of the many people who read a draft of this book.

A special word of thanks to Seamus McCann, College Farm Road, Letterkenny, for the use of his father's diary. This diary was again a very useful source in drafting this publication and gave great details of the Truce period and accounts of Newbridge Internment Camp. Thanks to Rory McCann for assistance in this regard also.

I am also indebted to Pat and Mary Dawson, Letterkenny, for giving me documentation relating to this period and for the use of a space to compile and write this publication, which made this process so much easier. Thanks to you both for all your help and for your friendship over the years.

I am very grateful and owe a special word of thanks to Niall McGinley for being so generous with his time to read through a draft highlighting the many grammatical errors, etc. I would also like to thank Niall for permission to use certain information from his book *Dr McGinley and His Times* and for the use of images from that book.

I would also like to thank Conall Cunningham, Spiddal, County Galway, for the story of his uncle and his family's involvement in this period.

Thanks to Declan O'Carroll for the use of photographs and for pieces of information that were of great significance. Declan was also very helpful when he read an early draft and thanks for permission to use information from his books on Finner Camp and Rockhill House.

I would like to thank the *Derry Journal* for permission to use information from the *Derry Journal* archives, which proved a very useful source when writing this book. The *Derry People and Tirconaill News* archives were also a useful resource and I would like to thank the staff at the *Donegal News* for bringing the archives from Omagh to Letterkenny for my research. Thanks to the editor Columba Gill and to Harry Walsh for all your help during this time. Thanks to Bernie Campbell and the staff at the Donegal Central Library, Letterkenny. Best wishes to Bernie in her retirement.

A special thank you to Pádraig Ó Baoighill for permission to use information from his book *Óglach na Rossan – Niall Pluincéad Ó Baoighill* and for travelling from Monaghan to provide me with very helpful information. Thanks also to Father Pádraig Ó Baoighill for permission to use information from his book *Cardinal Patrick O'Donnell*. To all publishers, libraries and archives who gave permission to reproduce information and photographs in this book: thank you all.

Thanks to Seán Beatty (Culdaff) for reading a very early draft and for permission to use information and images from the *Donegal Annual*. Sean was also very helpful with advice on various aspects of the book. Thanks to Jonnie Patton who was another reader of a very early draft. Thanks to May McClintock for a detailed list of townlands in north-west Donegal, which was a great help.

I would also like to thank Dr Brenda Niall for providing me with the papers of Father William Hackett and to Father Michael Head and Father Steve Curtin, Jesuit Provincial of Australia, for permission to reproduce the information from these papers. Thanks to Ciaran and Val Kelly for your hospitality during my time in Dublin. I would also like to thank the following people who helped in different ways: Jack Britton, Donegal Town; Dr Fergal McCluskey, Tyrone; Dr Michael Hopkinson, Scotland; Cyril O'Boyle, Breenagh; P. H. Doherty, Carndonagh. Thanks to all the staff at Mercier Press: in particular Mary Feehan, Wendy Logue and Catherine Twibill, and thanks to Jenny Laing for the editing.

To all my family, for the encouragement and support during the writing of this book – thank you.

Introduction

The Irish Civil War officially commenced on 28 June 1922 and lasted for less than twelve months, ending on 24 May 1923 following the IRA's announcement of a ceasefire and an order to dump arms. This short chapter of Irish history was for many years a forbidden subject with many participants reluctant to speak of their involvement or of the events that occurred because civil war by its very nature first divides and then destroys the bond between family, friends and eventually a nation. Despite its short duration, the Irish Civil War created bitter divisions that reverberated for many years after the hostilities had ceased. This book traces the course of the Irish Civil War as it occurred in County Donegal with reference to other related episodes, particularly those from the War of Independence, which provide an important insight into the men and women of Donegal who were also involved in the Civil War.

Ireland was elevated onto the international stage, attracting the attention of influential nations, when the founding of an indigenous government – Dáil Éireann – was closely followed, in January 1919, with the beginning of the War of Independence. It has been suggested that this was the second phase of the War of Independence and that the first phase began with the Easter Rising of 1916.

After almost three years of conflict, the British government realised that there was no possibility of defeating the IRA and a truce was called between Irish and British political leaders on Monday 11 July 1921. However, unknown to them, the IRA campaign was all but exhausted through the wholesale arrests and internment of volunteers from both Óglaigh na hÉireann and Cumann na mBan. The lack of adequate supplies of weapons and ammunition was another worrying factor for the IRA leaders. During this period the British used every means at their disposal

– informers, the Black and Tans, the Auxiliaries, internment camps, etc. – to defeat their Irish opponents, but by 1921 were resigned to the fact that the only opportunity for the resolution of the war was to engage in talks with the Irish political leaders.

The British insistence on holding the talks in London gave them the upper hand by forcing the Irish into an alien environment. This created friction between the delegation in London and the political leaders at home, mostly due to problems with communication. The British used their experience from previous negotiations to outmanoeuvre the inexperienced Irish negotiators and warned of a return to war 'within three days', threatening a more intensive and ruthless campaign. The Treaty that resulted from the talks failed to meet the expectations of many people in Ireland with the result that the country was thrust into a period of great uncertainty and tension that led to the outbreak of the Civil War. Some people believed the Treaty was effectively the abandonment of republican principles that had been widely supported and fought for in previous years – this was the primary reason for the divisions that developed between the IRA, Sinn Féin and the general public.

These divisions led Ireland into a vicious conflict: vicious in the sense that families, friends and communities were divided into two different factions – those opposed to and those in support of the Treaty and Articles of Agreement signed by the Irish and British delegations. One example of the divisions that occurred between families and friends was that of the Cunningham family. Edward Cunningham was an anti-Treaty prisoner who was held at Drumboe Castle following his arrest by Free State forces. From Carrick in south Donegal, he was a schoolteacher at Ballyconnell School, Ray, near Rathmullan, at the time, while his first cousin Joseph Cunningham was a member of the Free State Army and Edward's guard at Drumboe. Edward Cunningham had five brothers who were members of the IRA during the War of Independence, but at the outbreak of the Civil War the family was divided with three brothers opposing the Treaty and three supporting it.[1] Various terms were used to distinguish between the two factions including Dáil forces, Free State forces and regulars for the pro-Treaty faction, and irregulars, republican forces or the IRA for the anti-Treaty side.

Introduction

The Treaty that divided the island was first put to the elected representatives of Dáil Éireann, where it was ratified on 7 January 1922, and then to the people in the election of June that year. However, it could be argued that the will of the people was not fairly ascertained from this election due to the use of inaccurate electoral registers, the absence of a plebiscite in seven constituencies where the elected representatives were returned unopposed, and the promise of a republican constitution that ultimately failed to materialise.

In the weeks following the ratification of the Treaty, the Donegal IRA began occupying various barracks and other buildings that had been evacuated by the Royal Irish Constabulary (RIC) and the British military. After the split of the IRA into pro- and anti-Treaty groups, the different factions established these premises as headquarters and billets. In Donegal, in terms of equipment and numbers, the section of the IRA supporting the Treaty was much superior to that opposed to it, which was largely made up of men from other counties. The pro-Treaty faction in Donegal was also bolstered by the overwhelming support of the local Sinn Féin organisation. Before the outbreak of the Civil War the IRA's Executive anti-Treaty forces in the county were chiefly made up of men from other counties whose primary objective was to continue the war against the forces of the Belfast government (who still occupied the Six Counties of Northern Ireland which had split from Ireland after the Government of Ireland Act 1920): the Special Constabulary (a paramilitary quasi-police force), the British military, and later the Royal Ulster Constabulary. The Special Constabulary was founded following major outbreaks of sectarian violence in Banbridge, Lisburn, Belfast and other areas in the north-eastern counties during the summer of 1920. The membership of the Special Constabulary consisted chiefly of Ulster Volunteer Force (UVF) members who, with others, had perpetrated acts of vicious sectarian violence and murder. The Constabulary was established in the paranoid belief that the IRA would avenge these horrors and therefore, paradoxically, it was essentially a body tasked with protecting the perpetrators of violence.

The continuation of the war in the Six Counties against the forces of the newly established Belfast government received guarantees of support from leaders of the divided republican army including Liam Lynch, Michael Collins and Richard Mulcahy. Initially the pro-Treaty forces under the control of the Provisional Government did not impede the IRA in what became known as the northern offensive. This was adhered to for the first few months of 1922, and throughout this period, Michael Collins and Richard Mulcahy were operating behind the scenes with, among others, IRA Chief of Staff Liam Lynch, to organise an assault on the Six Counties. Plans were put in place from early March 1922 for a united force to attack and undermine the authority of the Belfast government. However, pressure from other quarters, namely the Belfast and British governments, soon forced the Provisional Government to suppress the actions of republican forces, which contributed to further friction between the two sides.

In June 1922 Field Marshal Henry Wilson was assassinated in London, an event which served as the catalyst for setting Ireland on another collision course, but this time it was the Irish against the Irish in a bitter and vicious Civil War which began following a now infamous attack on the Four Courts in Dublin on 28 June 1922. The British government blamed the Wilson assassination on the IRA Executive forces based at the Four Courts, when in fact the plan and execution originated with Michael Collins. The subsequent Civil War reintroduced familiar scenes to the Irish countryside and urban areas with ambushes, round-ups, internments and executions. The ramifications of this short chapter of Irish history resonated through Irish society for many years.

The Civil War in Donegal was unique in that over 90 per cent of the Irish Volunteers joined the newly established Provisional Government forces or Free State Army while the majority of those fighting on the republican side were from the southern counties of Cork and Kerry with many others coming from the border counties of Derry, Tyrone, Fermanagh and Monaghan. Many were reluctant participants as a large proportion had relocated to County Donegal at the behest of Michael Collins and Liam Lynch to be part of the northern offensive.

When the hostilities began the republican forces based in County Donegal were greatly outnumbered and struggled to even exist as the Civil

War dragged on possibly longer than it should have. As with every episode in history different versions of events and incidents have been recounted by opposing sides. It has always been said that the victor or the hangman will usually be best placed to present a version or an analysis, but there are always two sides to the story and the truth lies somewhere in between.

Chapter 1

A Brief Review of the War of Independence in Donegal

The Irish War of Independence began in theory with the Easter Rising of 1916, which followed several years of planning and organisation throughout the country. The Rising itself did not deliver the decisive strike against the British that the leaders had anticipated and ended in failure and confusion due to a series of unforeseen events, including efforts by senior figures to cancel it. The general population was by no means enamoured by the actions of the men and women who took part in the Rising and they subsequently became the target of anger at the devastation and deaths that resulted from the fighting. However, the Easter Rising served as the launch-pad for the next phase of the conflict against the British establishment in Ireland. When the leaders of the Easter Rising were executed, people's attitudes changed from one of disdain to one of respect and support for the revolutionaries.

The next phase of the revolutionaries' plan to win independence was to become organised along military and political lines with a view to taking over the governance of the country and launching a full-scale war on the British in Ireland. The leaders who were imprisoned at the internment camp at Frongoch in North Wales for their involvement in the Easter Rising used their time there to such good effect that it later became known as the 'University of Revolution'. It was there they set about organising and training men from the various counties in Ireland so that on their release they would be able to establish fighting units, intelligence departments and political branches of the Sinn Féin party. When many prisoners and internees were released in late 1916 and early 1917, the Irish Volunteers and the Sinn Féin party established military and political branches throughout the country as planned, including County Donegal.

The political and military organisations worked independently of each other. Sinn Féin operated in the political arena, with the Irish Volunteers (later known as the Army of the Irish Republic, the Irish Republican Army or the IRA) being a physical resistance movement that challenged the Royal Irish Constabulary and British military in open warfare. However, the two organisations were interlinked, with some Volunteers being elected as TDs in the election of December 1918 and later on, in 1920, some being elected to the local councils. The two groups also had a similar objective, which, in the early stages, was primarily to spread the principles of the Republic and prepare for the elections of 1918. As the Sinn Féin party grew in popularity, the British sought to stem this development with a miscalculated propaganda stunt. In May 1918 they declared that they had uncovered evidence that the leaders of Sinn Féin were involved in the importation of arms from Germany. In what became known as the 'German Plot', seventy-three leaders and activists of the Sinn Féin party were arrested and transported to jails in England. Despite the arrests, the party secured seventy-three seats in the election of December 1918 with three Teachtaí Dála (TDs) being returned to the Donegal constituencies: Joseph O'Doherty for North Donegal, Joe Sweeney for West Donegal and P. J. Ward for South Donegal. This election also witnessed the demise of the political domination enjoyed by the Irish Parliamentary Party and unionist politicians.

Those newly elected TDs who had not been jailed or were not on the run met at the Mansion House, Dublin, on 21 January 1919 as Dáil Éireann. While the First Dáil was in progress, reports were received in Dublin of an ambush in County Tipperary. The No. 3 Tipperary Brigade, led by Seamus Robinson and including Dan Breen, Seán Treacy, Tadhg Crowe, Patrick McCormack and Paddy Dwyer, had carried out a surprise attack. A two-man RIC party was escorting a cart of gelignite when the Volunteers ambushed them at Soloheadbeg, resulting in the deaths of the two policemen. The news of this incident was met with trepidation in Dublin and was condemned by a number of the Sinn Féin leaders, but to the Irish Volunteers this was the start of the next phase in the fight for Irish independence and the event that marked the start of the War of Independence.

However, although Soloheadbeg is considered to be the official start of the war, the Volunteers had been active before this, building up arms and experience of action. The first recorded actions by the Irish Volunteers in County Donegal occurred at Meenbanad Railway Station in west Donegal on 4 January 1918 and involved a party of Volunteers, under the command of Joe Sweeney, in the rescue of two British army deserters who had been arrested by the RIC. The deserters were from the local area but this action had more to do with the seizure of a rifle than the liberation of two British army deserters. The operation was a success with the deserters and rifle being taken into the custody of the Irish Volunteers without a single shot being fired.

Following the early activity of the West Donegal Volunteers the focus of the local organisation was the elections of December 1918. With the elections out of the way the attentions of the Donegal Volunteers then switched to procuring weapons and the general disruption of local infrastructure through the destruction of railway lines and roads to hamper the movements of the RIC and military in the county. In the early part of the campaign the Donegal IRA was prevented from taking on the crown forces due to the lack of adequate arms and Volunteers. The first opportunity for the Donegal IRA to engage with crown forces only came about on 12 December 1919 with an ambush near Dungloe. The target was a four-man RIC escort party which had conveyed a number of prisoners to a court in Letterkenny that day; the Volunteers organised the attack for their return to Dungloe. On that occasion, the West Donegal Volunteers had only three weapons, but this was enough to inflict the first casualties of the War of Independence in the county. The four RIC men received injuries with one later having to have his leg amputated. The West Donegal Volunteers continued to be very active throughout the war, and were adept at holding up RIC patrols, relieving them of weapons, ammunition and other equipment. The main protagonist in this unit was Frank O'Donnell, brother of Peadar O'Donnell – an organiser for the Irish Transport and General Workers' Union in County Monaghan in 1919. It was in that county that Peadar was inducted into the IRA and he soon became a leading figure in the Donegal republican movement. He spread himself between the two organisations before becoming a full-time Volunteer in 1920.

In early 1920 the Sinn Féin party enjoyed further successes in the local elections, securing majorities in twenty-nine out of the thirty-three county councils and 172 out of 206 rural district councils. In Donegal Sinn Féin won majorities in two out of the three municipal councils and in six out of the ten county council electoral areas. The progress of the new native government was further enhanced with the establishment of the republican justice system and the Sinn Féin or Dáil courts, which eventually rendered the British legal system redundant.

In April 1920 the Volunteers of the 1st Ulster or, as they later became known, the 1st Northern Division, burned fourteen unoccupied RIC barracks in County Donegal as well as a number of offices belonging to the Customs and Inland Revenue. This complied with a general order from GHQ to burn all unoccupied RIC barracks and offices of the revenue, and coincided with the fourth anniversary of the 1916 Rising.

The Volunteers of the 1st Northern Division were also credited with what was said to be the first arms raid to be carried out during daylight hours in the country. This incident occurred at an RIC barracks in Drumquinn, County Tyrone, where a substantial amount of weaponry, ammunition and other equipment was captured in a highly successful operation in August 1920. The Donegal Volunteers quickly followed up these actions with raids on the coastguard station at Fanad and the RIC barracks at Belleek. (Belleek straddles the border with Donegal, but the barracks were situated in County Fermanagh.) However, each major operation by the IRA was followed by an intense response from the British forces of raids and arrests, with their focus being mostly on the general population. With the increased support for Dáil Éireann, the Volunteers were under further pressure due to their new responsibilities for policing and various other civic duties.

With the increased activities of the Volunteers came an upsurge in raids by the RIC and military. The introduction of the Black and Tans in the spring of 1920 and the Auxiliary Division of the RIC in July of that year changed the nature of the war. The Black and Tans were neither police nor military and ignored the usual code of warfare. They were a band of ill-trained mercenaries, mostly made up of former soldiers and unemployed workers from England, deployed to create devastation in Ireland. These forces embarked on a vicious assault on the public as a means of deterring support for the IRA. In the late 1920s the British also introduced internment camps to house the growing numbers of known and suspected members of the IRA and Sinn Féin who were being arrested in their hundreds.

Events elsewhere also impinged on the efforts of the Donegal Volunteers. In November 1920 the British military made an important discovery in Dublin: following a raid on a safe house a briefcase belonging to Richard Mulcahy, IRA Chief of Staff, was discovered. It contained valuable information on many aspects of the IRA's organisation and more importantly a list of officers and men in every part of the country. An intense campaign of raids and arrests by the British military followed. The officers and Volunteers received prior warning, which many heeded, but some Donegal Volunteers were arrested and transferred to Ballykinlar internment camp in County Down.

The IRA in Donegal also had to contend with the annual migration of its members to England and Scotland for work on the harvest or in the mines. This occurred throughout the summer and autumn, causing upheaval in the local IRA companies, which had to be reorganised. The war effort was affected as the experienced men were forced to leave to earn much-needed income for their families. However, this also had its advantages as many of the men who went to Scotland or England joined the ranks of the local IRA units there and sent essential arms and ammunition to Ireland. The IRA GHQ in Dublin eventually addressed the yearly dilemma of emigration by making finances available to the most affected areas to ensure experienced men would not have to emigrate.

At the beginning of 1921 Donegal acquired the services of a full-time flying column of seasoned and experienced Volunteers, with the aim of increasing the war effort in the county. This was under the command of Peadar O'Donnell from Meenmore near Dungloe. Shortly after their arrival in west Donegal, members of the flying column were ordered to arrest a suspicious stranger who had arrived in Dungloe. The man, a British military lieutenant called Bracen of the Dorset Regiment, was arrested and held for questioning. He insisted that he was a mere civil servant investigating claims for damage or loss caused by members of the military while stationed in west Donegal. Bracen was released following a warning from a commercial traveller that the area would be saturated with military and that the village would be wrecked if he was held any longer. It soon transpired that he was actually an intelligence officer.

Within a week of Bracen's release, the West Donegal Volunteers received intelligence from two railway employees that a fish train was to travel from Derry to Dungloe. They were highly suspicious as there was no fishing in the area at the time and they believed that there was a very different cargo, i.e. British military. The local officer commanding (OC), Joe Sweeney, organised the Volunteers and the flying column to ambush the train near Meenbanad in the early hours of the morning of its scheduled arrival. The train duly arrived on Wednesday 12 January and was derailed by boulders on the line as it passed the ambush site. Rapid fire was then opened on the carriages until the passengers recovered from the crash and began to return fire. There was no official report regarding casualties, but it was believed that many military were killed and wounded and there were reports of blood being seen pouring out of some carriages. The arrival of the train and military was the direct result of Lieutenant Bracen's visit to the area – it was later discovered that he was among the passengers. Another train ambush at Crolly followed, but failed to have the same impact.

Despite this, the West Donegal Volunteers had been more active than others in attacks against crown forces. Their area had been almost cleared of RIC barracks and they had inflicted many casualties among the crown forces. Such was the scale of the IRA activity in this area that some in the British government described west Donegal as operating a 'Miniature

Republic'. On a national level, the sustained IRA campaign led to contact between the IRA and British leaders, who began a series of secret talks with a view to ending the conflict.

Following the train ambushes the British conducted sustained raids throughout Donegal, resulting in the arrests of large numbers of civilians as well as some IRA volunteers. These operations put enormous strain on the IRA and continued for weeks, with the British using ships and aeroplanes in their endeavour to capture the men. The round-up was very well organised with military and police covering all approaches to west Donegal. As a means of confusing these authorities the other 1st Northern Division brigades were instructed to increase engagements in their areas to give the impression that the flying column was operating outside the west Donegal area. This proved successful, with the military and police eventually turning their attention to other areas of the county.

The men of the 1st Northern Division were further burdened when friction developed between some of the officers. The hostility initially involved the divisional OC Frank Carney and the No. 2 Brigade and flying column OC Peadar O'Donnell, but it filtered through the ranks and served as a distraction. This internal tension required intervention from GHQ in Dublin and an officer was sent to Donegal to resolve the issue. However, with the arrest of Frank Carney at Burtonport when a British destroyer landed there much to the surprise of the local Volunteers, the situation was easily resolved, as Joe Sweeney was then appointed to the position of divisional OC.

The result of the contacts between the Irish and British leaders concluded with an announcement by the President of Sinn Féin, Éamon de Valera, in early July 1921 that a platform for negotiations had been established and that he intended to meet with the British Prime Minister, David Lloyd George, to discuss a peace settlement. This was followed by an announcement from GHQ that all operations by the IRA were to be suspended from Monday 11 July. This was a big surprise to the Volunteers and many felt cheated as they had not been consulted: nor had there been any indication of talks taking place between the two sides.[1]

Chapter 2

1921 – The Truce and Breathing Space

A 'Truce' between Ireland and Britain was signed at midday, Monday 11 July 1921, ending – or for some, suspending – the War of Independence. It was presented as an opportunity for all the men 'on the run' to return home; for many this was the first time since the start of the war in 1919.

The IRA's GHQ was conscious that the Truce would give the Volunteers a sense of comfort and men who became too comfortable might be reluctant to return to war should the Truce fail. Their immediate concern was to keep the men active and a decision was taken to start a course of military training for all Volunteers on various aspects of essential military techniques.

In west Donegal the joy and relief of the Truce interval was interrupted by the sad news of the sudden death of Willie Sharkey, 1st Lieutenant of the Dungloe Company IRA. Sharkey was only eighteen years old when he died following a short illness. He was an active Volunteer from the age of sixteen and played a lead role in all major activities of the No. 1 Brigade. He was known as heroic and fearless, and was involved in a series of ambushes where RIC patrols were held up and relieved of their weapons as well as other equipment.[1]

The first IRA training camp in Donegal was established at Dungloe in mid-September where all brigade, battalion and company officers were called for a course based on close order drill, open order drill, manoeuvres, attacking and defending positions, engineering and the use of explosives. The training officer sent to Donegal by Emmet Dalton, Director of

Training, was C. S. 'Todd' Andrews, a young Dublin man. Andrews was only nineteen years old and was a little daunted by his new appointment, informing Dalton that he only had experience of training at company level. Dalton told him that a former British army sergeant called Dixon would act as his adjutant and assist him. Andrews' first impressions of Dixon were not good, but the two travelled from Amiens Street Station, arriving late on Monday evening, 19 September, at Letterkenny Station where they spent the night. They continued on their journey the following day and arrived at Dungloe Road Station where they were met by Joe Sweeney, OC 1st Northern Division. Sweeney remembered Andrews from his days at Pádraig Pearse's school, St Enda's, in Dublin, where they had both been students.

Andrews and Dixon were taken to Sweeney's Hotel where they were to stay for the duration of their time in Donegal. On arrival the adjutant immediately made his way to the bar. Andrews did not think the man displayed any qualities to be expected of an IRA Volunteer and his general attitude displeased him. Later that evening Sweeney took Andrews to a small village hall where he met the Donegal commandants. Andrews immediately delved into the GHQ curriculum and delivered the first of his lectures based on the organisation of companies and communications. On finishing the talk, he looked around the room and began to wonder if the countrymen of west Donegal could be induced to discuss aspects of the subjects mentioned. He invited one individual to comment and the man immediately stood and began pouring out a stream of words arranged in fluent, well-balanced sentences full of striking imagery. Unknown to Andrews, the speaker was Peadar O'Donnell. Andrews was surprised and a little unnerved, thinking that if all those present possessed similar qualities of knowledge, assurance and fluency he would not have the face to complete the two-week course. However, Todd Andrews was among the good people of Donegal and Peadar O'Donnell recognised the young captain's unease and was sensitive to his predicament. After their initial meeting O'Donnell took Andrews under his wing and assisted him in many ways during the next fortnight. O'Donnell also recognised that Andrews' adjutant was of little assistance to him in delivering the GHQ curriculum and advised him to raise the issue with Joe Sweeney. Andrews suggested that Dixon should be sent back to Dublin and Sweeney agreed. After a few days, Andrews told Dixon to return to Dublin and sent a note to GHQ saying he found him unsuitable.

Peadar O'Donnell showed Todd Andrews much of the countryside around the Rosses and told him of its history and the hardships endured by the people. When the course had been successfully completed, O'Donnell took Andrews to his home where he met O'Donnell's mother. Andrews said of this meeting:

> It was easy to see where Peadar got his intelligence and his warmth. She gave me a great welcome showing a good deal more interest in me and my family than in the problems of the locality or of the nation. I was not used to being treated in so flattering or even so adult a fashion. She appeared to me to be a woman of very fine quality, shrewd and full of common sense, who was content with life despite what must have been a hard struggle to rear her children.[2]

While the training was in progress at Dungloe, another camp had been established at Drimarone, south Donegal, to cater for the No. 3 Brigade. The GHQ curriculum was also applied there with added emphasis on engineering. The IRA engineers were given instruction on explosives and in the manufacture of landmines, etc.[3]

The training camp for the No. 2 Brigade was held at Breenagh, on the main Letterkenny to Glenties road. This was held between 3 and 8 October with Todd Andrews again delivering the GHQ curriculum. On this occasion, the officers of No. 2 Brigade included Frank O'Donnell, Seamus McCann and John Mullan with Peadar O'Donnell assisting Andrews. During the course of training, some of the officers decided to test the men in what they called a 'shirt tail parade' – a mock attack on the camp in the middle of the night to assess the Volunteers' reaction. They made some blank ammunition by taking the lead out of the .303 shells and replacing it with paper. Later that night some of the officers surrounded the camp and selected positions before opening fire on all sides with the blanks. There was a scramble which caused much confusion. John Mullan shouted, 'for God sake get down on your bellies' as the noise of the powder blasting the paper crackled over their heads. The 'shirt tail parade' referred to the sight of the men running in all directions with their long shirt tails hanging out.

Sometime later, the officers decided to get some wild deer from Glenveagh estate as a treat for the men at the camp. A number of volunteers were sent out, a couple of deer were brought back, cut up and boiled with barley, and they made a great meal. That day there was meat and soup for everyone with some declaring that it looked very much like Christmas, such was the feast. There was another 'shirt tail parade' that night as the venison and soup proved a little too rich for most of the men![4]

At the conclusion of each training camp Captain Todd Andrews forwarded his report on the training period to the Director of Training, Emmet Dalton, including his observations on the competence of all personnel in Donegal. In the report on No. 1 Brigade at Dungloe, Andrews was critical of the camp's facilities as it lacked both a parade ground and accommodation for the officers. He was also critical of the weapons: 'The arms in the camp were in a bad condition of neglect and in one or two cases the rifles were in a condition dangerous to the user.' However, he was satisfied that the training had served its purpose: 'I am glad to report that on the conclusion of the camp there has been a very great and obvious improvement in the men.'

Andrews also mentioned the frustrations felt by the Donegal Volunteers: 'A debate on "Our War and Methods" developed into a criticism of GHQ for not paying more attention to the possibilities of County Donegal as a field for intensifying action in order to relieve pressure on the south.'

In his report on the Breenagh camp, Andrews commended Peadar O'Donnell for extending its duration for an extra week:

> At the end of the camp there was an improvement in the discipline and military bearing of the men ... there is however, plenty of scope for further improvement; with this end in view Brigadier O'Donnell proposes to keep the men in camp for another week ... there is no

doubt that Brigadier O'Donnell is acting very wisely in keeping the men for another week as it will do them an immensity of good.[5]

While the training camps were in progress, the IRA was called on to tackle civil disorder and carry out other civic duties. In an effort to address the issues, some of the Volunteers were dismissed from the camps and ordered to return to their command areas to address the various problems arising. Their principal duties during this period focused on upholding order and their primary target was the disruption of the growing poitín industry. In rural areas, poitín was creating serious anti-social problems and the Inishowen area was particularly affected. At that time it was almost impossible to go along certain mountain roads without passing poitín stills in full working order. Young boys were known to club together to purchase a bottle of the alcoholic beverage. There were stories at the time of men having to be physically restrained with ropes and of others found lying along the roadside at night so bereft of reason that they were eating grass and twigs from the hedges. Fifteen stills were discovered in the Clonmany area and on Tuesday 18 October the Carndonagh Company discovered and dismantled six poitín stills in the Malin area. In most cases the stills were surrendered without incident with one being discovered down the face of a precipice which was located approximately 600 feet from the open ocean.

Forty stills were discovered by the IRA over a two-week period throughout the Inishowen peninsula.[6] All known poitín stillers were visited and the Volunteers arrested those attempting to resist seizure of their equipment. The detentions acted as a deterrent to others, who surrendered their stills without resistance. In one instance when a man was ordered to hand over his still he produced an old one that was no longer in use. He was instructed to surrender his new still and he set off to comply with the order. He was then observed attempting to escape on a bicycle and was pursued by the Volunteers with the bike then being used as an exchange for the new still.[7]

Chapter 3

Eithne Coyle and the Mountjoy Escape

Whereas many of the plaudits of the War of Independence were directed at the IRA Volunteers, very little was apportioned to the women of Cumann na mBan, which belies their contribution during that period. The work of Cumann na mBan was important and carried equivalent risk to the IRA's activity of that time. Women risked arrest and even death when carrying important correspondence, weapons, etc.

Eithne Coyle was possibly the most prominent Donegal woman to have served in Cumann na mBan during the War of Independence and the Civil War. She became an active member of Cumann na mBan as soon as the organisation established branches in Donegal in 1917. She was engaged in raising funds for the purchase of arms and other equipment as well as being involved in the anti-conscription campaign in Donegal and later the election campaign of 1918. Following this she was sent to Dungannon, County Tyrone, having been appointed as an organiser for the Gaelic League, an organisation set up in 1893 to promote Gaelic culture and teach the Irish language. She relocated to County Longford in 1919 where she was responsible for founding branches of Cumann na mBan. In about February 1920 she was asked to move to County Roscommon to organise and teach on behalf of the Gaelic League. She had not been long there when she came to the attention of the local RIC, who began making her life difficult, and her house was the focus of many raids by the police and military. In July 1920, while she was on holiday in Donegal, a mixed party of police and military raided and set fire to her home destroying all her possessions. The local Volunteers secured another house for her near Roscommon town.

On her return to Roscommon Eithne Coyle focused on organising feiseanna and other events to raise funds for arms, etc. She was also very active in intelligence work for the local Volunteers. Following an ambush on 12 October, in which four RIC members were killed and others injured, a mixed party of twenty-five military, police and Black and Tans targeted Coyle's house. They smashed up the interior and piled all her belongings and furniture in the middle of the floor before pouring petrol over them. They threatened to set it on fire if she did not cooperate and answer their questions. Coyle encouraged them to light it, but told them that they would have to explain themselves to the owner, a local loyalist. This had the desired effect and they left soon after. The harassment continued and on Friday 31 December 1920 more than twenty-five soldiers, police and Black and Tans returned and again smashed up the house, while some dug up sections of the surrounding grounds, but failed to find anything incriminating. They returned the following morning with a warrant for Coyle's arrest and she was taken to the Roscommon Town Police Barracks. She was held there in a cold damp cell and was subjected to continuous verbal abuse by the Black and Tans until the next day when she was transferred to Athlone Barracks. She was detained there for approximately one month before being transferred to Mountjoy Jail in Dublin. She was subsequently tried in February 1921 and sentenced to three years' penal servitude, which was later reduced to one year.[1]

The Truce period brought many changes: prison rules were relaxed at various jails including Mountjoy, and visitors were allowed in. About this time, another Cumann na mBan member, Linda Kearns, was repatriated from Walton Prison in Liverpool, England. A nurse by profession, Kearns had served with Cumann na mBan in County Sligo. She was arrested on Saturday 20 November 1920, approximately one mile outside Sligo town, when she drove into a military checkpoint in a car which contained all the rifles and ammunition of the local IRA column. She was first taken to Sligo Jail, spending one week there before being transferred to Derry Jail, and eventually to the female prison at Armagh. Kearns was tried in

May 1921 and sentenced to ten years' imprisonment. She was subsequently transferred to Walton Prison in Liverpool where she was held until the Truce of July 1921 after which she was taken to Mountjoy Jail. Throughout her time in various prisons in Ireland and England Kearns' main thoughts were of escape. Sometime in late September 1921 she had a visit from another Cumann na mBan nurse called Josie O'Connor, who by the end of their conversation realised that Kearns was contemplating escape.

O'Connor returned some days later bringing a thermos flask of hot tea containing a large piece of dental wax to allow Kearns to get an impression of a key for a door leading to the grounds of the prison. A few days later Kearns received a parcel with a cake that contained a plan of the back of the prison and a note suggesting that a rope ladder could be thrown over the wall if she could make it into the prison yard. Kearns wrote down her ideas for the escape on notepaper and sewed both the note and the wax impression of the key into some clothes, which were sent out of the jail. Sometime later Josie O'Connor returned with a cooked chicken and inside it was the key. However, when Kearns tried the key it would not fit and needed to be filed in places. At this point she confided in Eithne Coyle, who informed her that some of the warders were sympathetic and would help. The two women began making plans for their escape and approached a friendly warder who agreed to assist and told them that on whatever night they decided to escape the door to the prison yard would be unlocked. A map was then sent out with an 'X' marked at the location where their rescuers would be waiting and the date for the escape was selected.

After consultation with the other prisoners, two more decided to join them: Mary (May) Burke who was serving two years and Aileen Keogh who was serving one year. The escape plan was set for Monday 31 October – Halloween night – but they had one final obstacle to overcome. A two-man military patrol would be continuously walking around the prison, so the escapees timed the patrol, estimating they would have enough time for three, maybe four, to make it over the wall. They discussed their difficulty and Eithne Coyle decided that she would go out into the yard with the others to hold the ladder and if she could not make the escape, she would create a distraction for the soldiers giving the others time to get away.

On the designated night, the women decided to have a football match in the corridor of the prison wing to create as much noise as possible. They had discovered from previous occasions that when they did this, the staff did not inspect their wing. However, on that night a wardress decided to watch and sat on a stool in front of the door the escapees had planned to go through. Coyle kicked the ball in her direction and the ball struck her, knocking her off the stool. This raised great cheers and laughter from the women and when the wardress decided that it was no longer safe to watch the game, she left, giving them the opportunity to make their way to the designated escape point. Three other prisoners on their wing were instructed to continue playing football in the corridor and occasionally call on the escapees to come out of their cells as if they were still there. The four moved out into the prison grounds closing the door behind them and made their way to the wall. Linda Kearns threw a stone over and a short time later a weight attached to a string was thrown back from the outside. At that moment they heard the footsteps of a soldier and they moved to the wall of the prison building, crouching in the shadows. When the man had passed, they moved back to the outer wall and found the string.

They then began pulling the rope ladder over the wall, but forgot to take account of the square-cut limestone on the top. Pulling against this eventually cut the string and the ladder fell back down on the other side. They again had to run to the shadows of the building when they heard the footsteps and voices of two soldiers. When the patrol had passed, the women returned to the wall and suddenly a string came over, weighted down by a penknife. This time they pulled the rope away from the cut limestone and the ladder soon dropped over the wall. Linda Kearns started to climb followed by Mary Burke and then Aileen Keogh while Eithne Coyle held the ladder out from the wall. Kearns got to the top but with the dark night could not see a thing at the bottom. She felt a rope and then heard Josie O'Connor whisper: 'Slither, Linda, slither.' She slithered down the rope and was quickly taken away by Tim Ryan who walked her over the canal and on to the bridge at Berkeley Road. Dr St John Gogarty was waiting there in a car and a few minutes later Burke arrived, escorted by a young Fianna Éireann member named Donnelly. They immediately drove away and made their way to Earlsfort Terrace to the house of a Miss O'Rourke, a relative of the doctor's wife.

Meanwhile, at the prison, Eithne Coyle began climbing the ladder, but as no one was holding it at the bottom she had a difficult time climbing, with her knuckles bashing against the wall. She eventually reached the top and slid down the other side to the street. Coyle and Keogh walked arm-in-arm to a waiting car which took them to Dr McLaverty's house in Merrion Square where they remained for several days.

One day Mrs McLaverty thought that the women could do with some exercise and decided to take them for a walk. They had not been out very long when they met Dr Paddy McCartan, who told them that a G-man was following them and advised them not to return to Merrion Square. Instead, having lost the G-man, they went to Maud Gonne MacBride's house in St Stephen's Green. When they got there Dorothy Macardle and MacBride's French maid Marie dressed in their clothes and walked to McLaverty's on Merrion Square.

They were not long at MacBride's when Seamus Burke arrived to say the house was no longer safe for them. He took them to the Cross and Passion Convent in Kilcullen, County Kildare, where they met up with Linda Kearns and Mary Burke. A short time later Aileen Keogh decided to return to her native area of Gorey in County Wexford. The others were only at the convent a few days when Tim Ryan arrived on a motorbike with a message from Michael Collins. It transpired that Seamus Burke was a paid British spy who had planned to get all four women in the one place where they could be arrested together. They were immediately escorted from the area by local Volunteers and taken to an IRA training camp at Duckett's Grove in County Carlow where they remained until after the signing of the Treaty.[2]

Eithne Coyle returned to Donegal after the Truce and a short time later was appointed as Cumann na mBan organiser for Donegal and Tyrone.

Chapter 4

The IRA Civic Police

The Truce period presented various law-and-order-related problems in many areas across the county. This period saw the IRA's transition from the role of a guerrilla army to that of a civic police force, as a lawless vacuum quickly developed. The problem was that the civilian population continued to ignore the authority of the RIC and the role of the IRA had not been ascertained with regard to civic duties. Despite this the IRA was always on hand to deal with any issues relating to law and order that came to its attention. They were kept particularly busy in this way in Inishowen. One example occurred on Sunday night, 30 October 1921, when a serious stabbing incident took place in the Culdaff area and was reported to the local IRA. A number of Volunteers were directed to carry out an investigation into the incident. The details were that Michael Kelly from Derry had been stabbed about the face and neck by his brother-in-law at Gleneely, Culdaff. The assailant was arrested by the IRA in Letterkenny the following Tuesday and claimed that he had acted in self-defence. He said Kelly brought the object with which the injuries were inflicted to his home. He was released following a full investigation and later that evening was taken to his home. He expressed his gratitude for the treatment he received and for the manner in which the IRA dealt with the matter.[1]

The Inishowen Volunteers also remained busy in the suppression of the local poitín industry, succeeding in capturing many stills in late October and destroying a number in the Culdaff area. 'Tools' captured comprised six or seven worms. Made from copper, the worm was always the most prized and most zealously guarded part of the still outfit.[2]

About the same time, a party of around thirty IRA volunteers took up quarters in the Inishowen workhouse where they established a camp. Their occupation did not interfere with the work of the house or with the other business of the district council, which was also performed there. However, the occurrence prompted a question in the British parliamentary papers when Colonel Gretton asked the Chief Secretary, Hamar Greenwood, what measures were being taken against the occupation by the Volunteers. These issues were relayed to the liaison officers appointed to each divisional area, who for the 1st Northern Division encompassing County Donegal and parts of Counties Derry, Tyrone and Fermanagh, was Commandant Patrick Sheils of Derry. The post of liaison officer was established as part of the Truce agreement and the individual appointed was tasked with addressing the issues and concerns arising between the IRA, British military and police in his area, which were relayed to GHQ for resolution.[3]

In early November the police barracks at Malin, Moville and Muff were closed and members of the RIC quartered there were transferred to larger stations. During the second week of November the following RIC barracks were shut down: Milford, Malin, Malin Head, Carrigart, Clonmany, Muff, Bundoran, Inver, Glenties and Falcarragh.[4]

With the IRA taking on the role of civic police, it was only a matter of time before they would clash with the RIC. The first conflict occurred at a Fair Day in the village of Ramelton on Tuesday 15 November. What started out as a relatively peaceful day suddenly became one of great tension following the appearance of the RIC under the command of District Inspector Hodge. Shortly after 1 p.m. a number of RIC members took charge of part of the town and it then transpired that a business house was under observation by members of the IRA. About 2 p.m. a number of RIC proceeded to the premises in question and ordered the IRA to disperse. This order was ignored, with the result that the IRA members on duty were arrested – Michael Jordan, Patrick Jordan and James McKendrick. The three were taken to the local barracks, where they were briefly detained. Immediately after the arrest of the three Volunteers, other members took their place and despite various threats from the RIC that they would be dispersed by force, remained in position. Diplomacy prevailed and no further arrests were made with the detained Volunteers being released after four hours without charge.[5]

Another problem soon developed for the IRA, when people started to use its name as a means of threatening and extorting money from others. The IRA authority in north Donegal was forced to take appropriate action and ordered the deportation of two men from the Kerrykeel area for entering a house and demanding money in the name of the IRA. A Presbyterian farmer in Convoy received a threatening letter, supposedly signed by the IRA, which ordered him to pay within seven days a sum of money allegedly owed to a resident in the Ballybofey area. The farmer promptly made his way to the headquarters of the local IRA officer and complained. Pending the arrest of the person on whose behalf the threatening letter was supposed to have been written, a local IRA company patrolled the vicinity of the farmer's house. The matter was satisfactorily settled and the IRA later issued a statement declaring that if anyone received similar notices they should inform the local IRA officers.[6]

The Sinn Féin courts continued to administer justice and the Carndonagh District Arbitration Court was held on Wednesday 23 November. Proceedings were interrupted when RIC District Inspector Geelan of Buncrana and a party of RIC men entered the court shortly after 11 a.m. The first case was in session when the police inspector, addressing the president of the court, stated that the gathering was not a court of arbitration and alleged that the people present had been brought by force and against their will. The president of the court refuted the accusation and said the people were present voluntarily after signing a request to have their cases submitted to arbitration. The court then continued, with the RIC remaining for the hearing of all cases, which lasted until 3.30 p.m. that day.[7]

The integrity and equality of the Sinn Féin courts was recognised and commended by every section of the community. An example of this was observed when an unsigned letter from a Donegal businessman appeared in the *Derry Journal* on Friday 25 November:

When I followed my father I followed his rule of always obliging a neighbour, be it with a mowing machine, or a ten-pound note, that was needed to tide over a difficulty. I found, when making up my books this year that I had £370 out amongst my neighbours. Polite requests were followed by registered letters, without result. Threats – the futility of which no one knew better than the recipients – to 'put the matter into my solicitor's hands', were also fruitless. Then I startled my family by announcing that I was going to the Sinn Féin Court. 'Never,' they said with one voice, 'A man in your position could not possibly countenance these irregular assemblies.'

'Why not,' I said, 'I want my money, and I see no other way of getting it.'

'But think of the effect on your appearance there will have [sic],' they entreated.

'I can think of nothing,' I retorted, 'but the effect on my finances, if I lose the money.'

The court sat in the workhouse. On the bench were six local laymen of standing. The resident – or parish judge – as he is called – was a doctor, the registrar was a local solicitor. We were all well known to each other. I stated my case, proved the debts, and got orders for payment to be made within fourteen days.

If a native of Ceylon is owed money and cannot obtain payment, he goes to his debtors and threatens to kill himself if not instantly paid. As it is known that he would carry out his threat, if humanly possible the debtor pays up, for, according to native law, anyone causing another to lose his life must forfeit his own. I do not know what was the method used by the Tribunal which sat in our parish – local opinion, 'what the neighbours would say' is a mighty power in rural Ireland – but this I do know – ten days ago I got paying orders for £370 and since then the post has brought me £345.[8]

Chapter 5

The Treaty Signed, but not Sealed

The Irish delegation travelled to London in early October 1921 to negotiate on behalf of Dáil Éireann the basis of a treaty with the British government. The Irish delegation included Arthur Griffith, Michael Collins, Robert Barton, George Gavan Duffy, Éamonn Duggan, Emmet Dalton, John Chartres, Ned Broy, Seán MacBride and Erskine Childers. The British delegation included David Lloyd George, Lord Birkenhead, Austen Chamberlain, Winston Churchill, Hamar Greenwood and Gordon Hewart. The negotiations reached stalemate at times and the talks almost failed on occasion. However, the Irish delegation were outmanoeuvred at the conference table resulting in the Anglo-Irish Treaty being signed on Tuesday 6 December. The last day of the talks was Monday 5 December and the British Prime Minister, David Lloyd George, pressed them to sign, but not all were prepared to do so. Lloyd George was reluctant to allow the negotiators time to consult with Dublin and insisted that the document be signed that night. The delegation was presented with two letters – one was the acceptance of the Treaty and the other was a rejection and the threat of a return to war 'within three days'. They were given two hours to decide. After the deadline, and following further discussion, the Irish signed the agreement at 2.10 a.m. on Tuesday 6 December 1921. There was no official record of the negotiations due to Arthur Griffith's agreement to a British proposal not to use official stenographers.[1]

The British used various tricks and dubious methods during the negotiations and at times split the Irish negotiating team by meeting for discussions with some members to the exclusion of the others. The signed agreement was accompanied by the Treaty document entitled: 'Articles of Agreement for a Treaty between Britain and Ireland' and contained two schedules. The First Schedule was known as 'The Constitution of the Irish Free State – Saorstát Éireann', which was to be drafted in accordance with the Second Schedule, which was the Treaty agreement or 'The Articles of Agreement'. In particular, words, laws or amendments would be void if found to be repugnant to any provision of the Second Schedule.

The document fell short of creating the Republic proclaimed by Pádraig Pearse in 1916; many quarters felt that it scarcely improved on the Home Rule Bill of 1914 (which allowed for an Irish parliament to make decisions on national affairs, as a devolved government within the British Empire) and were extremely dissatisfied with the Treaty offered to them. Because partition had been firmly entrenched six months earlier, no such republic could have been negotiated in London as the Belfast government refused to play any part in the talks.[2] Partition had been in existence since December 1920 through the Government of Ireland Act and was firmly established on Wednesday 22 June 1921 when the first session of the northern parliament in Belfast was officially opened by the British monarch George V. Partition had been cast in stone at that point, signalling a victory for the unionists of the Six Counties of Derry, Antrim, Armagh, Down, Fermanagh and Tyrone.[3]

At one stage, when the Treaty talks looked like they might collapse, word was received by the Derry IRA to arrange the escape of all IRA prisoners from Derry Jail; the IRA sent word to the prison and began preparing. In the days leading up to the breakout an officer of the 1st Northern Division IRA, Daniel Kelly, met with some of the local Volunteers in Paddy McGee's public house at Bishop Street, Derry. McGee showed them a bottle of chloroform and explained that this was to be used on the two policemen who were on guard duty at the prison gates. The anaesthetic was to be smuggled in by one of two friendly warders – Patrick Leonard and George Lloyd – who were frequent visitors to the public house. Another warder called Michael Finnegan also agreed to help.

There was also the question of smuggling guns into the prison, but

The Treaty Signed, but not Sealed

Daniel Kelly advised against this and the use of the chloroform. The Volunteers decided against the use of weapons, as this could have put the lives of all prisoners at risk, but did decide to smuggle the chloroform into the prison. The prisoners in Derry Jail had received instructions that Tuesday 6 December was the night for the escape attempt. There were several Donegal prisoners among the escape party and two were officers of the south Donegal IRA No. 4 Brigade: Thomas McShea and Patrick Johnston. (They had been sentenced to two years' hard labour in May 1921 having been previously charged with possession of a document relating to the affairs of the Irish Volunteers. The paper was a charge against a Volunteer for disobeying orders and was discovered on McShea: it had been signed by Johnston.) The men had made wax impressions of their cell keys and sent them out to have replicas made. However, the new keys did not fit the locks and Patrick Johnston had to make some minor adjustments for them to work. At about 11.30 p.m. Johnston was able to open his cell door and release twelve other prisoners: Patrick Tully (Clones, County Monaghan), Francis Gallagher (Ardara, County Donegal), Patrick Maguire (Newtownstewart, County Tyrone), Peter O'Donnell (Ballybay, County Monaghan), Patrick O'Reilly (Ardara, County Donegal), Francis Sheridan (Wattlesbridge, County Fermanagh), James J. Fitzpatrick (Newtownbutler, County Fermanagh), Bernard Sweeney (Burtonport, County Donegal), James McNulty (Creeslough, County Donegal), Patrick McAteer (Ballybofey, County Donegal), Hugh J. Timmins (Newtownbutler, County Fermanagh) and Henry O'Loan (County Antrim).

Warder Finnegan then unlocked the door and entered the cell block. McShea and Johnston immediately overpowered him, which initially shocked him, but he accepted that it was part of the plan. The men then questioned him about the guard situation and he told them there were two armed RIC constables on duty. Five men, including Thomas McShea and Bernard Sweeney, then set off to overpower the two RIC men (named Gorman and Lyttle), who were in a room and had their revolvers and a bottle of whiskey on the table. McShea and Sweeney went for the smaller of the pair while the others jumped the bigger man. Despite their opponent's appearance, McShea and Sweeney struggled to overcome him until McShea used the whiskey bottle to hit him over the head, knocking him out. The overpowered policemen were gagged and had their arms and legs tied before being dragged into the prison corridor. The prisoners then administered chloroform to them both. The majority of the escapees proceeded to the outside wall where a rope ladder was thrown over by Volunteers on the outside. However, at the same time a member of the Special Constabulary was walking down Bishop Street and when he approached opposite the end of Bennett Street he observed the two cars waiting for the fugitives. He became suspicious, immediately raising the alarm, and a detachment of soldiers was soon rushing towards the jail. The men inside heard the commotion and then came the general alarm. Johnston and McShea immediately tied up Leonard, who had brought in the chloroform for them, and put him and Finnegan into a cell. They then went into their own cells and locked the doors. The remaining escapees were still in the prison yard where they were rounded up and returned to their cells.

Due to the commotion it was some time before the two RIC men were found – both were dead. Johnston and McShea initially escaped suspicion as they were discovered to be still in their cells. However, Finnegan and Leonard were charged with the murder of the constables and, to clear his name, Finnegan quickly made a statement giving details of the whole affair. The other warder, George Lloyd, was not on duty that night and escaped suspicion. Both Johnston and McShea were subsequently charged with murdering the RIC men. Finnegan was to be the key witness in the case against them and was moved to protective custody at a military camp in Belfast.[4]

The release of internees and those regarded as convicted prisoners had been one of the principal issues at the negotiations in London. The Irish delegates had stressed the importance of the release of both internees and prisoners as paramount for the acceptance by Dáil Éireann of the Articles of Agreement between Ireland and Britain. In response, the British cabinet had met on Wednesday morning, 7 December, to discuss the topic. The British military Commander-in-Chief in Ireland, General Neville Macready informed the cabinet, 'that there would be no objection from the military point of view to the immediate release of the 4,000 internees'. The actual number of internees at that time was 3,627 with 4,368 internment orders having been issued up to the Truce of July 1921. The British government was fully aware that to comply with the request to release all internees immediately would strengthen the Irish delegation's position when advocating the acceptance of the terms of the Articles of Agreement to the members of Dáil Éireann. This was raised at the British cabinet meeting where it was stated 'that it would be more difficult for the Irish Parliament to reject the Articles of Agreement if the internees had been released as an act of clemency immediately after the signature of the agreement'. The issue of convicted prisoners was also discussed and arrangements were made to review each prisoner's sentence by a judicial tribunal, with special consideration to be given to those under sentence of death.[5]

Many in Donegal first read the full details of the Treaty on Wednesday 7 December when the daily newspapers arrived. The OC 1st Northern Division and TD for West Donegal, Joe Sweeney, read the details when the newspapers arrived at Burtonport on the morning train. His initial reaction was, 'To hell with this, this is not what we were fighting for', but he decided that he would travel to Dublin to gauge the full extent of the agreement and the reaction of others there before making a decision.[6]

The British honoured their commitment regarding the amnesty for all internees and all had been released from the various internment camps on Saturday 10 December. The arrival of those freed from Letterkenny and surrounding areas was signalled by loud cheering when their train arrived at the station. A number of prominent figures addressed the gathering including the IRA's No. 2 Brigade OC Peadar O'Donnell. He extended a hearty welcome not only to the internees returning locally, but also to all the prisoners returning to other areas of the county. On the subject of the Treaty he stated that he did not wish to say anything that would strike a wrong note, but it would be well to be frank since the terms would come in for comment, especially as many of those present were Volunteers. 'The boys will remember those nights when behind an old hedge here and there we swore an oath of allegiance to the Irish Republic.' O'Donnell was opposed to the Treaty and said that he could not reconcile the oath of allegiance to King George and England, declaring that the civilian population had a right to a say in the matter:

> [Some] will pronounce that we fought behind a cover of civilians. If the civilians are anxious to let down those who, in pursuit of greater things, obtained such terms as are offered today, it's a pity they could not let us have known that sooner. The Donegal Highlands are lovely spots and if the civilians are sick of being used as more or less of a base by us, most of us are ready again to don uniform and die fighting to uphold and maintain the Republic, to which we have freely given our loyalty. I have a message for the IRA 'stand fast'. Our HQ is intact and we will stand by our army chiefs as they stood by us and carry on as we are ordered. Let there be no recriminations. Some of the best brains in Ireland have taken more or less opposite sides regarding the terms and we must each respect the other's sincerity. We as a unit are not influenced by hate.[7]

The south Donegal internees arrived at Donegal Town Railway Station later that day. They were from the town itself, Killybegs, Kilcar, Carrick, Dunkineely and surrounding areas. Hundreds thronged the platform, Tricolours were waved and cheers filled the air. The Donegal Fife and Drum Band played the 'Soldier's Song' followed by 'Wrap the Green Flag Round Me' as the train conveying the men steered into the station. As they stepped from the compartments the handshakes were warm, the welcome sincere and the enthusiasm unbounded. That night members of the Volunteers, Sinn Féin and Cumann na mBan, together with the Fife and Drum Band, formed into procession order a short distance from the railway station and walked through the town.

Large crowds also met the Volunteers from the Inishowen area when they arrived in Carndonagh. People from Clonmany, Malin, Culdaff and other areas had gathered to greet the former internees. Long before dusk, every house was brilliantly illuminated with various lights, while in the surrounding hills bonfires were lit. The local IRA Volunteers had been preparing to greet their comrades from an early hour. Shortly after seven o'clock the steady tramp, tramp of the Volunteers under command broke the stillness of the evening and a cheer rang out informing the crowd that the former internees were home. One of them, James Lanigan, addressed the crowd, thanking them on behalf of himself and his comrades. He said the demonstration was an appreciation of the Irish cause of which they (the internees) were but a humble exponent and it was also a tribute to those leaders who were giving their all to the martyred dead who died for Ireland.[8]

Meanwhile Joe Sweeney arrived in Dublin endeavouring to gauge the true extent of the Treaty agreement and made his way to the Wicklow Hotel in the hope of meeting Michael Collins there. He met him as he was leaving the hotel. Sweeney described him as someone who was very depressed and discontented. Eoin O'Duffy was accompanying Collins, so Sweeney approached him to find out how members of the IRB (Irish Republican Brotherhood) featured in it all. O'Duffy replied that the head centre (of the IRB) had given permission to all members to make up their own minds. The IRB head centre happened to be Michael Collins. With that, Sweeney decided to return to Donegal to discuss the terms of the Treaty with the members of Sinn Féin and the Volunteers in west Donegal.[9]

Chapter 6

Donegal Debates the Treaty

The early indications were that a majority of the elected representatives of Donegal were prepared to support the Treaty and the message was for the Donegal TDs to accept the terms of the Treaty at the debates in Dublin. Throughout December 1921 the various Sinn Féin cumainn (branches) and comhairle ceantair (area councils) held meetings to discuss the Treaty and to seek the views of their members. At a special meeting of the Inishowen Rural District Council on Monday 26 December, the members unanimously passed a motion:

> We the Inishowen Rural District Council appeal to the TDs for North Donegal to ratify the treaty as the desire of the people is quietness and in the belief that the further war which is threatened as the consequences of non-ratification would result in the loss to Ireland of these people who, judged by their disinterested and intelligent labours hitherto are the very ones needed to complete the independence of the nation and believing that this consideration should outweigh any scruple about an avowal of allegiance exacted under duress.[1]

The North Donegal Comhairle Ceantar held a special meeting the following evening at St Mary's Hall, Buncrana, with twelve of the fourteen Sinn Féin cumainn in the area being fully represented. The following branches were represented: Moville, Milford, Killygarvan, Fahan, Desertegney, Clonmany, Carndonagh, Culdaff, Malin, Malin Head, Iskaheen and Buncrana. The chairman briefly but clearly explained that the purpose of the meeting was to ascertain the views of the people of north Donegal on the Treaty and to convey their views to their deputies.

The delegates from each district described the state of feeling prevailing and it was found that in every single district of the constituency the opinion was absolutely in favour of ratification or as one delegate put it, '99.99 per cent of the population of North Donegal demanded immediate ratification'. The following resolution was proposed, seconded and unanimously passed:

> That the members of the North Donegal comhairle ceantar, having carefully considered the Treaty signed by Ireland's plenipotentiaries are thoroughly satisfied that it embodies the essentials of Ireland's freedom and safeguards Ireland's honour. At the election in May last, having taken united action with other comhairle ceantair in the county and assumed joint responsibility with them for the selection, nomination and return of six deputies to An Dáil, we hereby call upon those six deputies not only to vote for the ratification of the Treaty, but to use all their influences with their fellow deputies to secure ratification. Failure to do so must be regarded as a betrayal of the best interests of their country and gross contempt for the opinions of their constituents.

The secretary was then instructed to send copies of the resolution to Éamon de Valera, Arthur Griffith and the six deputies for the county: Dr J. P. McGinley, P. J. McGoldrick, Sam O'Flaherty, Joe Sweeney, Joseph O'Doherty and P. J. Ward. As the meeting was concluding, the delegates from Kindrum Cumann arrived, having driven all the way from north Fanad as a storm prevented them from crossing Lough Swilly. They reported that the support of the people in their district was overwhelmingly in favour of ratification and they endorsed the resolution adopted by the meeting.

The Buncrana Urban District Council convened a special meeting on Wednesday 28 December and the following resolution was proposed by William Doherty and seconded by John Porter. It was passed unanimously:

> That this urban council believing that the plenipotentiaries secured all that was essential and more than was thought possible at the conference in London, declare for the ratification of the Treaty without further delay and urge An Dáil to establish forthwith the Provisional Government provided for thereunder and get to business without further speechmaking and we hereby direct our six deputies to record their votes in favour of such ratification.

The meeting of the East Donegal Comhairle Ceantar was held at the Literary Institute in Letterkenny on Thursday 29 December. Delegates were present from Letterkenny, Glenswilly, Drumoghill, Cloghan, Castlefinn, Murlog, Killygordon, Lismullaghduff, Raphoe and Ramelton. They all reported that their areas were in favour of ratifying the Treaty. The following resolution was proposed, seconded and passed unanimously:

> We the delegates present at this meeting of East Tirconaill comhairle ceantar are of opinion that the Treaty signed by our plenipotentiaries is consistent with the basis on which the conference took place. On this basis, association with the free nations forming the British commonwealth was defined and accepted by Dáil Éireann and as the people of East Tirconaill who we represent see no alternative but chaos, we hereby call on the deputies for Tirconaill to vote for the Treaty or resign forthwith. But we earnestly pray and hope that with the same unselfish patriotism that won for our leaders our love and trust, they in this circumstance will bury all differences and work in unity for our country's good.[2]

It was obvious from the outcome of meetings in the various areas that the consensus was in support of the Treaty. Whether this was due to the desire for peace by a war-weary population or to the knowledge that the county would not form part of a separate state under British rule, the ranks of the IRA would have to be consulted on the matter and their response would not be as straightforward.

Chapter 7

1922 – The Treaty Debates and Vote

The elected representatives of Dáil Éireann assembled at the UCD buildings on Earlsfort Terrace in Dublin on Wednesday 14 December 1921 to begin the marathon discussions on the pros and cons of the Treaty. With the debates now under way, Donegal County Council sought to have the issue dealt with at local level. Such was the immediacy of the situation the county council held a special meeting on Sunday 1 January 1922. A motion instructing the Donegal Dáil representatives to vote in favour of the Treaty was unanimously passed. However, the signing by the Irish plenipotentiaries of the Articles of Agreement for a Treaty between Ireland and Britain had created a sharp difference of opinion in the ranks of both Sinn Féin and the IRA. Immediately after the signing of the agreement this division became apparent and old comrades began to take opposite sides – those in favour of the Treaty and those opposed.[1]

The confused state of affairs continued within the ranks of the IRA and it was decided that the question of accepting or rejecting the Treaty should be put to each individual Volunteer in all brigade areas. Michael Collins as head centre of the IRB had earlier given instructions that all individual members of the IRB were to make up their own minds on whether to accept or reject the Treaty and this also applied to the individual members of the IRA.

The six Donegal TDs attended the debates and some addressed the Dáil, putting their views to the assembled gathering. Dr J. P. McGinley, speaking on Saturday 7 January 1922, stated:

It might be said that our men might have got better terms in London. Perhaps they might, but I can tell you that the people of Donegal anyhow have the very greatest confidence in the ability of Arthur Griffith and the sincerity of Michael Collins; and they believe that taking all the circumstances of the case into account they did what was best for Ireland. Now President de Valera has stated that rather than sign this Treaty he was prepared to see the Irish people live in subjection until God would redeem them. I may as well say at once that that is not my creed; that is a doctrine that never was preached in the history of the world before; that a country, if it could not get absolutely what it was out for, should fight to the extermination of its people. I, as one man, can't take the responsibility for committing the men and women who sent me here to a war of extermination, which I think would result if this Treaty were rejected. I have no qualms about the oath which I took in coming into this assembly; the people sent me here to get absolute separation if I could – I am for absolute separation if I could see a way out – but they sent me here to use my own free will; and if I could not get absolute separation at the present time I was to take something by which we could work out our own independence in the long run. I think in voting for this Treaty I am voting according to the mandate which my constituents gave me when sending me here.[2]

The South Donegal TD, P. J. Ward, addressing the assembly, said it was a bitter pill to swallow, but under the circumstances, they could not do anything else in the interests of the people. There would be no lasting peace with England, he considered, until Ireland was separated from it and the British Empire. He said he was willing to take the Treaty, but only as a stepping-stone to the independence of the nation and he would explain to his constituents the reason for his actions and would make no apologies to any man for his actions. He did not believe that what was in the Treaty meant the ultimate end of what he and others set out to fight for. He had formed his own opinion on the matter and his opinions had not been formed for him. When he stood for election he said he had stood for the complete independence of Ireland and the placards 'Vote for Ward – Vote for Independence' were still on the walls in Tír Conaill. All the time they had only one thing before them: the fight for the Republic was ongoing and would go on in the future.[3]

In contrast, the Donegal North TD, Joseph O'Doherty, who was opposed to the Treaty, also spoke at the debates. When he read the terms of the Treaty signed in London everything that was good in him revolted against it. Like his co-deputy from Tír Conaill he came to Dáil Éireann with an open mind, but no argument by those in favour of the Treaty had any influence on him: he saw it as giving away the whole case of Irish independence and saw them coming not nearer the day but further away from it. He would not be on the side of those swallowing pills and taking a backward step in the hope that they would find themselves in a better position. When he consented to stand for the Donegal North constituency he consented to stand for the Republic. At the first public meeting in the constituency the chairman of the comhairle ceantar told him that there was only one way to win the election and that was to not mention the word 'republic'. 'Very well,' he said to the chairman, 'they are entitled to their opinion, but they can get another candidate.' He was prepared to admit that the mandate of the election was one of self-determination, but it was a terrible crime to interpret that mandate against the interests of the people. He knew the people of north Donegal would accept the Treaty, but they would accept it under duress at the point of the bayonet. They would accept it as a stepping-stone to war. It was not peace and liberty they were getting.[4]

While the Treaty debates were in progress, two other Donegal TDs told Joe Sweeney that Éamon de Valera wanted to speak to him about his stance on the Treaty, but Sweeney informed them that he did not wish to speak to de Valera as he had already made up his mind. However, the two men later met and Sweeney described de Valera's attitude as 'rather school-masterly' when he approached him and said, 'I hear you're voting for the Treaty.' Sweeney said he was and that he did not consider the British threat of a return to war as an idle threat, and with that walked away.[5]

Some commentators have suggested that Michael Collins signed the Treaty for essentially pragmatic reasons as he certainly had his doubts about it long before the negotiations with the British. He realised that the Treaty agreement was the best available deal and the prospects of a reopening of the intelligence and guerrilla wars were not promising. He was aware that the Treaty could not alter the constitutional status of the north-eastern counties and the Government of Ireland Act, and had plans to achieve reunification by other means. Collins at that time had to be seen to be abiding by the Treaty terms although he was secretly following very different policies and was bent on undermining the new Belfast government and attempting to reassure old republican colleagues.[6]

The debates continued until 8.35 p.m. on Saturday 7 January, when the Articles of Agreement for a Treaty between Britain and Ireland were approved by Dáil Éireann. This signalled a victory for the pro-Treaty side with a narrow margin of sixty-four votes to fifty-seven, giving Ireland independence at the end of a thread.

The final moments of the debates and vote were recorded in the journals of Fr William Hackett. He was a member of the Jesuit Order, had played a major part in the War of Independence as a courier for the IRA, and was well known by many of the prominent figures of that time. Hackett gave a profound portrayal of the closing moments:

> Beside me was Peadar O'Donnell, an anti-ratifier as I judged from his groans. Then the long series of answers ended. The silence grew tense. We waited for the official tellers. Suddenly a loud cheer broke out from the assembled crowd … there was a majority of 7 for ratification. Collins was on his feet at once; 'There is no victory in this – there can be no victory over fellow Irish men'. De Valera responded to Collins saying, 'We must have peace. The army has been under perfect control and …' He paused, collapsed [into his seat] and the assembly broke up. Many men wept. They had hoped to see Ireland rise triumphantly from the tomb. The soldiers still guarded the portals. The resurrection was deferred.[7]

The difficulties some people had in accepting the Articles of Agreement or the Agreement and subsequent Constitution of Saorstát Éireann were not confined to any single element, but contained several areas inhibiting, among other things, complete self-determination.

The pro-Treaty TDs met a week later at the Mansion House where they ratified the Treaty and established a Provisional Government in accordance with Article 17. A Constitutional Committee was also established about this time and was tasked with drafting a constitution with Michael Collins and David Lloyd George agreeing that the draft constitution would be shown to the British cabinet for approval before being published by the Provisional Government.

The partition of Ireland, through the Government of Ireland Act 1920 and the subsequent acceptance of the Treaty, isolated Donegal to the extent that the county was now bordered by 140 km of the separated Six Counties and only 9 km of the newly established Free State: this practically cut Donegal off from the remainder of the twenty-six counties.

The *Derry People and Tirconaill News* carried a letter in its edition of Saturday 7 January from B. O'Donnell, Ballylar, Fanad, County Donegal, which gave an indication of the frustration within the rank and file of the Irish Republican Army and the desire for all Volunteers to have their voices heard:

> A chara – As an IRA man who was loyal to the Republic both in the field and the prison, may I point out the grave dangers involved in the muzzling of the men who won the position Ireland holds today. We may be only 5 per cent of the people as Mr Griffith says, or we may be more, but it was we who made Lloyd George call the Truce, and we have the right to be heard, whoever is silenced. Now GHQ may go wrong, and may try to dupe us with promises of fresh efforts for the Republic later, but men of the rank and file demand the right to be heard. If it is refused and a political arrangement reached without our concurrence, and maybe misrepresentation, the outcome will be not peace but chaos. So I voice the opinion of scores of my comrades in demanding that the ban on the rank and file be raised

and Volunteers listened to before this bogus peace be ratified. Let a Volunteer convention be held and the views of the men who fought be heard before any politicians pretend to speak for them.[8]

The issue of army unity following the Treaty vote led to much focus on holding a convention to decide on what direction should be taken by the IRA. The Volunteers of the IRA, or at least the majority, were of the opinion that they were fighting for an Irish Republic and not a partitioned state, which was the outcome of the Treaty. To address the many issues arising from the Treaty vote, meetings were planned, chiefly by those opposed to it, with a view to organising a convention to decide on what policy to adopt in light of the new developments. The priority for the anti-Treaty IRA was to establish an Army Council, which was formed on Wednesday 11 January and continued allegiance to the Republic was declared. The prominent members of the IRA responsible for forming the Army Council included Liam Lynch, Rory O'Connor, Ernie O'Malley and James O'Donovan. These individuals were also to the fore in advocating for an Army Convention to decide what policy the IRA would adopt regarding the Treaty.

In contrast Frank Aiken, OC 4th Northern Division, Louth and south Armagh, was opposed to a convention because it would create a definite split in the IRA. Aiken was of the opinion that a division would create a situation where passions would be roused and guns would go off. He opposed holding a convention until after the publication of the promised republican constitution on the basis that the army would be divided and its influence on the situation would be reduced to nil. Aiken's opinion was that this would create two armies in the country and that it would only be a matter of time before 'some fool' would do something which would start a civil war. However, the anti-Treaty IRA Army Council was prepared to put its faith in the electorate and decided that no action would be taken against the pro-Treaty side, no matter what the outcome of the Army Convention was, until the publication of the Saorstát Éireann Constitution and the holding of a general election.

The divisional commandants of the anti-Treaty IRA met at the

Mansion House, Dublin, on Monday 9 January. The atmosphere was tense and passions were raised with Liam Lynch addressing the meeting in what was described as the most impressive speech of the day, although he broke down, overcome with emotion, in the course of it. The general feeling was that a disastrous position had been reached in the army and that was the end of unity. Aiken's argument was that by waiting to hold a convention after the publication of the Constitution, 'we can all see clearly whether we have to split and with whom we have to split'. With the exception of Frank Aiken, all other officers agreed that an Army Convention should be held and instructions were given to begin organising it.[9]

Chapter 8

1922 – The Released Prisoners and the Condemned Prisoners

The British continued to honour their commitment regarding convicted prisoners and began releasing all pre-Truce detainees on Thursday 12 January. Many arrived home on Monday 16 January to enthusiastic receptions. The names of the men from Donegal and the 1st Northern Division were M. McRory, Buncrana; Patrick O'Donnell, Magheraban, Buncrana; D. McLaughlin, Buncrana; John Bradley, Glebe, Buncrana; John Doherty, Cornershesk, Killygordon; James Creaney, Buncrana; Joe McCranahan, Meeting House, Strabane; Dan McRory, Minagh, Buncrana; Neil Blaney, Rossnakill, Fanad and C. Corr, Tullymore.[1]

There were great celebrations throughout Fanad on the return of Neil Blaney from Dartmoor Prison, where he had been serving a term of five years' penal servitude. A large contingent of his old comrades travelled to Letterkenny to meet him. Bonfires illuminated the sky and crowds of cheering people met them at different locations along the route to Rossnakill, Fanad.[2]

These releases coincided with attempts to thwart the trial in Belfast of Patrick Johnston, Thomas McShea and Patrick Leonard, who were charged with the murder of the two policemen, Gorman and Lyttle, following the botched escape attempt from Derry Jail. The Belfast IRA received orders to kidnap the chief witness, Warder Michael Finnegan, who aided the prisoners' escape attempt. It was surmised that if he was prevented from attending the court, the prosecution could not prove a case against the two Volunteers. Finding ways to kidnap him proved difficult, so it was decided that his brother should be contacted and instructed to visit and take him for a walk to a location within the camp that would make it easier to carry out the kidnap. Finnegan's brother lived near Carrickmacross, County Monaghan and agreed to take part in the plan.

The operation proved successful due to the daring of a Belfast IRA officer named Seamus Timmoney who planned and executed it. On Thursday 12 January, McShea, Johnston and Leonard were taken from Crumlin Road Jail to the courthouse through its underground tunnel, for their hearing. The three men were just entering the dock when the Attorney General for the Belfast government, Richard Best, informed the court that the principal witness had disappeared from the military camp. However, his absence would not disrupt the trial of the prisoners as his evidence was on record in the form of affidavits and his non-appearance would only prevent the prisoners' legal team from cross-examining him. This information was quickly conveyed to the IRA who immediately released Finnegan with instructions to make his way to the courthouse.

At the very moment when the judge was ordering the removal of the prisoners back to the jail, someone entered the court stating that Finnegan had been seen nearby. The judge then ordered the trial to continue. However, the prosecution considered Finnegan a hostile witness due to his refusal to identify Leonard, McShea or Johnston. Despite this, the three men were convicted and sentenced to death by hanging, with the executions being scheduled for Thursday 9 February.[3] The other prisoners involved in the escape attempt and initially charged with the murders of Constables Gorman and Lyttle were Patrick Tully, Francis Gallagher, Patrick Maguire, Peter O'Donnell, Patrick O'Reilly, Francis Sheridan, James J. Fitzpatrick, Bernard Sweeney, James McNulty, Patrick McAteer, Hugh J. Timmins and Henry O'Loan. All twelve were present in the court and were acquitted when the prosecution entered a *nolle prosequi* (a formal notice of the abandonment of the trial against the men).

At the conclusion of the hearing the three condemned men were returned to Crumlin Road Jail and transferred by special train to Derry Jail on Saturday 14 January. As an additional security measure armed policemen were posted at every railway station the special train passed through. On arrival at Derry Railway Station, the prisoners were put into an armoured car and escorted to Derry Jail. Each man was put into separate cells in a section of the jail reserved for condemned men, conveniently located near where the scaffold was to be erected. Each prisoner was allocated a full-time warder by day and two at night. On Monday 16 January the men could hear the prison workman beginning the construction of the scaffold; this continued every day for the next few weeks. Within days of the men's sentencing Michael Collins appealed to James Craig, the leader of the Belfast parliament, to reverse or commute the death sentences, but his initial efforts fell on deaf ears.

In contemplation of the sentences being carried out Collins had been considering other options and was involved with senior IRA officers in both Ireland and England to ensure they did not take place. Anticipating that the sentence of death would be handed down, the IRA planned to liberate the three men from Derry Jail.

The escape party was *en route* to Derry on the day the condemned men were transferred back to Derry Jail. However, the would-be rescuers were arrested in what became known as the 'Monaghan Footballers' incident. The players and supporters of the Monaghan Football Club were on their way to Derry to play Derry County in the final of the Ulster Championship when the Special Constabulary held up their convoy of several cars at Dromore, County Tyrone, in a planned operation. All men were removed from the vehicles and arrested. Subsequent searches revealed documents relating to the escape, several revolvers and ammunition. In all, ten men were arrested including Daniel Hogan, OC 5th Northern Division, six other officers of that division, and members of the Monaghan football team. In an ironic twist, the ten were transferred to the same jail on Monday 16 January. The new IRA Chief of Staff, Eoin O'Duffy, responded to the arrests in an article published in the *Freeman's Journal*, in which he described the actions of the Special Constabulary as provocative. O'Duffy stated that the manner in which the detentions were made suggested that information had been sent from another station in County Tyrone. He claimed the men were only carrying the weapons as they were passing through hostile unionist areas and were travelling by car owing to the likelihood of a railway stoppage. O'Duffy took the matter up directly with the British authorities and said that unless they were released forthwith he would take retaliatory action.[4] With the arrest of the rescue party, the outlook for Leonard, McShea and Johnston remained bleak.

In the weeks following the Treaty ratification by Dáil Éireann the senior IRA personnel in the Six Counties formed an 'Ulster Council', which was made up of senior officers from the various divisional areas. These included Frank Aiken, who acted as chairman, and Major General Seán MacEoin, Deputy Director of Operations at GHQ Dublin. The first actions of the 'Ulster Council' were to counter the ongoing aggression of the Special Constabulary and the arrests of the officers of the 5th Northern Division. A decision was taken to mount a large-scale kidnap operation in the Six Counties with the targets being prominent unionists and senior members of the Special Constabulary. Before the abductions took place the full proposals, including the arrangements for detention, etc., were presented to General Eoin O'Duffy, Chief of Staff, Dáil forces, and General Richard Mulcahy, Minister for Defence; Michael Collins and Liam Lynch were also involved. Some amendments were made to the proposal regarding the detention of prisoners, but the plan was sanctioned at the highest level. The kidnap raids were to be carried out between 7 and 9 February with some fifty unionist politicians and members of the Special Constabulary targeted. The kidnap targets were then to be transferred to barracks in the twenty-six counties, including Drumboe Castle in Stranorlar. A number of prominent unionists were also targeted for abduction in County Donegal, including Major J. S. Myles from Ballyshannon, William Hamilton from Ballintra and Blacker Doughlas from Kinlough in County Leitrim. The house of T. J. Atkinson was visited, but he was not at home. Major Moore of Cliff House, Belleek, was also visited, but managed to evade capture.[5]

The sectarian violence that was primarily focused on the Six Counties spilled over into Donegal on Saturday evening, 21 January. On that occasion an inoffensive nationalist man was, without provocation, attacked by a unionist mob in the border village of Pettigo. This village is unique in that part of it lies in County Donegal and part in County

Fermanagh. The incident occurred in the Donegal portion and a number of Catholic residents attempted to intervene to save the man, but were prevented from doing so by a group of unionists who were described as 'the tolerant and respectable element of the population'. The attack escalated and five nationalists received severe beatings from the unionist mob. They could not ascertain any reason for the unionist attack except that the perpetrators had been drinking in a local public house during the evening. Some policemen arrived, but walked away again without doing anything. A priest and an officer of the republican police were sent for and they requested that the constabulary members arrest the attackers, but they declined to do so stating that they had no accommodation for them in the police barracks.[6]

The developing divisions within the IRA on the Treaty issue and the call for an IRA Convention were addressed in the January edition of *An t-Óglach*, the official newsletter of the IRA. The article endeavoured to quell divisions and stated that the ongoing issues had left the army absolutely unchanged:

> The Irish Volunteers were established 'to safeguard the rights and liberties of all people of Ireland'. They were always and are still the servants of Independence of the Irish nation. The Irish Republic was established by the vote of the Irish people at a general election and until the Irish people decide otherwise the Army of Ireland continues to be the Army of the Irish Republic. One of the outstanding characteristics of a good soldier is steadiness, he does not lose his head in any sudden emergency, he is not affected by any political propaganda from his duty or his discipline, he realises the safety of the nation at a time of national unsettlement depends upon the discipline, solidarity, steadiness of its army. He obeys his orders and preserves the same outlook that he brought us through so many dangers, the outlook of a true soldier is being steady and loyal to the nation. The soldiers of Ireland have been the friends and defenders of the Irish nation in the past they were always and remains [sic] so; they are of the people, for the people, they have not taken arms to bully and cow

1922 – The Released Prisoners and the Condemned Prisoners

the people, but to help and defend them. Their strength lies in the fact that they interpret the national will, constitutionally expressed. The army continues under the same command, the personnel of its officers is unchanged. The differences of opinion with regard to the question of political expediency will not be allowed to affect the fine spirit and common discipline for which our army is renowned.[7]

The month of February brought new problems for the new Provisional Government with Cumann na mBan rejecting the Treaty, in contrast to the majority within Sinn Féin who elected to support it. The national organisation of Cumann na mBan arranged a special convention in Dublin on Sunday 5 February to discuss the terms of the Treaty. At the conclusion of the meeting, the delegates voted 419 to 63 to reaffirm their allegiance to the Republic and against the Treaty; all female TDs voted against its acceptance.[8]

The planned kidnappings of what turned out to be forty-two prominent unionists and members of the Special Constabulary began on Wednesday 8 February: most were carried out successfully with the exception of operations at Lisnaskea and Enniskillen in County Fermanagh. A party of IRA men was making its way to Donegal with three hostages when their car was involved in a minor accident with another vehicle. The vehicle belonged to John McCarroll from Lisnaskea, who was later traced and arrested. In the operation at Enniskillen, the Special Constabulary surprised the kidnap party and all twelve men were arrested, later being convicted and receiving sentences of five to ten years' penal servitude.[9]

The kidnappings provoked a vicious reaction from the Special Constabulary in County Tyrone. The village of Clady on the Tyrone/Donegal border was the scene of an assault by the sectarian police in the early hours of Friday 10 February. During clashes with the Special Constabulary, numerous residents were injured and one of the constables was killed. In anticipation of reprisals, many of the residents evacuated the village later that day. The nationalist community in the village, some of whom were prominent republicans, received notices with the Castlederg postmark: 'Prepare for death if Baird and Yorke are not released – Red

Hand Gang'. John Baird and Albert Yorke were among the forty-two prominent unionists: both were from the Clady area, but had been kidnapped in Strabane.[10]

The kidnappings of the unionists created great unease between James Craig and Michael Collins. The Belfast government was incensed and considered sending raiding parties into Donegal and Monaghan to rescue the kidnapped men. James Craig put to Winston Churchill the question of whether there was 'any legal obstacle to our sending a flying column of 5,000 Constabulary to recover the kidnapped unionists'. He suggested that a response to the actions in the Six Counties could have been a British military invasion of portions of Donegal that would then be occupied until the kidnapped were returned. However, Churchill warned against such action, arguing that it could create a situation whereby the Provisional Government would resign and authority would pass to the IRA Executive.[11]

The plight of Thomas McShea, Patrick Johnston and Patrick Leonard remained high on Michael Collins' agenda. The failed plan to liberate the men, which had led to the kidnappings of the prominent unionists, remained at the forefront of his mind. The staff at GHQ in Dublin had been considering another plan to prevent the death sentences being carried out and their attention switched to England. About that time Patrick Daly, OC Liverpool IRA, was in Dublin to meet with Collins and during a meeting at the Gresham Hotel it was suggested that the two hangmen, who both lived in England, should be either kidnapped or executed. Collins was in favour of execution and instructed Daly to return to England to carry out the operation. This task had a Donegal connection as James Cunningham from Carrick in the south of the county was one of the men chosen to be involved in the operation. Cunningham, OC Birmingham IRA, had been very active from 1919 to 1921 in procuring weapons and ammunition for use in Ireland. He happened to be in Liverpool in early February with a consignment of weapons and found himself in the middle of the operation to prevent either of the English hangmen from travelling to Ireland. Paddy Daly was in charge and had instructions to put both John Ellis and William Willis, two of the government's official hangmen, under surveillance – and at the appropriate opportunity to assassinate them.

Daly began making enquiries about the two hangmen and discovered that Ellis lived in Rochdale, near Manchester, and Willis lived in Manchester. He was also informed that a photograph of them both with a former colleague was displayed in the 'snug' of a public house in Rochdale. The men of the Liverpool Company travelled to Rochdale and visited the pub to familiarise themselves with the appearance of the pair. Two teams of Volunteers were then sent to Rochdale and Manchester. The Rochdale party arrived at its destination and called at Ellis' home, but he was not there. Meanwhile the other party's car broke down *en route* to Manchester. It transpired that Ellis had already left for Belfast.[12]

A few days before the execution date, Thomas McShea had a visit from a friend called John Conlon. As McShea was being taken from his cell to the visiting area, he observed a man being admitted to the prison. He said to the warder escorting him, 'That man coming in is Ellis the executioner?' but the warder did not answer. Thomas McShea's visit with John Conlon was very emotional. Conlon said to McShea in a trembling voice: 'I have called out to your place to see your mother and I found her bearing up against all her worries and troubles with remarkable fortitude.' He then added: 'I have come here to tell you that in case I do not see you again your mother will be in my special care whilst she lives and whilst I live. As long as I have a shilling she will get half of it.' Conlon then completely broke down and had to be helped away by two prison warders.[13]

Frantic efforts were being made by people from all over the country to secure a reprieve for the condemned men. The Derry City Corporation held a meeting in the days leading up to the execution, which was presided over by Hugh C. O'Doherty, nationalist mayor. The issue of the condemned men was discussed and a deputation was selected to go to Dublin to petition Collins and Griffith, who told them to leave the matter with them as they were due to travel to London where they would raise the matter with the British government. While in London, Collins championed the cause of Leonard, McShea and Johnston and secured reprieves for them. The kidnappings of the prominent unionists obviously played a part in this. The three prisoners were later taken from Derry Jail under heavily armed escort and transferred to Larne. From there, they were taken to Stanraer in Scotland by boat and then on to Peterhead Jail. They remained prisoners there until their release in August 1925.[14]

Meanwhile back in Donegal a tragedy occurred late on Monday 13 February resulting in the deaths of an IRA officer and a Volunteer. Captain Hugh Britton and Volunteers James Gallagher and Malachy Doherty were in a public house belonging to John Gallagher, Donegal Town, when they were approached by a man claiming to be a British soldier based at Finner Camp. He introduced himself as Alfred Thompson, from Rotherhythe in London, and said that he had deserted from the camp. He claimed that when he absconded he took some weapons and ammunition with him, concealing them outside Ballyshannon. He asked them, if he handed the arms over to them, would they hand them over to the military, but Hugh Britton said they had nothing to do with that. Thompson said if they got a car, he would take them to the place where they would get the arms and ammunition. The Volunteers decided to look at Thompson's arms cache and made their way up the street to get a loan of a car from Patrick Meehan, which was driven by James Brogan. Before they set off, Thompson asked if either of the men were armed, to which Malachy Doherty said it did not matter whether they were or not. Britton then asked Thompson if he was armed and he pulled out a revolver and fired at Britton, who leapt to the side and the bullet struck James Gallagher. Doherty produced a revolver, pointed at Thompson and pulled the trigger, but it failed to fire.

Doherty and Britton then jumped Thompson and a struggle ensued with Thompson firing off a further four shots before he was disarmed. Thompson then made a run for it and got away. Britton was wounded during the struggle and crawled along the street knocking on doors for help. Several doors were opened but quickly closed again, before the residents of one house came to his aid and carried him on a makeshift stretcher to the infirmary at the local workhouse. The injured men were attended by three doctors from the area, but to no avail as both later died from their wounds. The IRA Volunteers later arrested Thompson on the evening of Wednesday 15 February when John Travers and Hugh Gallagher discovered him near Laghey village, several miles from Donegal Town, and took him to Drumboe Castle, then in the charge of the IRA. Thompson was subsequently handed over to the British military on Friday 24 February.

In a follow-up to the shooting incident the IRA also arrested Ernest Lawson, a former British soldier, on 15 February. Lawson co-managed a public house with his mother in Donegal Town. When the IRA arrived at his home, he produced a revolver, but surrendered when he was informed that he was being arrested on suspicion of having information regarding the whereabouts of Thompson and the shooting.

The funerals of Captain Hugh Britton and James Gallagher of E Company, 2nd Battalion, No. 4 Brigade, 1st Northern Division took place on Thursday 16 February in Donegal Town. The townspeople witnessed impressive scenes with approximately 3,000 attending. The coffins, draped in Tricolours, were carried on the shoulders of their comrades while members of Cumann na mBan carried floral tributes and recited the rosary in Irish. Following interment at the Old Abbey graveyard, three volleys were fired over the graves and the 'Last Post' sounded.

Ernest Lawson was charged before a republican court in Donegal Town with unlawful possession of a revolver. He pleaded guilty and was ordered to pay a fine of £2 and costs of £3. Presiding over the court, P. J. McGoldrick, IRA brigade officer, said no irresponsible persons would be allowed to have revolvers. It did not matter whether a man was a Protestant or a Catholic, he would get fair play at republican courts. Replying to McGoldrick, the unionist Lawson said he had no objection to the manner in which he had been treated since his arrest.[15] The inquest into the deaths of Hugh Britton and James Gallagher returned a verdict of wilful murder against Alfred Thompson.[16]

The end of the kidnapping saga was confirmed at a meeting of the British cabinet on Thursday 16 February, which was told that James Craig 'had offered to give favourable consideration to the question of the release of certain Irish Republican Army officers recently arrested in Ulster, after the Irish Provisional Government had secured the release of the Ulster residents recently kidnapped'. Craig's softening position was short-lived and had conditions attached. The release of republican prisoners was on condition that the Provisional Government would recognise the validity of the decisions of the Northern Irish courts and that no further requests for the release of prisoners would be made on political grounds.[17] Craig honoured the agreement reached with Michael Collins, and the ten IRA men arrested at Dromore in County Tyrone in January were released into the custody of the British military and driven to County Donegal.[18]

In anticipation of further IRA activity and attacks along the border areas a large number of Special Constabulary men were deployed to locations close to the Donegal border. On Friday 17 February, large numbers of A-Specials were moved into Garrison in County Fermanagh, approximately three miles from Belleek. Another company of Specials commandeered Clonelly House near Pettigo.[19] Commandant General Joe Sweeney raised this new development along the Donegal border in correspondence to the Provisional Government's Minister for Defence, Richard Mulcahy:

> We hold Lifford and Clady bridges but we have not the arms to protect our people in Pettigo and Belleek. In the latter area the RIC, Black and Tans and Specials are intolerable and unless your Liaison can get these forces withdrawn from their present position on the Donegal side there will be serious trouble. The Barracks they now occupy is a regular fortress and possession of it would give us control of the whole town …[20]

Throughout February the RIC continued to evacuate some of the rural barracks in County Donegal, which were subsequently taken over by the IRA. However, the barracks were being taken over by the two different sides of the IRA: those opposed and those in support of the Treaty. Despite this, the Tricolour was immediately hoisted from the windows of each station under occupation. The evacuations were witnessed by large numbers of people who cheered loudly when the flags were raised. On Monday evening, 20 February, 150 members of the RIC from various stations in Donegal arrived in Derry for demobilisation.[21]

1922 – The Released Prisoners and the Condemned Prisoners

The Truce period was marred with further tragedy on Tuesday night, 21 February 1922. On that occasion an IRA party from the Milford area, under the command of Captain Joseph Duffy of Lough Road, Milford, was in the process of carrying out a raid on the house of Leslie Huddlestone, a former British army officer, at the Cairn, Ramelton. The party approached the house, knocked on the door, and a voice was heard from inside, asking, 'Who is there?' A member of the raiding party said he had a message and someone from inside instructed him to slip it under the door. At that moment Captain Duffy arrived to take charge of the situation and as he was approaching the door a shot was fired from inside the house striking him in the abdomen. He stumbled back into the arms of his comrades and died almost immediately.[22]

News of the incident was relayed to Peadar O'Donnell later that night as he and Seamus McCann were sitting by the fire at a hotel in Lifford. An IRA man from Milford named McCafferty walked in to report the shooting. O'Donnell was very upset and said that Duffy was one of his best company captains during the War of Independence. O'Donnell issued an order for the seizure of all weapons held by civilians in the Milford area.[23] The following day an estimated 1,000 IRA men arrived in Milford for Captain Duffy's funeral. At the inquest held in Milford the following Thursday, 2 March, the jury found that Duffy died from shock and haemorrhage due to a gunshot wound. It also found that he was acting officially when he was killed, owing to the failure of the his subordinate to command admission in the proper manner.

The Milford parish court was held in the schoolroom at Milford workhouse on Thursday 9 March and at the conclusion of the cases before it, the court passed a resolution of condolence to Joseph Duffy's mother and family. The chairman, Anthony McElwee, said:

> As this is our first meeting since the lamented death of our much respected townsman, Captain Joseph Duffy, I am sure I am voicing the feelings of my brother magistrates and of those present when I say we were deeply grieved and shocked to hear of his untimely end, and to extend our sincerest sympathy to his mother and other members of

the family. I have known Joseph Duffy since he was a child, and it tells well of his character that no one can point to a single act of his that his friends need to be ashamed of. He was identified with Sinn Féin from the beginning and continued to uphold it in the dark and stormy days when it was very unsafe to be even suspected to be in sympathy with the movement. I hope in the New Ireland there will be many boys like him – good, faithful and true. He said but little, but if there was duty to be done and risks to be run, no more staunch or fearless comrade was to be found than Captain Duffy. He was the sole support of his mother, a woman far advanced in years and I trust it can never be said of the people of Milford, the members of Sinn Féin and IRA that they were so ungrateful as to allow her to suffer want or discomfort during the few remaining years of her life.[24]

The acceptance of the Treaty and the formation of the Provisional Government in mid-January had further diminished the authority of the RIC in the new state. The transfer of powers from London to Dublin created a period of confusion as to policing – a lawless vacuum had been created in which unrestrained gangs of criminals roamed certain areas of Donegal. The initial targets of these bands were unionist shopkeepers and farmers. There was great uncertainty as to who would ensure order and to whom crimes were to be reported.

The issue of policing had been addressed by the Provisional and British governments in January. However, this only related to the disbandment of the RIC. The Provisional Government had subsequently convened a meeting at the Gresham Hotel in Dublin on 9 February where it was decided that a civic guard would be established. In the interim, the function of policing was to continue under the authority of the local IRA. However, with the IRA split over the Treaty, both sides assumed authority and this created problems.[25]

This issue was brought to the fore in County Donegal in February following a series of robberies in many areas including Stranorlar and Killygordon. The IRA men based in Ballybofey were made aware of the crime spree and immediately conducted investigations resulting in a series of arrests. In Donegal Town and surrounding areas the residents and business community first addressed the issue of criminal activity and policing by convening a meeting to address the rise in criminal activity in the area. On Wednesday 22 February it was decided to establish a volunteer police guard for the area until other arrangements were made. A committee was appointed made up of local businessmen and clergy. Patrick Gallagher, solicitor and president of the Richard Bonner Sinn Féin Cumann, presided and instructed the group to raise voluntary subscriptions for the temporary maintenance of the IRA police to be based at the former RIC barracks.[26]

The following day a party of IRA men under the command of Commandant James Walsh was on patrol at the Milford Fair with instructions to stop and search all vehicles entering the town. Three IRA men spotted two men running up the street away from their post and going into Alcorn's grocery shop. The IRA men pursued them, entered the shop and ordered the two to raise their hands: but one man did not obey. The order was given again and then a third time but the other man put his hand into his coat pocket, drawing a weapon and was immediately shot dead by Patrick Connolly. The deceased was Charles Herbert Burns, a former British soldier who came from Kilmacrennan. It was not known why the pair ran away from the IRA patrol.[27]

On Wednesday 22 and Thursday 23 February an Extraordinary Sinn Féin Ard Fheis was held at the Mansion House, Dublin, to interpret the constitution of the organisation in view of Dáil Éireann's acceptance of the Treaty. The two-thirds majority required for an amendment provided for a tense encounter. Resolutions were presented by de Valera, Collins and Griffith on the Treaty, elections and the Saorstát Éireann Constitution. Efforts were made to hold a vote on aspects of the three topics, but fears of a split brought about the postponement of a vote on the Treaty and instead it was agreed that the elections should be delayed for three months after the publication of the Constitution. The ard fheis was then adjourned for three months.[28]

Chapter 9

The Special Powers Bill and the Six-County Policy

The partition of Ireland posed an uncertain future for the nationalist population of the Six Counties. Having endured the wrath of the unionist population through the pogroms of 1920 in Banbridge, Lisburn, Belfast and elsewhere, they now found themselves under the control of a unionist government. Their situation deteriorated further following the introduction of the Special Powers Bill in March 1922. This piece of legislation by the Belfast government was a firm indication that the nationalist population would be subjected to the autocratic authority of the unionist government. The bill would supersede trial by jury, abolish inquests and introduce the use of flogging, imprisonment and the death penalty. Possession of weapons and ammunition could result in a jail term of three years' penal servitude and ten lashes with the cat-o'-nine-tails, which was a whip of nine narrow pieces of leather tipped with metal balls. The absurdity was that unionists were granted permits to carry guns and in many instances accompanied the Special Constabulary in sectarian attacks, while nationalists found with weapons as a defensive measure were subjected to a jail term and flogging with the 'cat'. The Special Powers Bill was criticised by some English newspapers. An article published in the *Manchester Guardian* and later quoted in the *Irish Independent* on Monday 27 March stated:

> Whilst envenomed politicians in the Ulster Parliament are voting themselves power to use torture and capital punishment against

citizens whom they forbid to defend themselves while they scarcely attempt to protect them from massacre, some of their own partisans in Belfast carry wholesale murder to refinements of barbarity hardly surpassed in the Turkish atrocities in America and Constantinople.

The Civil Authorities (Special Powers) Act received the royal assent on Friday 7 April effectively giving the Belfast government dictatorship laws.[1]

While the nationalists of the Six Counties were faced with such dire prospects, some at the highest echelons of the Provisional Government were galvanising support for the continuation of war against the northern state. In February 1922 Richard Mulcahy told the North Eastern Advisory Committee, which had been established to communicate nationalist opinion to the Provisional Government, that his relationship with the Belfast government gave a perception of accepting the Treaty, a necessary façade to present in order to allow him the opportunity to destroy it. Michael Collins told the IRA's 2nd Northern Division at a meeting in Dublin that although the Treaty might have seemed like an outward acceptance of partition, the government had decided that they would make it impossible for the partition to continue in existence. He claimed partition would never be recognised even though it might mean smashing the Treaty.[2]

Meanwhile, the Treaty continued to cause much disquiet among the ranks of the Irish Republican Army. The lack of adequate leadership in addressing the issues prompted the anti-Treaty IRA to take the initiative in organising a convention, which would allow representatives from the various IRA divisions an opportunity to express their views and concerns. As part of this process, notifications, which included instructions for copies to be sent to all companies for the selection of delegates, were distributed to all divisional areas on Wednesday 1 March:

> A General Convention of the Irish Republican Army will be held on the 26th March 1922 … As a preliminary to this Convention you will arrange to summon a special meeting of your Company not later than

the 12th March 1922. At this meeting Delegates will be elected by ballot to represent the Company at a Brigade Convention to be held not later than the 17th March 1922 ...[3]

Despite the tension escalating between the pro- and anti-Treaty sides on the surface, behind the scenes a cooperative approach to the problem of partition was developing under the direction of leading figures from both sides including Michael Collins, Richard Mulcahy and Liam Lynch. Planning for the northern campaign also involved Eoin O'Duffy, who was directed by Collins to begin discreetly organising for an offensive on the Six Counties using the bordering counties, including Donegal, as a base. The operation began in late February with conferences held at which Liam Lynch and his staff and Michael Collins and his chief advisors were present. At one of these meetings it was decided that both the pro- and anti-Treaty IRA would select officers for the campaign in Ulster. It was agreed that IRA officers from Munster would be appointed with a staff of officers to assist them and that they were to proceed to Counties Donegal, Louth, Monaghan and Cavan. Michael Collins insisted on one thing: when things got going in earnest all activities were to be in the name of the anti-Treaty IRA.

Another element of the agreement was the exchange of weapons recently received from the British with those from the Cork brigades to avoid embarrassment for Collins when dealing with the British government in the event of a rifle falling into the hands of the British.[4] Liam Lynch was heavily involved with Michael Collins in the plan to dispatch north a large consignment of arms.[5] In the meantime Collins sent a messenger to Joe Sweeney to say he was sending arms to Donegal and that they were to be handed over to a certain person. He did not say who the individual was, but that someone would come to Donegal later with credentials. As soon as the weapons arrived, the local IRA spent a couple of days removing the serial numbers with hammers and chisels – to prevent the guns being identified later. Sometime later Joe Sweeney received a dispatch from Johnny Haughey requesting to meet him at Greencastle in the hills above Omagh and it transpired that Haughey was the contact. Over 400 rifles were taken into the Six Counties by Dan McKenna and Johnny Haughey shortly afterwards.[6]

One of the officers selected to go to Donegal was Seán Lehane from County Cork, who had served under Tom Barry during the War of Independence. Lehane was to serve as the officer commanding the 1st Northern Division comprising Donegal and portions of Tyrone and Fermanagh. A short time later Charlie Daly from County Kerry and former OC 2nd Northern Division, County Tyrone, was appointed as Lehane's second in command, with many other officers and volunteers from the southern divisions also being directed to Donegal.[7] There was another major consideration behind the joint IRA offensive – it was hoped that agreement on a common IRA strategy would halt the widening divisions and therefore avoid the outbreak of civil war.[8]

Charlie Daly had been opposed to the Treaty from the outset, which had consequently led to his demotion. This was communicated to him through correspondence from the pro-Treaty IRA Chief of Staff Eoin O'Duffy at GHQ Beggars Bush. The correspondence, dated 4 March 1922, stated that following a meeting of the 2nd Northern Division and brigade officers held on Thursday 2 March, O'Duffy had decided to transfer Daly from the position of divisional commandant to that of organiser with the director of organisation's staff. Daly had held this position before being appointed to command the 2nd Northern Division. O'Duffy said that Daly's appointment as OC 2nd Northern Division was only on a temporary basis as there was no local man capable of taking on the role in the absence of Commandant Morris who had been imprisoned in Dartmoor Prison in England:

> I always considered that local men were better suited for such positions in every part of Ireland where proper men could be secured. It was not possible to get a local man capable of filling this position in the 2nd Northern Area until the return from Dartmoor of Commandant Morris. Immediately on his return I considered that he should be placed in a responsible position on the staff with a view to eventually putting him in charge of the division.

O'Duffy also referred to complaints made by officers of that division and said that some had declared they had no confidence in Daly's abilities as OC. Charlie Daly's response questioned the basis of the complaints and stated that he regarded his demotion as bizarre when his appointment as organiser was considered. He sent his reply from Whelan's Hotel, Eccles Street, Dublin, on Wednesday 8 March:

> After what occurred at the meeting of the Divisional and Brigade officers of the 2nd Northern Division at Beggars Bush on the 2nd inst., this communication has given me no small amount of surprise. If the statements made by you there were accurate I should not be fit to be offered any position of responsibility in the Army. After hearing all sorts of ridiculous complaints, which you tried to make the most out of, you accused me of being the only divisional commandant in Ireland who brought politics into my Army; of being insubordinate, of trying to obstruct GHQ and of putting my removal to what you called traitorous motives of GHQ. Notwithstanding all these grave accusations you now offer me a position on the director of organisation's staff.

Daly brought it to O'Duffy's attention that his correspondence was misleading and dishonest regarding the reasons why he was demoted. Daly had obviously received reports from some of those attending the meeting when he pointed out certain inaccuracies in O'Duffy's correspondence:

> In this communication you give a different reason for my removal to the ones you gave at the meeting at Beggars Bush. There you tried at first to make it appear before my staff and Brigade officers that it would be because of certain complaints which you received. When these, as a means, failed, you stated 'twas because of my youth and inexperience. Now you give an altogether different reason.

Charlie Daly believed his demotion was because of his opposition to the Treaty and the possibility that he could have secured the support of many men in the 2nd Northern Division to that end. Eoin O'Duffy had communicated his intentions to Richard Mulcahy, Minister for Defence, in a letter dated 21 February 1922. In the letter O'Duffy said he was not satisfied that Daly was capable of continuing in the position of divisional commandant. He had suggested Tom Morris as a suitable replacement. O'Duffy had earlier undermined Daly's authority by redirecting weapons destined for the 2nd Northern Division from Dundalk to his own command area of County Monaghan.[9] In the end Daly refused his new commission and subsequently resigned.

Meanwhile, with the plans for the Six Counties offensive in progress, efforts for the procurement of sufficient weapons and ammunition were increased. The IRA in England continued to obtain those items despite the strict terms laid down by the Truce. The Birmingham IRA, under the command of Donegal man James Cunningham, who had served as a gunrunner during the War of Independence, played a pivotal role in procuring weapons and ammunition. A Volunteer under Cunningham's command, Dan O'Malley, discovered an endless supply of .303 ammunition for Lee-Enfield rifles – the weapons of choice for the IRA. O'Malley had found a factory which had been set up on the outskirts of Birmingham for breaking down the surplus .303 ammunition to extract the brass and nickel content. The result was a weekly supply of between 800 and 1,000 rounds.

The Birmingham Company received orders from Dublin to raid the factory and remove as much of the ammunition as possible. James Cunningham selected twenty men for the mission, with a lorry and car also commandeered. The arrangement was that Cunningham was to meet O'Malley's contact at the factory gates, which were off the main thoroughfare. Cunningham was to wait there to admit the men at different intervals, as he was the only one who could identify the individual members. On the night of the planned raid, Cunningham knew something was not right when he met the contact at the front gate of the factory. When the gate was opened the contact refused to go into the factory grounds to open the doors of the building, insisting that he remain at the gate with Cunningham. After some time Cunningham persuaded him to walk towards the factory but he immediately started walking down the road in the opposite direction from which the other men had been told to approach. Suddenly two armed, plainclothes policemen jumped over a wall and arrested Cunningham. He was knocked to the ground and roughly handled before being taken to an office in the grounds of the factory.

The plan was for the other men to approach the factory gates in pairs at different intervals. Patrick Daly, the Liverpool IRA OC, was moving towards the factory gate with another man, but became suspicious when Cunningham was not there to admit them as arranged. The two men walked a short distance away from the gate and awaited developments. A little time later, a figure climbed over the gate and ran up the road. Daly knew things were not right and the two decided to leave the area. As they walked through the adjoining streets they noticed uniformed policemen, and plainclothes police, identifiable by white armbands, standing at various locations along the road. The two men began talking loudly about current topics in their best English accents and succeeded in getting through undetected. Other IRA men were arrested when they approached the factory and, within two hours, six members of the raiding party were brought into the office where Cunningham was being held. They were then bundled into a lorry and taken to Steel House Lane Police Station in Birmingham. There was a general round-up that night with raids in Hanley, Liverpool, Manchester, Newcastle and Dewsbury. Meanwhile, Daly and the other IRA man decided to make their way to Cunningham's boarding house and wait there for the night. A party of detectives raided the house at approximately 2 a.m. the following morning and the two men were ordered downstairs to be questioned. After a long period of interrogation, the pair successfully convinced the detectives that they were labourers and were allowed to return to their rooms. As they did so, one of the detectives shouted after them, 'You are lucky you are not with your friend Jim tonight.'

In the days following the arrests, Patrick Daly organised legal assistance for the prisoners and made his way to London to secure the necessary funds from the Irish Self-Determination League. This organisation was responsible for raising funds for the Irish government. Daly met with Art O'Brien, who was chairman of the organisation, and the necessary arrangements were made. Daly then reported to Sam Maguire, Head Centre of the IRB in England, to inform him of the circumstances relating to the arrests. The IRA men were held until 8 June when they were released on bail raised by the Irish Self-Determination League. They immediately returned to Ireland, forfeiting the bail, and reported to the Four Courts where an inquiry was established in an attempt to discover the circumstances of their arrests and the general round-up, but the inquiry failed to identify the source of the leak.[10]

Meanwhile back in Donegal an unidentified group carried out an attack on the old constabulary barracks at Newtowncunningham, then occupied by pro-Treaty forces. Shortly after 11 p.m. on Saturday 25 March a number of cars arrived in the village and soon afterwards their occupants launched an attack on the barracks. The assailants opened with a few intermittent rifle shots, developing into something in the nature of a pitched battle. The attacking party occupied points of vantage overlooking the building on which they opened up with heavy gunfire, the Dáil troops vigorously replying in kind. The inhabitants of the village were terror-struck as the noise of rifle and revolver fire continued for almost two hours. Although they were unidentified, it was suspected that the attacking party was a group of the Special Constabulary who had travelled from their base in Derry. The barracks were evacuated a short time later and were then occupied by anti-Treaty IRA forces.

The escalating sectarian violence that was sweeping through the Six Counties brought further tragedy to County Donegal. Edward McKinney from Desertegney near Buncrana was employed by the McMahon family as a barman and was staying in their family home at 3 Kinnaird Gardens, off the Antrim Road in north Belfast, when he was murdered in the incident known as the McMahon family massacre. The killing of the McMahon family took place in the early hours of Friday 24 March during the hours of curfew. The murder gang, consisting of one man dressed in civilian clothing accompanied by four others dressed in RIC caps and waterproof coats, attacked the McMahon family home with a sledgehammer. It was approximately 1.20 a.m. when the hall door was smashed in. The four men in police uniforms rushed up the stairs and ordered all the male members of the family including Edward McKinney downstairs to the dining room. The women of the house, Mrs McMahon, her daughter and her niece (Mary Downey) were taken into the kitchen. Mrs McMahon got down on her knees and pleaded for mercy, but was struck on the side of the head and fell to the floor. Meanwhile the seven men were told to say their prayers. Owen McMahon asked why they were being singled out, to which a gang member said he was a papist – a respected papist – and looked upon as a leader among papists in the city. With that, the gang proceeded to shoot the seven boys and men. Four were killed instantly and another succumbed to his injuries later in hospital. The dead were: Owen McMahon (50), Francis McMahon (24), Patrick McMahon (22), Gerald McMahon (15) and Edward McKinney. One of the other McMahon children was seriously injured and was removed to hospital. John McMahon was shot in the neck and later recalled the incident from his hospital bed: 'The leader said, "you boys say your prayers" and at that same moment he and the others fired volley after volley at us. I think I lay on the floor for half an hour before the ambulance came. Three or four regular RIC came too.'

Twelve-year-old Michael McMahon also survived the massacre, though fired at several times. He did this by dodging between his father and brothers and finally by creeping under a sofa. The funerals of the four McMahons were held on the afternoon of Sunday 26 March under a heavy British military presence. In anticipation of attacks on the funeral cortège, the British military lined the streets from north Belfast to Milltown Cemetery in west Belfast.

Unknown to the loyalist mob or the McMahon family at the time, Edward McKinney was an IRA Volunteer and this was later confirmed by IRA GHQ. His membership of the IRA was concealed after the killing as it would have given the police and loyalist mob an opportunity to justify their actions. Winston Churchill described the murders as 'worse than cannibalism'. The murders of Edward McKinney and the McMahon family members were said to be in reprisal for the killings of two Special Constables earlier that day and were carried out by their colleagues. McKinney's remains arrived at Buncrana on Saturday morning, 25

The Special Powers Bill and the Six-County Policy

March, and his funeral took place at Cockhill Chapel at 11.30 a.m. the following morning and was very largely attended by the local population. A resolution of sympathy to the family of Edward McKinney was issued by the unionist community of Desertegney the following Friday, 31 March.[11]

In the aftermath of the McMahon massacre, the anti-Treaty IRA GHQ issued a statement to the effect that if further attacks against nationalists in the Six Counties took place, immediate reprisals would follow. Around the same time, the Provisional Government was coming under increasing pressure from the British government on the issue of the IRA and the plans for an Army Convention to be held in late March. The British declared that the IRA was under the control of the Provisional Government and therefore answerable for the continuation of the boycott policy and skirmishes along the Donegal 'border'. The boycott policy had been introduced during the War of Independence, and involved a boycott of products from English and unionist firms. In many cases this meant the commandeering and often destruction of products to prevent their sale in shops in Donegal. In mid-March, Arthur Griffith, on behalf of the Dáil Éireann cabinet, declared the impending IRA Convention illegal. Despite the announcement of the ban, the leaders of both sides continued to engage in negotiations in an attempt to heal the rift. Terms, designed to prevent a split in the IRA, agreed between Richard Mulcahy and Liam Lynch were rejected by the Dáil on Tuesday 21 March.[12]

Around this time, while much of the public's attention was focused on the political situation in the country, many areas of County Donegal were experiencing great economic distress. The situation in west Donegal was extremely bad, caused by a lack of local employment and failed crops, exacerbated by the lack of work in England and Scotland, which was generally a good source of employment for many people in the county. About this time Maud Gonne MacBride was travelling throughout Donegal on behalf of the White Cross, an organisation formed in America for the purpose of raising and distributing funds to the poor in Ireland. MacBride's mission was to gauge the hardships being experienced by the people of the county. She endeavoured to draw the attention of the political leaders to the miserable conditions being endured in some parts of County Donegal. In a letter to Arthur Griffith she wrote:

> I returned from Donegal on Wednesday evening. The situation in the Rosses and in some of the islands and local lands along the coast is very serious and will be so till the end of July when the potato harvest will ease things. There is actual famine in some districts and a few people have already died from want …

MacBride informed Griffith that the White Cross had allocated several thousand pounds to the worst affected areas and considered that a further amount of £20–25,000 would be needed. Her letter concluded with the harrowing story of the death of a man due to starvation:

> The Donegal people are very proud. I saw no beggars, but in one house where a man had died … I was told there was not a scrap of food to be found, people in Dungloe only knew of his great need when his wife crawled into town to beg for a priest.[13]

The government's response to this is unknown, but a further £2,175 was distributed to the worst affected areas by the White Cross.

Chapter 10

The IRA Convention and Split

The anti-Treaty IRA Convention was held in Dublin on Sunday 26 March 1922. There was great dissension among the ranks on the political issue of the Republic versus the Free State. Over 200 delegates attended, representing forty-nine brigades as well as officers from eight divisional staffs. The convention was held in defiance of the prohibition issued by Arthur Griffith and of an announcement by Richard Mulcahy, Minister for Defence, that every officer and Volunteer taking part in it would pay the penalty of suspension from the army. A letter to this effect was distributed to all divisional and brigade commandants in the days before the convention: 'All officers and men who attend the Convention on Sunday next … automatically sever their connection with the IRA. You are simply to regard them as suspended, and report on each case separately to GHQ'.[1]

The delegates met at the Mansion House for the private session and security was very tight, with a line of twenty men stationed at each entrance. A number of officers from the 1st Northern Division were in attendance, including Charlie Daly, Peadar O'Donnell, Seán Lehane, Frank O'Donnell, Joe O'Donnell, Seamus McCann and Alfie McCallion. The convention reaffirmed the IRA's allegiance to the Republic. In the gathering were a few grey beards, but the majority were young men in their late teens or early twenties. Very few wore uniforms, but the majority were clad in the familiar type of trench coat. They arrived in Dublin from all over the country with the session lasting for over twelve hours. Another convention was planned to discuss outstanding issues.² The convention also brought the anti-Treaty IRA under the control of an Executive Council whose members were selected by the delegates. The IRA dissolved its allegiance to Dáil Éireann and the following resolution was passed unanimously:

> That the Army re-affirms its allegiance to the Irish Republic; that it shall be maintained as the Army of the Irish Republic, under an Executive appointed by the Convention; that the Army shall be under the supreme control of such Executive, which shall draft a Constitution for and submission to, a subsequent Convention.³

An Executive of sixteen was elected to control the army. One of the decisions taken at the convention was to continue enforcing the boycott, which would contribute to the policy of undermining the authority of the Belfast government.

On Tuesday 28 March the Executive Council of the Irish Republican Army issued an order to all officers and other ranks at that time in the 'regular army' and members of the civic guard, which had been set up to take over policing duties, to return to their respective units and declared that recruiting for these forces should cease immediately. A policy of boycott was to apply to those who remained in the civic guard. The order also alleged that the Minister for Defence of Dáil Éireann and his staff were guilty of acts inimical to the Irish Republic. The council's order declared that from that date neither the Minister nor his chiefs of staff exercised any control over the IRA.⁴

Following the convention, Seán Lehane travelled to his former command area in west Cork to recruit experienced officers to go to Donegal in preparation for an assault on the Six Counties, which was to go ahead despite the widening split between the pro- and anti-Treaty sides. He secured the services of a large number of men, including Moss Donegan, Jack Fitzgerald, Seamus Cotter, Denis Galvin, Jim Lane, Denis O'Leary, Seán Fitzgerald, Billy O'Sullivan, Tom Mullins, John O'Donovan and Mick O'Donoghue, all experienced officers from the West Cork Brigade.⁵ Charlie Daly had also secured the services of over twenty men from Kerry, including Martin Quille, Daniel Enright, Timothy O'Sullivan, Michael McElligott, Patrick Clifford and Christie Broden.

The southern contingent travelled by lorry to Dublin and reported to the Four Courts where they were briefed by Liam Lynch, Joe McKelvey, Rory O'Connor and Liam Mellows. Starting on the Donegal/Derry border and using Donegal as a base, with cooperation from the pro-Treaty forces there, they were to make war on the crown forces along and inside the border. The pro-Treaty authorities – Collins in particular was mentioned – were to supply material help by way of equipment, arms, etc. The southern IRA left the Four Courts briefing with the impression that by creating war along the border, and with support from the pro-Treaty forces, the situation would revert to the pre-Truce pattern with both factions of the IRA fighting the crown forces.[6]

While the IRA was making preparations for the northern offensive there were indications that the British military was preparing to support the Special Constabulary, since troops formally based in County Tipperary were transferred to Enniskillen in February. The 1st Battalion of the Lincolnshires were initially deployed to Belleek Fort, in Donegal territory, but they abandoned the fort again in March and moved to Belleek village, which is in County Fermanagh. The fort was then occupied by a company of Dáil troops whose numbers were later strengthened by a large number of IRA Executive forces.[7]

Chapter 11

Changing of the Guard and the Belfast Boycott

The acceptance of the Treaty in January had signalled the official end of British military and RIC authority in the twenty-six counties. The wholesale evacuation of County Donegal had begun shortly afterwards, with military based in Letterkenny and Buncrana returning to Derry, and military based at Finner Camp sent to Strabane, Belleek and Enniskillen. The first move occurred in early February with 200 Royal Marines evacuating Buncrana. The RIC also left the county, leaving the various barracks and other premises open to occupation by the IRA Executive forces (anti-Treaty) or by Dáil forces (pro-Treaty). The Donegal Treaty liaison officer, Commandant Patrick Sheils, supervised the handover of barracks from the RIC. However, neither the military nor the RIC were familiar with who supported or who opposed the Treaty and they were mere spectators when the various barracks and buildings were seized by the different factions.

One of the first towns in County Donegal to be officially evacuated was Buncrana, where enthusiastic scenes were witnessed, with the barracks being evacuated on Monday 27 March. The police barracks were vacated by the RIC and immediately taken over by Dáil troops, under Commandant Joseph McLaughlin, with a large crowd assembling to witness the transfer. Loud cheers were heard when the Tricolour was hoisted from one of the upper windows. The following day Lifford and Raphoe Barracks were evacuated by the RIC, who were replaced by Dáil troops. There were similar scenes when the Tricolour was hoisted from the windows of both barracks to great cheers and applause. On the same day, the two RIC barracks in Letterkenny were evacuated and handed over to Commandant Tom Glennon of the Dáil troops at 7 a.m. The old coat of arms or British insignia was taken down from the main entrances by Daniel Gillen and large Tricolours were hoisted.[1]

The first obvious split in the IRA was observed at Carndonagh, Moville and Muff when, under the direction of Peadar O'Donnell, police barracks were taken over by the IRA Executive forces. However, the republican troops in the county were at a disadvantage in terms of strategic barracks evacuated by the RIC and British military. The only strategic outposts occupied by the Executive forces were the former RIC barracks in Ballyshannon and Finner Camp, near Bundoran. The issue of strategic posts for IRA forces based in County Donegal was of the utmost importance in their primary objective – the 'northern offensive'.

The IRA Executive's policy of boycotting goods from unionist firms in the Six Counties continued apace when the train from Derry to Burtonport was held up on Friday 31 March at Newtowncunningham. The IRA Executive ordered the guard to throw out copies of the *Derry Journal*, which were then burned. When news of the occurrence reached the office of the *Derry Journal*, fresh copies were printed off and promptly dispatched, but these, with other newspapers, were also destroyed when the second train arrived at Newtowncunningham. Road-blocks were set up at Newtowncunningham as part of the Belfast boycott and all traffic was stopped and searched. All lorries belonging to unionist firms from Derry had their contents seized. Roads leading to west Donegal were also patrolled and a lorry belonging to S. Cochrane, Waterside, Derry, was held up and the driver compelled to transport it to another part of the county.[2]

In early April, Seán Lehane's new recruits went to Dublin to meet with the other officers of the 1st Northern Division to receive instructions on the northern offensive and finalise plans. Alfie McCallion then drove some of the men back to Donegal in a large touring car via Longford, Carrick-on-Shannon, Sligo and then on to Bundoran where they stopped for the night at O'Gorman's Hotel. They arrived in Letterkenny the next day and held a divisional staff meeting in McCarry's Hotel later that evening.

Those present were Seán Lehane, OC; Charlie Daly, vice-OC; Peadar O'Donnell, Divisional Adjutant; Joe McGurk, Divisional Quartermaster; Mick O'Donoghue, Divisional Engineer; Jack Fitzgerald, Brigadier; Mossy Donegan, Brigadier; Denis Galvin, Divisional Transport Officer and Captain Seamus McCann. A number of important decisions were made at the divisional IRA meeting, one of which was to seize and garrison the masonic hall in Raphoe and to occupy Glenveagh Castle in the Derryveagh Mountains, which was to be the principal base of the reorganised 1st Northern Division under the IRA Executive. The following day a party of ten took over the masonic hall and began preparing it for occupation as an IRA stronghold, fortifying it with sandbags, etc. A small garrison was then installed and the neighbouring premises belonging to the local solicitor were commandeered as quarters for the divisional officers. Receipts and written authorisation were then exchanged between the solicitor and the officers.

The divisional engineer, Mick O'Donoghue travelled to Glenveagh Castle and established engineering headquarters there, assembling special groups for each of the four brigade areas. Engineering officers were put through a rapid training course in military engineering and the engineering division was greatly improved with the arrival of Donncha MacNelis, a native of Glencolmcille.

Meanwhile the divisional OC, Seán Lehane, travelled throughout the county accompanied by a number of officers, carrying out inspections in the various towns and parishes. A number of areas were reorganised and new staff appointed: Derry, OC Seán Hegarty; Lagan (east Donegal), OC Jack Fitzgerald; south Donegal, OC Brian Monaghan and north-west Donegal, OC Frank O'Donnell.[3]

The IRA Executive forces now got to work and a large party of IRA crossed into County Fermanagh on the evening of Tuesday 4 April and attacked the Special Constabulary based at Garrison. A Special Constable called Plumb was killed during the attack and three others were seriously wounded. The Special Constabulary, accompanied by British military, surveyed the scene of the attack the following morning and discovered that Plumb's body was missing. They followed up with reports that it had been removed by the IRA and taken to Kinlough where it was badly treated. However, the local Catholic priest and the local Church of Ireland minister (who were responsible for having the body removed) later contradicted these reports. They stated that the constable's wounds consisted of a single gunshot wound to the head and that no other injuries were evident.[4]

The activities of the IRA Executive forces in the exercise of the boycott policy attracted a number of complaints from the public, which prompted Peadar O'Donnell, Divisional Adjutant, to clarify matters with a letter that appeared in the *Derry Journal* on Wednesday 7 April:

You will please insert in a prominent place in Friday's issue (7th inst) the following statement of some recent happenings in Tirconaill. This letter you will please note, is not to be the basis of any newspaper controversy in your columns:

The seizure of motor cars in parts of Tirconaill other than the Lagan area was under permission other than from the new Executive.

The seizures of Friday last, 31st of March were under authority given in respect of the Convention decision that the Belfast boycott be drastically enforced and extended to the six county areas. The foodstuffs have been delivered in the case of the large consignments to the customers who had ordered them, but the money will be paid to the Belfast Expelled Workers Fund by shop-keepers concerned in Ramelton, Milford and Carrigart. In respect of the private cars taken, other than Belfast travellers, representations may be made to the OC, Churchill, this also applies to the motor lorries, except that these latter will be held pending an instruction from the Army Council. Many people seem to forget the Belfast boycott has never been off so far as the IRA is concerned. A pronouncement by the Provisional Government in no way affects the Army of the Republic. If Derry cuts itself off from Ireland politically the sooner Derry recognises such a step is commercial suicide the better for Derry. We have not really begun the boycott yet.[5]

The fact that the *Derry Journal* published the letter was a surprise, as the same newspaper had been a target of the boycott in previous weeks. However, the publication of the letter served to protect the *Derry Journal* from further attack in the boycott campaign.

The boycott continued that day with another train raid at Raphoe. When the midday train arrived at Raphoe a party of IRA removed the engine driver, guard, stationmaster and porters, who were then locked into the waiting room. An armed guard was put on them and the raiding party removed all goods and placed them on a commandeered lorry, which was driven away. All unionist newspapers were seized and burned on the street.[6]

The boycott policy was one of the issues prioritised at the anti-Treaty IRA Convention in March. The IRA Executive forces in the bordering counties were instructed to carry out an intense campaign against all trains and lorries carrying goods from unionist firms in the Six Counties.

In the early stages of the boycott campaign, Eithne Coyle was very active. She cycled to the Letterkenny Railway Station on Thursday 6 April and, as always, was very well dressed, wearing a type of grey uniform and a felt hat. On the arrival of the morning train, she held up the guard of the van with her reliable old triggerless revolver. She then ordered him to throw out all the morning papers, which she set on fire. She proceeded to Glenmaquin where she held up the midday train on the Strabane to Letterkenny line, destroying the Belfast newspapers.[7] The evening train was held up at Letterkenny Station on Saturday 8 April and was searched by Coyle, accompanied by another woman who removed and destroyed the Belfast newspapers. When the same train reached Dungloe, armed men searched it for Belfast goods, but there was nothing found on board.[8] On Saturday 8 April the last train from Derry was held up at a gatehouse near Dungloe and thoroughly searched for Belfast goods.[9]

When the train from Derry to west Donegal arrived at Creeslough on Monday morning, 10 April, Eithne Coyle was once again there to meet it: producing her revolver she held up the guard. Two other women accompanied her and they searched the van, removing parcels containing copies of the *Derry Standard* and Belfast newspapers, which were brought to the platform and set on fire. They targeted the same station later that night and the following morning, removing bundles of Belfast papers and the Derry unionist newspaper the *Sentinel* before setting them on fire. The following Tuesday several parcels of the *Sentinel* were taken off the morning train at Creeslough and burned.[10]

On Saturday 8 June a convention of the Dáil forces (pro-Treaty) was held in Ballybofey and attended by 250 officers of the divisional brigades, battalions and companies. The entire 1st Northern Divisional staff: commandant, adjutant, quartermaster and the directors of all the special services with the exception of engineering, declared loyalty to the Provisional Government and Dáil forces. Overall, approximately 90 per cent of the Donegal IRA declared loyalty to the Dáil forces. At the conclusion of the convention, a meeting was convened to select pro-Treaty candidates for the impending elections. They were Dr J. P. McGinley, TD; P. J. Ward, TD; P. J. McGoldrick, TD; Joe Sweeney, TD; Patrick Barry, County Councillor, Inver and John McLaughlin, Buncrana.[11]

In late March Michael Collins and James Craig had entered into a second pact at the behest of Winston Churchill. Collins agreed to prevent further action by the IRA against the military and Special Constabulary in the Six Counties. Craig agreed, among other things, to address the plight of the Catholics who lost their jobs at the Belfast shipyard and the release of the political prisoners who had been serving sentences relating to pre-Truce offences. However, Collins was also tasked with stopping the boycott of goods from the Six Counties. This continued in Donegal and Craig raised the issue with Collins within days of the pact:

> I learned at the meeting that the Boycott of goods from Northern Ireland was still in force, and that in County Donegal especially, there has been a ruthless destruction of the necessities of life and the seizure of motors and motor-lorries delivering in that county. And further, that agents have been expelled from certain towns in the South and West simply on the ground that they were representing Northern firms. I hope you will take instant action to rectify this state of affairs.[12]

As we have seen, in February 1922, the IRA had responded to the arrests of the IRA men of the 5th Northern Division through a series of kidnappings in Counties Tyrone and Fermanagh. The hostage situation provided Michael Collins with a bargaining opportunity, as many IRA men were imprisoned in jails in the Six Counties and Scotland. Many of the prisoners were sentenced or on remand for activities occurring before the Truce of July 1921, whilst others had been arrested under the Special Powers Act introduced by the Belfast government. Collins used the release of members of the Special Constabulary, kidnapped at Clones in February, as a test of good faith when he wrote to James Craig on Tuesday 11 April requesting the release of a Donegal prisoner on compassionate grounds. The telegram stated:

> Have received telegram from Glenties, County Donegal that father of Bernard Sweeney, prisoner, Derry Jail seriously ill. Would be glad if Bernard Sweeney given parole to go home. Michael Collins.

Craig's reply stated:

> In reply to your telegram of today I regret that I am unable to comply with your request regarding Bernard Sweeney as I am advised that release on parole is not allowed by law. Prime Minister, Northern Ireland.

The prisoner in question was a brother of Joe Sweeney, commander of the Dáil forces in Donegal. Collins had used his influence in having the members of the Special Constabulary released by the IRA in Monaghan and referred to this when he wrote to James Craig on Tuesday 11 April:

> I am very glad to be able to tell you that the prisoners who were captured at Clones were released last evening. Enquiries are being pursued regarding the other prisoners alleged to be detained in custody ... I should like to lay stress on the urgency for the release of Bernard Sweeney about whom I wired you yesterday. I note your legal difficulty about release on parole but his case comes under Clause 10 of the Agreement ...[13]

The correspondence also included a list of prisoners from Counties Tyrone, Fermanagh, Derry and Donegal. At that time there were seventy-two prisoners held at Derry Jail, including Donegal prisoners Edward Gallagher, Carrick; Charles Coll, Sheskinarone, Dungloe; Owen Sharkey, Kincasslagh; William McCusker, Stranorlar; Pat Lee, Eastport, Ballyshannon; Albert Griffin, Mountcharles; Joachim Murray, Kilcar and Patrick McAteer, Ballybofey. Thirteen prisoners being held at Peterhead Jail in Scotland included the Donegal men Patrick 'Poppy' Johnston and Thomas McShea. A total of eighty-four prisoners were incarcerated at Belfast Prison at the same time.[14] Some prisoners were released in the months that followed, while others were not released until much later, some as late as 1925.

There was trouble brewing in the ranks of the IRA Executive and divisions rose to the surface during a second convention held in Dublin on Wednesday 12 April. The splits developed following the proposal of a resolution, giving the British seventy-two hours to leave Ireland. At the time several thousand British troops remained in Dublin under the command of General Neville Macready. This resolution caused great confusion among the delegates, with some refusing to vote thinking they would not have sufficient time to return to their units before the time for the ultimatum expired. Divisions also developed between the officers of the IRA Executive regarding policy. This was observed for the first time when Rory O'Connor announced that he was going to the Four Courts and that this would be the new GHQ. He extended an invitation to all delegates who had voted for war against the British to meet him there the next day. This split the Executive Council and members of the IRA's southern divisions made their way to the Clarence Hotel, establishing a separate headquarters under the command of Liam Lynch.[15] The faction led by Rory O'Connor commandeered both the Four Courts and the Four Courts Hotel shortly after midnight on Thursday 13 April. O'Connor gave an interview to a reporter from the *Irish Independent* later that day. He declared emphatically that the occupation of the building should not be taken in any way as a *coup d'état* nor did it indicate the beginning of a revolution. 'There is going to be no revolution,' he said.[16]

Some of the anti-Treaty Donegal IRA, including Peadar O'Donnell, arrived at the Four Courts the following morning and remained there for some time. The IRA Executive garrisoned at the Four Courts appointed Joe McKelvey as their chief of staff. However, the garrison from the south occupying the Clarence Hotel held a meeting on the same morning for the purpose of asking Liam Lynch to resume the position of chief of staff. This was then communicated to the garrison at the Four Courts along with the fact that Lynch was going to the south to establish a GHQ there. This created further confusion with two commands being established: one in Dublin under Joe McKelvey and one under Liam Lynch of the 1st Southern Division, Cork.[17]

Meanwhile in County Donegal a member of the IRA Executive forces, Edward O'Flaherty, was arrested in the village of Clady on the Donegal/Tyrone border on the night of Thursday 13 April by members of the Special Constabulary. When searched, a revolver and ammunition were discovered in his coat. He was conveyed to the police barracks in Strabane and was scheduled to appear at a special court the following day charged with possession of an uncontrolled weapon. At approximately 9.30 a.m. the following morning his sister Molly O'Flaherty called to the station to visit him. After a short conversation she left, returning a short time later with a packet of cigarettes and then she went away again after approximately fifteen minutes. She returned with her mother and the two requested to see Edward to discuss private business and were escorted to a room off the barracks hall. Their mother left after a short discussion at which point Molly and Edward stood in the hall chatting. As soon as the constable in charge turned his back to attend to something, the two unchained the door and, opening it, burst out and jumped into a waiting car. They drove off at speed through the streets of Strabane with the police in hot pursuit in a Crossley car. The O'Flahertys sped through the town and successfully crossed the bridge at Lifford to safety.

The period of transition from the Truce to the Treaty was for some a time for settling old scores from the previous campaign. Those suspected of working for, or passing information to, the RIC were obvious targets. John Collins, a former British soldier, had been identified as a British agent and arrested by the IRA in July 1921. He had been interrogated and sentenced to death. However, the Truce intervened and his life was spared, but he was ordered to leave the county. Following the signing of the Treaty, Collins returned to live with his wife in Ramelton. At approximately 11 p.m. on Friday night, 14 April 1922, a party of IRA men called at his home. It was not known which faction the party of men represented. Collins was arrested and brought out of the house to be questioned on suspicion of being a British agent. He was taken along a road leading towards Fortstewart and placed against a wall. Collins suddenly made a run for it in an effort to escape and a volley of shots was fired hitting him five times. The IRA immediately left the scene. After about two hours, Collins managed to crawl back to his house where he received treatment, but later died from his wounds.[18]

The transition period posed many problems and one particular difficulty concerned the issue of which authority prevailed over the other – Dáil forces under the Provisional Government or the IRA under the Executive. With each side claiming to be the legitimate authority, it was only a matter of time before friction began to develop. Another problem was the fallout from the IRA Convention, which resulted in a declaration from the Minister for Defence, Richard Mulcahy, suspending finances to the IRA Executive because of their refusal to recognise GHQ under the Provisional Government. The IRA Executive Council responded to this with Rory O'Connor ordering all divisions under their control to seize bank notes from banks in their areas.

The conflicting authority would inevitably lead to confrontation and the first sign of this in the county occurred at Donegal Town on Saturday 15 April. In the early hours of the morning, a party of Dáil forces encountered a group of ten IRA Executive men preparing to break into the Ulster and Belfast Banks. The patrol fired a shot in the air, to which the IRA returned fire and a battle ensued for up to half an hour. The police in the local barracks on hearing the shooting took up positions at the windows and engaged with the IRA men, who were forced to make a hasty retreat in cars parked on the Ballyshannon Road.

There was further activity the following day at nearby Ballyshannon when the residents of the town were rudely awakened in the early hours of

Sunday morning by the IRA Executive forces erecting barricades. They were IRA men from the 3rd Western Division, which included Sligo, Leitrim and a portion of Donegal. The barricades were erected on the bridge and one at the East Port to control traffic coming from the Six Counties. The reason for this activity was to prevent the Dáil troops based at Drumboe Castle from travelling to Sligo Town, where Arthur Griffith was scheduled to address a meeting. The commandant of the IRA 3rd Western Division Executive forces, Billy Pilkington, issued a proclamation prohibiting the meeting; 'in the interests of peace' neither side was permitted to hold meetings. Despite this the meeting went ahead and Major General Seán MacEoin of the Dáil forces deployed over fifty well-armed men on various streets around the town and an armoured car was also present.[19]

The Special Powers legislation introduced by the Belfast government in early April led to a mass exodus of people from Counties Derry, Tyrone and Fermanagh into County Donegal. The mass exodus included many republicans and a party of IRA men from the 2nd Northern Division, Tyrone, crossed into Donegal on Sunday 23 April. The men of the 2nd Northern immediately reported to their former OC Charlie Daly at McCarry's Hotel in Letterkenny. McCarry's Hotel was often frequented by republicans and was the location of the Sinn Féin courts during the War of Independence. The men from the 2nd Northern Division included Neill Gillespie, James McElduff, Willie John Kelly, Archie McDonnell, Tom Kelly and many of the men from the Dungannon area. Seán Lehane, Charlie Daly and the new arrivals remained there for a few hours and had Sunday lunch, before evacuating the place and making their way to Foxhall near Churchill.[20]

Meanwhile Eithne Coyle's one-woman boycott campaign continued when she boarded the afternoon train at Buncrana Station on Tuesday 25 April. She seized all parcels containing newspapers and carried them into another carriage. The train continued on its journey to Carndonagh and on crossing a bridge Eithne Coyle threw the parcels into the river. In an earlier report from 18 April in the *Derry Sentinel*, a correspondent of the *Daily Mail* who had witnessed one of Eithne Coyle's displays described his experience:

Presently we drew up at one platform station in the heart of the mountains. 'This door is locked porter.' It was the voice of a girl … a few yards from my carriage, revolver in hand, stood a slim neatly dressed girl and a bewildered porter was eyeing her with ill-concealed nervousness. The guard hurried up – no questions asked – the doors of the van were simply thrown open. 'The boxes are in my way,' she said. The cool decided tones and a slight flourish of the revolver made the guard and the porter hasten to obey. A few large boxes were dragged out and laid on the platform; the girl stepped into the van and in a few seconds emerged with bundles of newspapers in her arms. 'You can put these boxes back now and proceed,' she said. Laying the revolver on the ground making sure that it was within reach she began stacking the newspapers in one large pile; then producing a small bottle of petrol and a box of matches from her pocket, she proceeded to set them on fire. As the train steamed out her bonfire was blazing merrily.[21]

Despite the general order to increase the Belfast boycott, Eithne Coyle considered the IRA Executive in Donegal to be somewhat unresponsive at that time in enforcing the boycott. However, she was persistent and travelled extensively throughout the county in continuance of the boycott policy. There was also the attention of the civic guard to contend with, who could have arrested her for her activities, but Coyle was relentless in this work. She had also trained some of the Cumann na mBan members in the local areas in an effort to intensify the embargo.[22] The Letterkenny to Burtonport train was held up at Foxhall Station on Tuesday 25 April and a number of products from Belfast traders were removed.[23]

In the early hours of Wednesday morning, an unidentified party of men attacked the Dáil forces' No. 1 barracks at Letterkenny. The assault began about 2.45 a.m. when they opened fire and a bomb was thrown, hitting the front of the building. All the windows in the barracks and in nearby houses were smashed. The garrison failed to reply to the sustained attack, but the attacking party was forced to retreat when fired on by troops from the No. 2 barracks at Lower Main Street. During this time the Special Constabulary was known to launch attacks in County Donegal and it was strongly believed that it was responsible for the attack in Letterkenny and other areas. However, as the assailants were not identified, suspicions were also cast on the IRA Executive forces, adding to the growing tensions between the two groups.[24]

This growing tension between the pro- and anti-Treaty factions was evidenced on Sunday night, 30 April. On that occasion a small party of Executive forces from Finner Camp was passing through Ballybofey in a Ford car and was held up by Dáil forces manning a barricade at the bridge between Ballybofey and Stranorlar. The IRA party consisted of seven men: three officers from the Six Counties and an escort of four Volunteers. They were removed from the car and taken to Drumboe Castle under escort. Food was prepared for them but they refused to eat it as a protest against their arrest while on duty. The seven were then placed in a single cell and were held until daybreak the following morning. They alleged that they were roughly handled and that a tool kit had been removed from the car by Commandant Tom Glennon.[25]

In an effort to avoid the growing tensions developing into confrontation in Donegal, Joe Sweeney, Commandant General of the Dáil forces in the county, summoned Seán Lehane and Charlie Daly to his headquarters at Drumboe Castle. Sweeney's second in command, Tom Glennon, was also present at the meeting and was described as 'very bitter', refusing to recognise the authority of either Lehane or Daly or the authority of the IRA Executive Council. Glennon even called Lehane and Daly enemies of the government. Lehane informed Sweeney that they would continue to launch attacks on the Special Constabulary in Counties Derry, Tyrone and Fermanagh, arguing that this was the reason they had been sent to Donegal. Although Sweeney was insistent that Lehane evacuate the county with his men, he wanted to avoid an all-out fight with the republican forces and was said to be apprehensive about the presence of so many seasoned IRA men from the Cork and Kerry divisions. The meeting ended without a resolution.

Lehane and Daly made their way to McCarry's Hotel in Letterkenny where later that evening a council of war was convened. A decision was taken at that meeting to begin planning war operations in Derry and

Tyrone as soon as columns could be organised. It was also decided that two attacks would be planned for Wednesday night, 3 May. One column, under the command of Charlie Daly, was to proceed to north Tyrone to attack a company of the Special Constabulary reported to be garrisoned at Melenon House. The other would be led by Seán Lehane with a force of approximately thirty riflemen, and would mount an attack on the British military camp near Derry City. They decided to return to Raphoe where they would make the final preparations.[26]

On Wednesday morning, 3 May, a meeting of the commanding officers of the IRA Executive and Dáil forces convened in Dublin to discuss the growing tensions. Following three hours of negotiations, a statement was issued setting out the terms of the agreement: 'A truce is declared as from 4 p.m. today until Monday with a view to giving the representatives of both sections of the Army an immediate opportunity of discovering a basis for army unification.'

Under the terms of the truce (1) all operations, except training and ordinary army routine would cease; (2) all penetrative reorganisation would cease; (3) both sections would cooperate to maintain order and prevent acts of aggression against person or property. The truce agreement was negotiated on behalf of the IRA Executive by Commandant General Liam Lynch, Chief of Staff, Commandant General Liam Mellows and Brigadier General Seán Moylan and on behalf of the Dáil forces by General Eoin O'Duffy, Chief of Staff, Major General Gearóid O'Sullivan and Adjutant General Seán MacEoin.[27] The truce period was later extended to the following Wednesday.

The allegiances of IRA men in Bundoran and Tullaghan were also decided on the same day. Ninety men attended a parade of the Bundoran Company, where all but three pledged allegiance to the IRA Executive. The majority of the Tullaghan Company also pledged allegiance to the Executive Council, with four supporting the Provisional Government. At the Bundoran Urban Council meeting earlier that week three members had been called on to resign because they no longer stood by the Republic.[28]

Chapter 12

The Northern Offensive and the Newtowncunningham Tragedy

The objective of the northern offensive was to undermine the Belfast government, but it was also a response to the escalating sectarian violence being meted out to the nationalist population in the Six Counties. The sectarian violence began in June 1920 following the assassinations of two senior RIC personnel: Colonel Smyth was a native of Banbridge and was assassinated in Cork, while District Inspector Swanzy was killed in Lisburn. The backlash from these killings witnessed the unionist populations of Banbridge, Lisburn, Dromore and later Belfast venting their anger on the nationalist population. The situation was made more desperate following the establishment of the separate state encompassing the six north-eastern counties through the Government of Ireland Act 1920. The Treaty further isolated the nationalist population and sectarian violence reached crisis point. In the period between 10 February and 21 April 1922, 127 nationalists were killed and over 300 were injured.[1]

This period coincided with efforts to maintain unity between the two factions of the pro- and anti-Treaty IRA. Both sides strove to avoid any confrontation. While negotiations were ongoing in Dublin to form the basis of a temporary truce, the IRA Executive forces in Donegal had gathered at Raphoe to make the final preparations for the dual attack on British military and the Special Constabulary in the Six Counties. The IRA Executive forces were unaware of the truce announcement earlier that day when shortly after dusk on Wednesday evening, 3 May, the two parties set off for their respective targets, one led by Seán Lehane, the other by Charlie Daly.

Seán Lehane's party drove to a location near Burnfoot Railway Station where they abandoned their vehicles and advanced on foot until they reached Burnfoot Cross. Two IRA men were instructed to go into Burnfoot village and dismantle all telegraph and telephone apparatus and cut all wires connecting the station with Derry. With the immediate area secured, and all civilians under armed guard in a nearby shed, Seán Lehane led the attack column in the direction of Derry.

The British military camp was located a few miles away on the outskirts of Derry City. Nearing the camp some of the party noticed a flickering light and thought it was the military signalling. They observed this for a while but could not decipher the signals. They assumed their plans were foiled, but carried on cautiously. Further on they discovered the flickering light was a camp fire and were reassured. The fire actually aided the attacking party as it served as a beacon, outlining the enemy position. The IRA party took up firing positions along a trench overlooking the camp. Seán Lehane inspected the line a number of times and when he was satisfied that all the men were in good positions he instructed them to open fire in the direction of the flickering camp fire and with a single whistle blast the still and quiet night was disturbed with an exploding volley of gunfire.

The first response from the British military was a series of Very lights (flares) being sent up illuminating up the whole area and then suddenly machine-gun fire opened up on the IRA's position. The British response was much quicker than anticipated, giving the impression they had received prior warning of the attack. Bullets passed over the IRA men's heads striking the wooden fence behind them, showering many with wood splinters. Rifle and machine-gun fire, exploding bullets and rifle grenades suddenly enveloped them. The IRA men, with their rifles and hand-deployed grenades, had no response to this aggressive onslaught. They were pinned down, such was the ferocity of the British response, and they had to counter the possibility of reinforcements arriving from Derry City. With that, Lehane quietly ordered all men to cease fire and retire back to Burnfoot. A rearguard remained for some time to secure the safe retreat of the main body of men, which discovered that some of the men had neglected to take all their arms and ammunition in their haste to retreat. This was considered a serious offence, since an IRA soldier was drilled to regard his weapon and ammunition as his most precious possessions. The items were collected by the members of the rearguard, who then fired one last volley of shots before they retreated and the British responded with another ferocious outburst of rifle and machine-gun fire. The rearguard crawled away under a hail of bullets and arrived safely back to Burnfoot. After a roll-call, it was discovered that five men were missing and two were slightly injured. The missing men arrived soon after and the entire column moved off in the direction of Newtowncunningham arriving there shortly before 6 a.m.

Later that morning Seán Lehane instructed a party of five men to proceed to Buncrana to seize the bank notes from the Belfast Bank in the town in accordance with the instructions issued by Rory O'Connor in March. Meanwhile the remaining IRA men set about selecting billets in the Newtowncunningham area. Some of the officers eyed a mansion on the outskirts of the village and decided to commandeer it for themselves. A man named Black, who was a loyalist and leader of the Black Preceptory in the Newtowncunningham area, owned the house. To their surprise, they were cordially received and their host gave them refreshments while engaging them in conversation about politics and the situation in the Six Counties. Before retiring to bed, sentries were posted outside the building and at various points in the village.

Meanwhile the five IRA men had arrived in Buncrana and had gone into the Belfast Bank where they seized approximately £800 in bank notes. A member of the Dáil troops, Johnnie Murphy, was making his way up the street on an errand when one of the Executive IRA men standing sentry outside the bank confronted him. Murphy was questioned before being allowed to leave and he returned to the barracks to inform his OC, Joseph McLaughlin. The Buncrana OC immediately organised the men at the barracks and they made their way in the direction of the bank. Johnnie Murphy remained at the barracks while Jack Doherty, Jim Hutton, Bill Burns, James Doherty, Pat McLaughlin and Joseph (Seán) MacLochlainn made their way to the bank by different routes. The sentry at the bank spotted the advancing Dáil troops and went inside to inform the others. Within a few moments, two of the IRA Executive forces emerged and were said to have started shooting at the approaching soldiers.

Other members of the IRA forces situated at the Market Square were said to have started firing at the Dáil troops, who were forced to take cover, and a short battle ensued. A local man named John Kavanagh rushed onto the street to get his eighteen-year-old daughter, Mary Ellen, when a stray bullet passed through his hand striking her in the back, with the bullet lodging in her left lung. Mary Ellen later died at the Derry Infirmary on Saturday 27 May. Esther Fletcher, nine years old, was also shot during the battle and died later that day at the Derry Infirmary. Two local men, Peter McGowan and Pat McGuire, were also wounded, as was Jack Doherty. The IRA suffered two casualties and, during a lull in the battle, evacuated the area with the wounded, making their way to Newtowncunningham. The Dáil forces in Buncrana were unable to contact their headquarters at Drumboe Castle as the lines were cut and Joseph MacLochlainn drove to Stranorlar to report the incident. He arrived at Drumboe at approximately 2 p.m. and a large party of soldiers was ordered to travel to Buncrana in an eight-vehicle convoy under the command of Commandant Tom Glennon.

Meanwhile IRA officers based at Newtowncunningham were only a few hours in their beds, resting from the previous night's operation, when a messenger looking for Seán Lehane awakened them. He informed Lehane of the shooting at Buncrana and that the men had just arrived back in the village. Lehane rushed to the village to receive a full report from Joe McGurk and immediately ordered the mobilisation of all available men. They ensured the two wounded men had received first aid and were preparing to have them removed to Lifford Hospital.

At that moment, Charlie Daly and his party arrived at Newtowncunningham from Tyrone, but their adventure had not been as exciting as that of the others. They had arrived at their intended target, Melenon House in north Tyrone, and found the place barricaded and fortified with steel shutters. They attempted to gain entry by using the butts of their rifles to break into the house. Failing to do so they then decided to abandon the operation and did not even discover if the place was inhabited or not.

The convoy of Dáil troops from Drumboe Castle had stopped at Letterkenny for some time and were joined by additional troops for the journey to Buncrana. Travelling at a fast rate the three Crossleys in the convoy were some distance ahead of the cars when approaching the outskirts of Newtowncunningham at approximately 6 p.m. According to republican sources, at the same time in the village of Newtowncunningham Seán Lehane OC and Charlie Daly vice-OC were contemplating whether or not to travel to Buncrana to speak to the officer in charge of the Dáil troops there. Suddenly someone shouted, 'Vehicles approaching!' and they could hear the humming of Crossley engines approaching the village. No one knew who was approaching and there was general confusion with many thinking it was the British or the Special Constabulary from Derry pursuing them in a counter-attack. A number of IRA men climbed over the walls on both sides of the village street. The remainder of the men were scattered on the road at different points in the village as the first Crossley in the convoy came into view. Packed with troops sitting back to back with rifles at the ready the first two lorries passed the IRA positioned on the walls at the entrance to the village. As the third lorry came along the street Commandant Tom Glennon stood up and aimed his revolver at Seán Lehane, who was standing in the doorway of a house, and fired a single shot hitting the fanlight above his head.[2]

There was silence for a couple of seconds and then the second lorry stopped dead in the street with two soldiers jumping off and taking cover behind a car. Sporadic gunfire began to ring out from all quarters, but no orders had been given and it seemed that every man was acting on his own initiative. Some of the IRA fired at the tyres of the vehicles as they began to speed away, by which time both sides had started to shoot at each other.

The Dáil troops were at a disadvantage, packed into the backs of the lorries, and a number of them were hit almost immediately. The cars taking up the rear of the convoy had arrived on the outskirts of the village and men took up positions along the road and in nearby fields before firing in the direction of the village. The IRA took cover before returning fire and succeeded in flanking the Dáil troops, but some of them had taken refuge in a nearby house from where the cries of a woman could be heard. The woman had five children in the house and the IRA decided to surround the house, but not to fire. The Dáil troops evacuated the house by the back and retreated through the fields towards the railway line and the remainder of the Dáil troops retreated leaving behind some of their cars, weapons and ammunition. Meanwhile the shooting continued from the three Crossleys as they sped out of the village leaving their two stranded comrades behind. The two soldiers soon realised they had been abandoned and immediately surrendered. One of them was slightly injured and when later questioned admitted that they had been instructed to stop and take up battle positions if they encountered any IRA.

Having gone some distance out of Newtowncunningham the Crossleys stopped and it was then discovered that one man had been killed outright and that eight others were wounded, three succumbing to their injuries soon after. They were taken to the residence of a farmer named Hamilton at a place called Stewarts Corner approximately two miles from Newtowncunningham on the Derry Road. The dead were Corporal John McGinley from Ardsbeg, Eddie Gallagher from Burtonport, Daniel McGill from Ardara and Edward Murray from Sion Mills, near Strabane, County Tyrone. The injured were Packy Bryson, Jim Dawson, Johnny Grant and two other soldiers, McCool and Sharkey.[3]

John Devenny, a member of the Dáil forces who lived on the outskirts of Newtowncunningham, heard of the shooting incident in the village, but was unaware of any serious casualties on either side. His first indication was when a motorist passing through the village shortly afterwards stopped to inform him that the convoy of Dáil troops had stopped at Stewarts Corner. Devenny immediately commandeered a passing lorry, made his way to Stewarts Corner, and was informed that no one would return to Newtowncunningham to seek medical assistance. Devenny went to the village and informed Fr Ward that his services were required. He sent Susan Haughey to inform Dr Rankin. When Devenny and Fr Ward returned to the Hamiltons they found the doctor there attending to the wounded.

This incident served to deepen the divisions of an already divided army in Donegal. When everything returned to normal in Newtowncunningham Seán Lehane ordered the collection of all captured vehicles, weapons and ammunition. They then abandoned the village and returned to Raphoe with the two prisoners. The captured soldiers informed Lehane that they had heard of the temporary truce when they stopped at Letterkenny and had been shown a wire from their GHQ in Dublin that stated a truce had been arranged. However, Seán Lehane had not received notification of the temporary truce, having spent the previous day and night organising the attack in Derry. On their return to Raphoe, a telegram was waiting for Lehane from Liam Lynch, IRA Chief of Staff. The telegram had originally been delivered to McCarry's Hotel in Letterkenny the previous evening and later forwarded to Raphoe. It was an official notification stating that a truce had been signed by Liam Lynch and General Eoin O'Duffy, Dáil troops, GOC effective from 6 p.m. the previous evening.[4] The Dáil troops at Drumboe Castle and Letterkenny were fully aware of the truce and in spite of this had gone on a mission to round up the IRA men involved in the Buncrana shootings, whereas the IRA Executive forces had not been aware of the temporary truce at that time. The overzealous officer, Tom Glennon, travelling on the third lorry had created the situation when he fired his weapon as they drove through the village, provoking the unnecessary fight.

Different versions of what actually happened at Newtowncunningham emerged, both at the time and in subsequent years. Some versions of this incident tell a different story – one which puts the IRA in ambush positions along the road entering Newtowncunningham village where they were said to have engaged in an unprovoked attack on the Dáil forces convoy as it passed by. The commanding officer of the Dáil forces in County Donegal, Joe Sweeney, gave an account of the incident, which was greatly at variance with the version of the Executive forces. Commandant General Sweeney stated that earlier that morning Joseph McLaughlin, the officer commanding the Dáil forces stationed at Buncrana, had received information that an armed party of twenty-five men was carrying out a raid on the Belfast Bank in the town. McLaughlin, accompanied by five other men, made their way to the bank and claimed that they were fired on by a man standing sentry outside the bank. It was stated that McLaughlin then ordered all civilians off the street before opening fire on the men as they left the bank and that a short battle ensued. The Dáil forces' account stated that word of this affair was received at Drumboe Castle, then GHQ of the Dáil forces in the county, and a large party of Dáil troops set off to Buncrana. This party was under the command of Commandant Tom Glennon.

The convoy of troops reached Newtowncunningham and on entering the village it was stated that the occupants of the first lorry noticed men in positions behind walls on either side of the street. At the entrance of the village a sudden call to 'Halt' was heard, quickly followed by gunfire directed at the second and third lorries. Sweeney also alleged that an officer of the Executive forces informed a brigadier of the Dáil forces that the ambush was planned. Additionally, there was the suggestion that local people in the village overheard conversations between IRA Executive forces that the ambush was prepared with the full knowledge as to who was to be ambushed.[5]

In the days following Newtowncunningham, orders were received from GHQ in Dublin requesting the attendance of the 1st Northern Division officers at the Four Courts. Seán Lehane, Charlie Daly, Jack Fitzgerald, Mick O'Donoghue, Peadar O'Donnell, Frank O'Donnell and Joe O'Donnell travelled to Dublin.[6]

The Newtowncunningham incident created much local debate at the time with both sides offering contradictory accounts of what actually instigated the shoot-out that led to the deaths of four young men of the Dáil forces and injury to several others on both sides. At the time reports of the event in the local press put the blame firmly on the republican forces in the county and stated that it was the result of a planned ambush. This concerned Charlie Daly to the extent that he felt it necessary to write to his mother in Kerry to ensure she received an accurate account of the incident. Daly put the blame on the Free State command in the county. He was in Dublin and staying at the Clarence Hotel when he wrote the letter: 'You have seen about the row in Donegal a few days ago. 'Twas a very tragic affair, but the blame lies wholly with Joe Sweeney, the F.S. div. OC.'

Daly also referred to the meeting between the commanding officers on both sides:

> So Lehane and I went to him [Sweeney] on this day week. We told him that we were not in Donegal to fight him, and that if his H.Q. were not going to fight in the six counties neither it nor he should interfere with us who were. He told us that he did not recognise us at all, and went on about his army being the army of the 'Government' and so on. We wanted him to face facts or there would be trouble, but he said he did not care and would carry out his orders no matter what happened. I knew Joe well. I did my best to try to make some arrangement so that we would not have the same things happening as there were in other parts. 'Twas no use and more than this his adjutant, a Belfast chap named Glennon, said we were their enemies ... No Donegal man feels this business worse than I do. I pray to God that I may never have to fire a shot against our own fellows. If such a thing would be likely to happen I would prefer crossing the border and get killed by the Specials ...[7]

Despite the tragedies at Buncrana and Newtowncunningham Michael Collins was pressing ahead with the northern offensive from his end. On Thursday 4 May he issued a circular directing all ministers of the Provisional Government to prepare schemes of non-cooperation with and obstruction of the functioning of the Belfast government, and in the circular he emphasised the importance of not losing sight of this matter.[8]

The majority of the republican officers of the 1st Northern Division had returned to Donegal to find the work of reorganising intensified. Arms, armaments and equipment had arrived from the southern divisions and were distributed to various strong points in the Lagan area and on the border. Charlie McGuinness had brought some new weapons into the country from Germany sometime earlier. McGuinness was known as a sailor and adventurer and had landed Mauser rifles with ammunition at

Passage East and Ardmore in County Waterford. He was one of a number of IRA men purchasing weapons and ammunition in Germany and had been involved in this work from August 1921.[9]

Around the same time the Derry Brigade, IRA Executive, under Brigadier Seán Hegarty, garrisoned several strategic points along Lough Swilly and Lough Foyle, including Inch Island, Fahan, Muff, Skeog House and Manorcunningham.

At this point, the IRA was also busy auctioning off the contents of facilities abandoned by the British navy to raise money for necessities for the men such as food. On Wednesday 10 May the IRA auctioned the contents of the British naval wireless station at Bunbeg in west Donegal. Items including furniture, fittings and bedsteads were purchased by people from the local area. The building was then set alight. As soon as the locals heard of the fire they hurried to the station and tried to remove anything of value, including doors, windows, etc. When the IRA men saw that the buildings were fully ablaze, they left the area and made their way to Glenveagh Castle. The naval wireless station had been commandeered sometime earlier and the British naval coastguards evicted. The station was fully equipped and the contents were estimated to be worth between £20,000 and £30,000.

Republican forces commandeered an unoccupied mansion later that week at Salthill, Mountcharles. The mansion was the property of the Marquis of Conyngham. The men then set about gathering provisions and a raid was carried out on the Mountcharles Railway Station, removing goods from unionist firms consigned for merchants in Mountcharles.[10]

The adverse publicity following the Newtowncunningham and Buncrana incidents prompted Seán Lehane, OC IRA Executive forces in Donegal, to write a response. Lehane's letter first appeared in the *Irish Independent* and was later published in the Friday 12 May edition of the *Derry Journal*. Lehane said that he had made every effort to establish friendly relations with the Dáil forces under Joe Sweeney: 'I did my utmost to arrange an interview with the OC representing Beggars Bush in Donegal area with a view to establishing friendly relations and arranging a basis of unity and cooperation between the two forces.' He said his reasons were to prevent tensions developing into confrontation and alluded to the aggressive tactics employed against his men: 'Pro-Treaty forces were continually holding up, searching, disarming, arresting, imprisoning and in some cases ill-treating my men. The relatives and comrades of these Volunteers were requesting that action would be taken to afford them protection.'

Lehane sympathised with the families of the deceased men and suggested that the cause of the tragedy lay with the Dáil forces' command in the county:

> My staff and I deeply regret the tragic results of the conflict and tender our sympathy to the relatives of the deceased soldiers. With the full facts now before them for the first time the people of Donegal are in a position to determine where the responsibility rests.[11]

A letter followed from Joe Sweeney. According to him, the incident at Newtowncunningham was a planned ambush by the IRA:

> At the entrance to the village there is a bend with trees, and a high hedge on each side of the road, concealing the village street. The occupants of the first tender on entering the street noticed men in positions behind the walls and in laneways, and one or two were out on the street. Suddenly 'Halt' was shouted and simultaneously fire was opened on the first and second tenders, which were in the street. It is a falsehood to say that the first shot was fired from the third lorry.

Joe Sweeney said that he had conducted a thorough investigation into the incident and concluded that the third lorry had not entered the street at the time the shooting started. He also cleverly pointed out that the majority of the IRA men were not natives of the county:

> With the exception of the non-natives of the county, practically every man who fired a shot during hostilities stands by GHQ... recognition of the latter fact is shown by the importation by Executive support of strangers to this county.

Joe Sweeney dismissed the claim that their convoy could have been mistaken for Special Constabulary retaliating for the previous night's attack in Derry. He also said that information from an Executive forces officer confirmed that it was a planned ambush. Sweeney also suggested that the IRA was responsible for attacks on his forces at Drumboe Castle, Letterkenny Police Barracks, Raphoe and Lifford Barracks. He also blamed the IRA for the recent crime spree in eastern Donegal:

> There were wholesale seizures of motor cars, shops were looted, trains raided and provisions seized and in cases cattle were taken from poor farmers and slaughtered for the use of Executive forces. Private houses were occupied in Raphoe and Castlefinn and the owners evicted.[12]

The friction and tension between the two forces diverted attention away from the growing criminal activity in the county. Seán Lehane was informed of the problem on his return from Dublin. A criminal gang or gangs had been responsible for a series of raids on private houses, businesses, trains and the seizure of vehicles with the name of the IRA being used to instil fear in the people. In response to the reports, Lehane issued the following warning:

> This statement is frankly made in view of the fact that we are forced to issue a Solemn Warning to individuals who are indulging in looting and theft. Taking from one person a personal convenience of another is hooliganism and merely copying the worst features of the times we live in. We should be glad if immediate notification of all seizures of motor cars, raids on private houses, trains, etc., were sent to this office at once, and a copy of all receipts held sent here for reference back to the OC of the units concerned. So serious has the menace of hooliganism threatened, to the simple justice of the official raids and seizures carried out by us that we will not hesitate to deal very sternly with offenders. Deportations have occurred already in this area. Even more stern measures will be taken if necessity demands they should.[13]

The manager of the Donegal Railways, in response to an appeal made by him, received the following telegram from Seán Lehane: 'Have taken steps to prevent indiscriminate seizures. Report unofficial seizures immediately.' Following this there was no further interference with traffic on the Donegal Railways in the Raphoe, Clady and Castlefinn areas.[14]

Another letter appeared in the local press to contradict an earlier report suggesting that the IRA was responsible for the death of an elderly resident of Ballindrait, near Lifford. The following letter, from William Knox Ellis, a nephew of the deceased, appeared in *The Irish Times*:

> I have read the account of the death of my uncle, Captain Knox, in *The Irish Times* and I think it somewhat misleading. A party of IRA Volunteers called at Clonleigh and asked Captain Knox for the loan of his motor car, promising to take good care of it and return it afterwards. Captain Knox granted their request. It is true that the excitement probably caused his death; but the IRA had no wish to do him any harm, as he was most popular with everyone. On learning the sad news, the IRA Volunteers at once sent back the car.[15]

The growing tension between the two factions was causing concern among the nationalist community in the Six Counties. A delegation made up of Frank Aiken, Armagh; Mr Walsh, Omagh; Pat Laverty, Newry; and Fr A. Smith, Newtownhamilton, met in early May to discuss the effect on the Six Counties should civil war break out. They considered what measures they could present to both sides to quell further divisions and bring about peace. They arranged a behind the scenes meeting with representatives from both sides, which was held on Tuesday 16 May at the Mansion House, Dublin. Those present included Arthur Griffith, Michael Collins, Éamon de Valera, Cathal Brugha, Richard Mulcahy, Eoin O'Duffy, Liam Lynch and Rory O'Connor. The delegation urged the importance of unity in the south particularly in view of the situation in the Six Counties. Michael Collins raised the concerns of the delegation the following day during a Dáil session where he put an emphasis on unity in government and the army as the basis of achieving a united Ireland. He stressed that

The Northern Offensive and the Newtowncunningham Tragedy

conflict in the south would be detrimental to the northern policy and the plight of the nationalist population.[16]

Meanwhile in Donegal, the northern offensive was intensified with attacks on British forces in the Foyle, Mourne and Derg Valley areas of Derry and Tyrone. The attacks were carried out by day and night. A police constable was killed in one attack near Castlederg, County Tyrone. He had been the driver of an armoured car leading a convoy of vehicles. There were other injuries, with the other occupants of the vehicles having to escape, leaving weapons and ammunition behind. The IRA later retrieved these. It was during this ambush that the IRA discovered its Mauser ammunition was armour piercing.

Although the IRA seldom suffered any serious casualties during these attacks, the Special Constabulary subjected their families and known republican supporters in the Six Counties to vicious reprisals. The Special Constabulary used a campaign of arrests, beatings and torture and on many occasions people were murdered. In one instance, the village of Desertmartin, two miles from Magherafelt in south County Derry, was attacked by a large party of Specials on Friday night, 19 May. They wrecked houses and premises, setting them on fire, and four nationalist men were taken from their beds and murdered in classic Black and Tan style. They were Henry McGeehan and his brother along with John Higgins and his nephew Francis. News of this atrocity reached the IRA in Raphoe the following day. It was very upsetting for Brigadier Seán Larkin of South Derry, as this was his former brigade area and he knew the victims. Larkin wanted to form a party of men from the Donegal garrisons to travel to the Desertmartin area and attack the Special Constabulary as a reprisal. However, Seán Lehane forbade any of the southern men to go, as he was reluctant to lose any of the men he had brought to Donegal. He gave Seán Larkin permission to form a party of Six-County men and they set off for County Derry, but they arrived back within a couple of days having failed to engage with the Special Constabulary.[17]

The date selected for the launch of the northern offensive was Friday 19 May, but some of the northern divisions failed to engage with the enemy as per orders, while the 3rd Northern Division jumped the gun. The

Belfast Brigade launched an attack on the Special Constabulary barracks at Musgrave Street, which was also the police headquarters. A party of approximately twenty IRA men was involved, resulting in the death of one Special Constable and injury to another. A number of bridges were also blown up in the general Belfast area and other areas of County Antrim. However, the 2nd and 4th Northern Divisions failed to act at all, so the campaign was destined to fail.[18]

The impending general election in the twenty-six counties was seen as another opportunity to unite the divided factions in the country. Michael Collins and Éamon de Valera signed an election pact on Saturday 20 May following long negotiations. The basis of the pact was that pro- and anti-Treaty candidates would contest the elections under the auspices of Sinn Féin. The agreement was approved by the Sinn Féin Ard Fheis in Dublin the following Tuesday, as both leaders had recommended it as a triumph not for one side or the other, but for the nation. Michael Collins said that the value of the pact was that it had secured not just unity in the Dáil, but unity in the nation: 'We must be united to face any situation that comes to us from outside or any quarter. It was not an attempt to deprive any elector from giving his vote to whomever he chose.' De Valera expressed the hope that the agreement would give them back a united Irish army. These statements gave great pleasure to the delegates, who numbered approximately 2,000 representing Sinn Féin cumainn from all parts of the country.[19] The pact was an agreement that the following elections should not be taken as deciding the issue of the Treaty, but as creating a government to preserve peace.

The news of the election pact was frowned upon by the British and was perceived as a threat by unionists. Unionists viewed a united front in the twenty-six counties as a threat to the existence of the northern government. However, the election pact failed, following pressure from the British, with pro-Treaty campaigners calling on people to vote for candidates and parties outside the pact such as Labour and the Farmers' Party. The election pact would have the result of electing some members to the Third Dáil who would sign the declaration swearing allegiance to the British monarch, while others would not. This was viewed by the British as a breach of the Treaty and the announcement of the pact was followed by renewed threats of a return to hostilities with British military being mobilised in Dublin and various areas of the Six Counties.[20]

The Special Constabulary and the new police force in the Six Counties, the Royal Ulster Constabulary (RUC), adopted countermeasures to IRA activities in Counties Tyrone and Fermanagh. On Monday 23 May they began a mass round-up for the internment of known IRA men in both counties and the general harassment of republicans and their families. This sparked a mass exodus of people from areas along the border into Donegal, with many being forced to leave their families and homes. The Special Constabulary was known for its brutality and people were badly mistreated in these raids, with many properties being ransacked and damaged. The brutality of the Specials spilled over into Donegal when refugees directed their frustrations at the unionist population in the county. One example was witnessed in Raphoe when the atmosphere in the town began to take a sinister sectarian twist. Fuelled by alcohol, the anger of some refugees boiled over, provoking the murder of a former head constable of the RIC in Raphoe. This particular incident originated in Raphoe town at a public house owned by Pat McGlinchey, which was a favourite meeting place for the IRA. McGlinchey had spent some years in America and had married an American woman called Kate who had very anti-English and anti-Protestant views, always carried a revolver and was described as a 'demon'. Kate McGlinchey was working the bar on this particular night and while talking with a number of refugees from the Six Counties encouraged them to exact revenge on the local Protestant community. She plied them with drink while inciting them to avenge their forced exile. Later that night she set off with a group of men to the home of retired RIC Head Constable Joseph Ballintine. He was found the following day and had been shot a number of times. This outrage prompted IRA officers at Raphoe to take immediate action and every IRA man was questioned about his membership, service and background. Anyone whose character or career was questionable or unsatisfactorily verified was disarmed and dismissed, with many of them reportedly joining the ranks of the Dáil forces.[21]

About the same time, Joe Sweeney was returning from Dublin and saw a large concentration of Specials gathering in Strabane as if preparing for an assault on the IRA at Lifford. He immediately made his way to Raphoe to inform Peadar O'Donnell, who happened to be in Letterkenny at the time. Sweeney told the IRA men present that the Specials were preparing to cross the border at Strabane into Lifford. Captain Seamus McCann organised all available men and they made their way to Lifford. That night there were about 200 men holding the bridge.

Men were then posted at Lifford and Clady bridges, and one night James Kelly and a party at Clady attacked a group of the Special Constabulary travelling in an armoured car. One of the Specials was killed and the remainder fled the scene leaving the body in the street. Shortly before midnight on Monday 29 May, republican forces stationed in Lifford again attacked the Special Constabulary stationed in Strabane. An intense and sustained gun battle continued until after 5 a.m. the next morning. Large machine guns and bombs were used in the battle and for many miles around the noise of the shooting could be heard. Women and children were panic-stricken and spent the night lying on the floors of their homes.[22]

The republican forces were also concentrated along the border from Castlefinn to Clady and during Sunday 28 and Monday 29 May farmhouses in that district occupied by loyalists were raided and commandeered. Those identified as militant loyalists received notice to clear out and the vast majority moved to Castlederg in County Tyrone.[23]

One of the IRA engineers, James McElduff, was travelling throughout Donegal in search of detonators for landmines to be used against the Specials along the border. He was travelling between Donegal Town and Ballybofey and gave a lift to Eithne Coyle, who was busy with her one-woman campaign in continuance of the boycott policy. Neither McElduff nor his travelling companion knew who she was. The car broke down on the outskirts of Ballybofey and they decided to walk into the town. They found the entire area under the control of Dáil troops. All three were arrested at the first barricade and brought to a barracks in the town. The men were put in a cell and a soldier said the woman must stay outside. 'Wherever the boys go, I go along too,' Eithne Coyle said. They were not long there when Seán Lehane heard about their arrests and sent a warning to the officer in command of the town, which secured their release a short time later.[24]

Sometime before the official launch of the northern offensive in mid-May, the OC 1st Northern Division IRA, Seán Lehane, had mobilised his men for a big offensive against the Special Constabulary in Castlederg, County Tyrone. However, he remained very secretive about this particular operation and did not disclose any information about the intended target. Lehane was perhaps reluctant to disclose too much information based on the previous major operation in Derry where there had been suspicions of a leak of information. He ordered the IRA men to bring explosives, landmines and other demolition equipment, suggesting an attack on the barracks in the town. They made their way in the direction of Castlefinn and then on to Castlederg. They were on the outskirts of Castlederg and making final preparations when a courier arrived with an urgent message for Lehane. Operations were immediately suspended and Lehane ordered all men back in the direction of Castlefinn. The courier brought them to a farmhouse near the junction at Doneyloop Chapel and inside Tom Barry, IRA Director of Operations, warmly welcomed them. The Cork men were delighted to be reunited with Barry, their former OC West Cork Brigade. He had travelled specially from GHQ at the Four Courts with an order to temporarily cease all actions against the British forces in the Six Counties. Barry informed them that preparations were at an advanced stage for a large combined offensive to be launched throughout the Six Counties and that fully equipped columns were to be sent to strengthen the IRA in the Six Counties and the bordering counties.

The column, with Tom Barry in tow, returned to Raphoe in very high spirits and looking forward to the combined offensive against the old enemy. A few days later Tom Barry returned to Dublin accompanied by Seán Lehane, Charlie Daly, Peadar O'Donnell, Jack Fitzgerald and Denis Galvin to finalise plans for the offensive. The majority of the Donegal party returned a week later to prepare for the impending offensive. There was now a more comradely spirit in evidence among the ranks of the IRA and Dáil forces. However, despite the order to temporarily cease action against the British, the men of the 1st Northern Division continued with small-scale activities against the British military and police from within Donegal territory. Trains travelling between Omagh and Derry had to enter Donegal territory and in one incident the IRA seized a train pulling four petrol wagons. The cargo of 16,000 gallons of petrol was destined for the 165th Infantry Brigade of the British army based in Derry. A number of IRA men boarded the train at Strabane Station and held it up as it was approaching Carrigans Station. The tanks were detached from the train and a heavily armed IRA section was posted to guard the captured fuel, night and day, in anticipation of a British attack to retrieve it. Sporadic raids and attacks flared up again along the border and a British armoured car was blown up by a landmine at the Camel's Hump between Lifford and Strabane.[25]

Chapter 13

The Battles at Pettigo and Belleek

The villages of Pettigo and Belleek, located on the border of Counties Donegal and Fermanagh, were the focus of much activity during the late spring and early summer of 1922. Pettigo was situated in a unique position with one street consisting of two churches and a few houses cut off by a small river lying in Fermanagh, while the portion of the village including the police barracks and railway station was in Donegal. At that time the village had a population of approximately 500 people and was predominantly unionist. The Dáil forces under the Provisional Government established a garrison on the Donegal side in late April under Commandant Danny Gallagher. About the same time many of the republican forces who were forced to abandon Counties Tyrone and Fermanagh had relocated to Pettigo and Belleek. This mass exodus of men was partly due to the Special Powers legislation and also a request to all active IRA men to undergo proper organisation and training.

Over the following month the Special Constabulary based in County Fermanagh was responsible for numerous acts of aggression against Dáil forces and the general population in Pettigo and the surrounding areas, possibly at the behest of unionists living in the area who did not want Dáil forces occupying the town. These actions took the form of intermittent sniping at the barracks in the village and in some instances at civilians, with members of the Special Constabulary crossing into Donegal. The battles in the days that followed were the IRA's last stand against the British involving both the Dáil forces under the Provisional Government and the IRA under the Executive Council.[1] The initial actions of the Special Constabulary were unprovoked, but later activities could possibly be viewed as a response to the ongoing campaign by the IRA along the border with Counties Derry, Tyrone and Fermanagh.

Members of the Belfast government had been engaged in a campaign for the British government to take action against the IRA and Dáil forces through a propaganda campaign and the over-dramatisation of certain events. Their tactics worked to some extent, with members of the British cabinet falling for the dramatic statements of the over-excited unionists. One example of this originated from Richard King, Dean of Derry, when he wrote to James Craig warning of an immediate attack by the IRA based in Donegal. The source of the information was a number of loyalists who claimed to have been forced to flee from the county. James Craig relayed this as fact to Winston Churchill in London stating: 'I have reliable information that a force is mobilising in Donegal to launch an attack when word is given from higher authority.' Churchill responded by sending naval ships to Derry.[2]

The fears of these over-eager individuals were not unfounded as the IRA based in Donegal continued to attack garrisons along the bordering counties. However, there was little cooperation by way of assistance from the Dáil forces' command in Donegal despite assurances from Michael Collins during initial discussions in Dublin outlining the northern policy. Joe Sweeney, the officer commanding Dáil forces in Donegal, always maintained that he was never instructed by his GHQ to assist their counterparts.

Finally, however, events on the Donegal border in May and June 1922 brought the forces of the divided IRA together in one last battle with the British military. The battles of the Pettigo/Belleek triangle (covering the area between Pettigo, Belleek and the northern shore of lower Lough Erne) were unique in that this was the only place in Ireland where the IRA engaged with British forces in a stand-up fight with a defined battle line.

The Special Constabulary launched their first mass assault against the Donegal IRA on Saturday 27 May. A large number of Specials crossed Lough Erne from Roscor, County Fermanagh, in a pleasure steamer called

The Lady of the Lake, towing several smaller boats. They landed near the village of Belleek and made their way to Magheramenagh Castle, then the residence of the local parish priest, Fr L. O'Kierans. He was evicted and the Special Constabulary took possession of the building. They immediately established defensive positions in the grounds and began firing at anyone perceived to be IRA forces. However, their only victim was a local loyalist who was struck in the eye by a wood splinter as he stood sheltering behind a tree. The Specials were only at the castle a short time before realising they had positioned themselves at an unsafe location where they could be easily attacked.

Over the same weekend a party of IRA men from the 2nd Battalion, No. 3 Brigade had occupied Cliff House, Belleek, which belonged to Major Moore, a commandant of the Special Constabulary in Derry. He was also Grand Master of the Derry Orange Order. The occupation of Cliff House was undertaken as a precaution against an anticipated invasion of Donegal by British military then stationed in large numbers in all Six-County border areas.

Due to the conditions of the Truce, the Dáil forces had to be confined to the Donegal side but the movements of the Executive forces were not restricted. Dáil troops abandoned Belleek Fort and were replaced by the IRA. Thirty IRA men advanced along the railway line towards Magheramenagh Castle. On their way there they came under attack from a party of Specials who then retreated to the castle, pursued by the IRA. The Specials then abandoned the castle and retreated to their boats on the lough. They withdrew to Boa Island on Lough Erne, where they were reinforced by another 100 Specials with medical attendants to treat their wounded. A small number of IRA men had also suffered minor injuries.

The IRA garrison at Pettigo received word on Sunday morning of the Special Constabulary's advance on Belleek village. The officers in charge at Pettigo ordered men to dig a trench across the road at Pettigo Bridge to prevent the Special Constabulary advancing by road from Fermanagh. As this work was in progress large numbers of the Specials were observed approaching from Fermanagh. This put the men digging the trench in a precarious position, so a cover party of fourteen men was ordered to positions overlooking the bridge. This put the digging party directly in the line of fire, so those men were subsequently ordered to abandon the trench. The two sides maintained their positions on either side of the bridge and there was a tense silence in the village for the next couple of hours. Suddenly a shot was fired by a British military sniper on the Fermanagh side, followed by three or four more, intermittently. Then both sides began firing. The IRA held positions overlooking the bridge and bullets struck the walls of houses and buildings nearby, in some instances causing large lumps of lead to fall on them. The air was quickly filled with the smell of cordite as both sides continued firing; their rifles soon became too hot to handle.

The disturbances at Pettigo and Belleek warranted a visit on the Sunday morning from the general officer in command of the Dáil forces in Donegal, General Joe Sweeney. Dressed in full military uniform he proceeded to Belleek to inspect the posts there and gauge the situation. He was approaching the barracks at Belleek when shots were fired from the Fermanagh side with several narrowly missing him as he walked up the hill. He was forced to take cover and had to run into the barracks while dodging the bullets as the firing continued.

While Pettigo was under siege there was further activity at Belleek with a large party of Specials arriving in the village from Enniskillen in a number of Crossley tenders accompanied by one armoured car to assist their comrades at Boa Island. They were ambushed by the IRA as they crossed into Donegal at Belleek, and a short but sharp engagement followed in which the driver of the armoured car was killed, causing it to crash, blocking the road. With the road impassable, the occupants of the other vehicles were forced to retreat on foot under heavy fire from the IRA at Magheramenagh Castle. Later that evening the combined forces in Pettigo received information that A- and B-Specials were converging on Pettigo and taking up defensive positions. Great rumours began circulating of a full-scale invasion of the area by the British military based at Enniskillen. These rumours created panic and soon the local unionist population began evacuating the area, crossing into County Fermanagh, while the local nationalists made their way to other areas of Donegal.

The Battles at Pettigo and Belleek

Later that night a large contingent of Specials advanced from their headquarters at Clonelly House, County Fermanagh, to Pettigo and on arrival immediately opened fire on IRA positions to secure a route through to their besieged comrades on Boa Island. The IRA returned fire and after a two-hour engagement the Specials retreated to their convoy of Crossleys. They then attempted an outflanking movement to reach their comrades on Boa Island through Lowery. To do this they would have to cross the narrow isthmus of Donegal territory known as the Waterfoot, which juts out into Lough Erne between Letter and Lowery, both situated in County Fermanagh.

The IRA based at Pettigo remained in position overlooking the bridge until 7 a.m. on Monday 29 May when the shooting had stopped. The IRA men were instructed to go in twos and threes for breakfast. Later that morning, as Danny Gallagher and Nicholas Smyth were making their way to their meal along the street in Pettigo, a shot was fired from the Fermanagh side, striking the ground just in front of them. They immediately lay down on the road and another IRA man, who had witnessed the incident, fired in the direction of the sniper with a Thompson machine gun. There was no response from the sniper after that.

A section of IRA men was sent to the isthmus at the Waterfoot on Monday morning, 29 May, where they entrenched themselves in an attempt to prevent the Specials from crossing Lough Erne. Over the next few days the Special Constabulary contented themselves with sporadic firing into the town from the surrounding countryside.[3]

As the battle of Pettigo progressed, Michael Collins and Arthur Griffith were attending a meeting at 10 Downing Street in London on Wednesday 31 May. To their embarrassment, Winston Churchill confronted them about the ongoing hostilities at Pettigo. Neither man knew if the actions were being carried out by the forces of the Provisional Government or the IRA. Collins at that time was unaware of the incident and immediately disclaimed any responsibility and repudiated the action. Later that afternoon Churchill addressed the British parliament and, on the basis of Collins' statement that morning, declared that the Provisional Government forces were not involved. He ordered the British forces based at Enniskillen to occupy Belleek and Pettigo. They were directed to take action against armed parties who fired at them from the Donegal side. Churchill later wrote to Collins warning him: 'if British troops entering or holding Belleek village are fired at either from Belleek Fort or adjoining Free State territory the military authorities have full discretion either to bombard or occupy'.

Collins was briefed on the background of the incident at Pettigo on his return to Dublin. He immediately sent a telegram to Churchill in London:

> Regret to say it makes the situation very much more serious. Must protest on behalf of the Provisional Government against your troops moving on our positions without any prior warning – Emphasise that inquiry essential as of course our men must defend their positions in our territory against any attackers ... You misunderstand the position and only immediate enquiry can put it right.[4]

Meanwhile back at Pettigo the shooting continued the following morning, Thursday 1 June. The British intensified the assault on Pettigo that day when a large convoy of British military, RUC and Special Constabulary advanced on the village. The IRA waited until the convoy was within range before opening fire. The British immediately took up defensive positions and replied with rapid gunfire, which continued for over an hour, and they were said to have suffered several casualties. They then retreated leaving a Special Constable sheltering behind a tree. He suddenly made a sprint up the road and the IRA men held their fire and cheered him on as he ran to safety.

The British forces continued sniping at Pettigo throughout Thursday and Friday night and then commandeered and assembled all available boats at Portonode from where a battalion of soldiers was transported to Boa Island. Carrying the boats across the island, they landed at Letter, two miles downstream of Pettigo. Another British military battalion advanced from Kesh to Lowery. The battalion at Letter attempted to join their comrades at Lowery. However, a number of IRA outposts had been positioned at the Waterfoot and a detachment of IRA under John Travers made its way to Letter to stem the enemy approach, with John Scallon leading reinforcements to the Waterfoot. Throughout Saturday night both battalions of British soldiers repeatedly attacked the IRA at the Waterfoot in the hope of dislodging them, but they failed. During the intensive fighting a section of the IRA under Nicholas Smyth cautiously made their way from Pettigo, a distance of a mile, to assist their comrades at the Waterfoot. They had to crawl for about 300 yards to get to the position held by Jim Scallon and his men who were coming under heavy fire from two British sections. Scallon suggested that they move into positions between the two enemy sections so that when firing began it would dupe the enemy to fire at each other. This worked: both British sections opened fire on each other and when they were thus engaged the IRA men crawled back into their positions. The British sections continued to fire at each other for some time before realising what had happened, and they eventually retreated to Boa Island. After the enemy retreat, the IRA men were able to get some much-needed sleep.

A detachment of the Lincolnshire Regiment had landed near Boa Island on Saturday morning, 3 June. At the same time a large party of Specials had invaded Donegal through Lettercran, which is five miles from Pettigo, and terrorised the local residents. As two young girls were returning from Lettercran Chapel, four Special Constables ran towards them with one shouting, 'We will have our own back now.' He fired at Bridget McGrath, who fell when she was hit. When Susan MacNeil attempted to help her, another Special Constable fired, striking her on the arm. The girls' injuries were superficial and they managed to escape by running up a lane with the Specials firing after them. They entered the house of John McGrath through a back window. There was nobody in the house apart from Mrs McGrath nursing her baby. She bandaged the girls' wounds before the Specials began firing at the house, forcing the two to run out the back door to escape to safety. Later that night a large number – about 200 – of Specials attempted to cross at Lettercran from Fermanagh into Donegal to attack Pettigo from the rear. An IRA post, foreseeing their intentions, intercepted them there and after a fierce engagement the Specials were forced to retreat having suffered casualties.[5]

Early on Sunday 4 June the IRA section at the Waterfoot was relieved by another section and the men made their way back to Pettigo where many attended the early morning mass. At 10 a.m. that morning another detachment of the Lincolnshire Regiment with two companies of the South Staffordshire Regiment and a section of the 4th Howitzer Battery moved on Pettigo village from the east under the command of Colonel Wyatt, Commandant of the 18th Infantry Brigade. While mass was in progress the British military crossed the bridge into Pettigo and began taking up positions. Heavy fire was opened on the village as mass was ending and the people were leaving the chapel. At the same time two officers of the Dáil forces, Commandant O'Farrell and Lieutenant Martin, were walking along the main street towards their headquarters at Martin's Hotel when British forces opened fire with machine guns. The British were located at the Belfast Bank which was in Six-County territory and situated at the top of High Street. O'Farrell and Martin shouted to the people to take cover and they had just reached Martin's Hotel when a howitzer 60-pound shell exploded near the barracks, shortly followed by two others, which flew over the town and landed in a nearby field. Colonel Wyatt, accompanied by other officers in an armoured car, approached the village along the Kesh Road and stopped at a barricade. Commandant Michael O'Farrell ordered Martin to approach the British officers, who were by that time standing beside the armoured car at the Kesh Road barricade. Martin walked over to Wyatt, who said, 'You have fifteen minutes to leave the town or get shot up.' Shells continued to fly overhead, landing near Dáil forces' posts. Martin returned to inform O'Farrell that the British officer had ordered them to leave town and they had fifteen minutes to do so.

The Dáil forces had two cars in the barracks yard, but the drivers had not yet returned from mass. O'Farrell and Martin approached the British officer and requested an extension of the time so that the outposts could be informed. The officer refused and immediately placed O'Farrell under arrest, asking Martin if he was the only remaining officer in charge, to which he said he was. He was allowed to leave and was told to have all his men cleared out of the area.[6] The British continued firing into the village that morning with three howitzer 60-pound shells fired in the direction of Billary Hill overlooking the village. A convoy of armoured cars then drove into the village covering both the roads and railway links for an area of three miles' radius around the village. However, gunfire from the IRA prevented them from clearing the way for some time. The British replied with intense and heavy gunfire, forcing the unit of the IRA covering the bridge to withdraw to new positions, which allowed the British to clear the barricade at the bridge and advance into the village. As this main thrust was in progress, two other columns of British troops which had been stationed at Letter and another approaching from the north by the Lough Derg road, attempted to join forces to encircle the village. The IRA kept them at bay and left the escape route open to the main body of both pro- and anti-Treaty IRA who withdrew to the hills. They kept up a running fire until 5 p.m., at which point they retreated. However, approximately eight IRA men at the machine-gun post which manned Drumhariff Hill covering the approach to the town held their positions until their ammunition was exhausted and the post was then surrounded and captured. Patrick Flood of Pettigo, Bernard McCanny and William Kearney of Drumquinn, County Tyrone were killed at their posts. Patrick Flood was killed by rifle fire on Drumhariff Hill, while the howitzer shells directed at Billary Hill killed Bernard McCanny and William Kearney.

A large-scale evacuation followed and the IRA men made their way to the hills to escape the bombardment. One group was caught out in the open when a howitzer shell exploded beside them. However, no one was injured: the men were only covered with mud and were able to continue over the hills in the direction of Ballintra. Some IRA men fled by boat and made their way across Lough Derg to the pilgrimage island. The prior of the pilgrimage, Dean Keown, fearing a British assault on the island, had the IRA men transferred by boat to the opposite shore where they were able to cross the mountains towards Donegal Town. Many of the evacuating IRA men were picked up along the road by passing motorists and over sixty men safely evacuated Pettigo and were temporarily housed in the old workhouse. Many were in bad shape physically and nearly all had lost clothing, money, etc. The local population showed great kindness to them and the parish priest organised a collection to provide men with clothes. In an incident at the workhouse William Deasley from Dromore, County Tyrone, who had been active in the battle at Pettigo before escaping to safety, was accidently shot and later died.

While the fighting was taking place in Pettigo, the IRA at the Waterfoot was heavily engaged by vastly superior numbers of British forces and forced to surrender after two hours. By four o'clock on Sunday 4 June, the shooting had ended and Pettigo was under the control of the British, thus ending the battle of Pettigo. The unionist population started to return to the village by that evening. The battalions of British military had been sent into the Six Counties in early May by Winston Churchill, the then Secretary of State for the Colonies, on the advice of Field Marshal Henry Wilson, military advisor to the Belfast government.

The British contingent was powerful compared with the IRA who numbered less than one hundred young men in their teens and early twenties who withstood that final week under continuous fire with no sleep or rest. This incident seemed to heal briefly the division between Provisional Government and IRA Executive forces. Unfortunately this temporary feeling of old time unity disappeared as soon as the military operations against the British forces ended.[7]

The parish priest of Pettigo, Fr Bernard Hackett, returned to the village on Sunday evening after the shelling had ended and discovered the village under the control of the British military. He approached the commanding officer to enquire if there were any dead or wounded. The British OC said there were no wounded and that the bodies of three men had been taken to Enniskillen. A large number of B-Specials directed abusive and insulting remarks towards the priest and he considered it unsafe to remain there. The following day John McHugh informed Fr Hackett that the body of young Patrick Flood was lying partially exposed on Billary Hill. The two men approached a British officer who was sitting outside Flood's Hotel. Beside him was a coffin leaning against the wall with a piece of paper pinned to it with the words 'Shinners accommodated' written on it. The priest informed the British officer about the body and he refuted the claim. When the priest introduced John McHugh, who confirmed the presence of a body,

British military evacuating Letterkenny *McGinley Collection*

Hugh Britton's remains entering the Old Abbey graveyard, Donegal Town
Courtesy of Jack Britton

Pettigo, scene of the battles between the IRA and British forces in May and June 1922
Courtesy of the National Library of Ireland

Joe Sweeney and Dr J. P. McGinley entering Treaty talks at UCD, Earlsfort Terrace, Dublin, January 1922
McGinley Collection

Mary (May) Burke, Eithne Coyle and Linda Kearns at Duckett's Grove, Co. Carlow, 1921
Courtesy of Prionnsíos Ó Duigneáin

The IRA take over Falcarragh Barracks, 1922
MacElhinney Collection

The IRA taking over Buncrana, 1922 — *MacElhinney Collection*

The IRA in Carndonagh, 1922 — *McGinley Collection*

The IRA police Donegal Town, 1922

Courtesy of Cyril O'Boyle

Seán Lehane, Charlie Daly, Jack Fitzgerald, Denis Galvin, Seán Fitzgerald
MacElhinney Collection

The burnt-out courthouse in Letterkenny *McGinley Collection*

Donncha MacNelis
Donegal Annual Archives

SS *Lady Wicklow*   *Courtesy of the National Library of Ireland*

IRA prisoners at Ballybofey   *MacElhinney Collection*

Hugh Britton	Bernard McCanny	Patrick Flood	William Kearney
William Deasley	Patrick Johnston	Thomas McShea	Neil 'Plunkett' O'Boyle
Seamus McCann	Peadar O'Donnell	Charlie McGinley	Jack Sweeney
Timothy O'Sullivan	Daniel Enright	Charlie Daly	Seán Larkin

the British officer instructed a sergeant to accompany the two men to the location, where they found the corpse of Patrick Flood partially covered with clay and sandbags. They returned to the town and asked permission to remove Flood's body and bury him, but the officer was reluctant to allow a funeral, stating that he did not want any trouble. After assurances from the priest, the officer gave them permission to remove the body and told them to use the coffin with the offensive note attached. The priest refused and said they would get one from the local undertakers. They eventually retrieved the body and with the help of other locals carried it down the hill through the town, where they were subjected to a torrent of abuse and jeers with someone throwing a Union Jack over the coffin.

In the days following the take-over of Pettigo, the homes and businesses of nationalists living in the area were broken into and looted by members of the military and B-Specials. Some residents were ordered by the Specials to leave the town and the local Catholic church was targeted, with several windows being broken.[8] The combined action in County Donegal was raised in the British House of Commons and shortly afterwards Michael Collins received a telegram requesting him to give an explanation about what forces were involved. Collins denied any involvement of Dáil troops and demanded an enquiry into the actions of the British soldiers and Specials, but the British government refused. This incident led Collins to reappraise his northern strategy and he later declared a policy of peaceful obstruction against the Belfast government for the foreseeable future. However, he also stated that the actions of the IRA along the border and in the Six Counties were merely for the protection of the nationalist minority. Collins blamed the provocative actions of the Special Constabulary for the whole thing. In contrast, Craig's propaganda machine put the blame exclusively on the IRA, suggesting that any actions of the Special Constabulary constituted a defensive measure.[9]

Unionist politicians had passed many dramatic reports to the British government (circulated between 24 May and 15 June by military advisor Major General Arthur Solly-Flood) about plans to attack British forces in the Six Counties. According to one report there was a secret deal 'between Collins and De Valera to build up strength under cover of the Free State until the situation was ripe for the two forces to unite and strike at the Empire'. The invasion of Pettigo and Belleek initiated by the British at the behest of James Craig's representations to Winston Churchill was based on similar information.

In an extract from one of these circulated reports, Major General Arthur Solly-Flood warned of a grand-scale assault on the British Empire with the aid of international support:

> The triumphant Republicans now boast that in a year's time they will be in such a strong military position that they can laugh at England, 'if', in the words of Cathal Brugha, 'there is still such a place on the map'. Throughout the whole of these proceedings, there is constant and abundant evidence that the Irish Republicans are in close touch with foreign communists, Bolshevists, and internationals to promote revolution in England and bring about the destruction of the Empire.[10]

The propagandists and the British government were giving the northern offensive more credit than it deserved as cooperation between the two sides in Donegal was less successful than suggested. The original starting date for the offensive in the Six Counties was 19 May 1922. However, commands and countermands led to great confusion, with some areas engaging with the enemy while others waited for further instructions. Overall the joint IRA offensive failed, with the breakdown in communications between various divisions and with others failing to take part for unexplained reasons.

The northern government was made aware of the plans and ordered a general round-up of all known IRA men. Internment was introduced in the Six Counties and large numbers of the Special Constabulary moved into south Armagh and south Down unopposed. An IRA memo at the time reported, 'after a period of over five weeks, demoralisation has practically completed its work'.[11]

Having secured Pettigo village, the British military turned their attention to the village of Belleek several miles away. They began with a reconnaissance of the village on Thursday 8 June with two columns of the

Manchester and Lincolnshire Regiments. One column approached from the north along the Pettigo Road and the other from the south along the Enniskillen Road. Shortly after midday, the British sent an armoured car ahead of the military column and as it arrived at the school on the Pettigo Road shots were fired from a location approximately 300 yards away. At the same time the other column, approaching on the Enniskillen Road, was fired on from Belleek Fort, which is situated in County Donegal. The British column approaching on the Pettigo Road engaged with the IRA and advanced in extended order to Belleek village. The shooting from the IRA at Belleek Fort was answered by the British with four rounds of howitzer 18-pounder shells. The IRA garrison soon evacuated the building. At approximately 1.30 p.m. a column of the Lincolnshire Regiment entered Belleek Fort without any resistance and soon the Tricolour was replaced with the Union Jack. Both Belleek and Pettigo were then in the hands of the British military and temporarily under the control of the Belfast government. The military operations at both Pettigo and Belleek were justified by the British military as necessary measures to clear the area of republican forces. The British military remained in the area and stated that they had no intentions to advance any further provided their troops were not fired on.[12]

The parish priest of Belleek, Fr O'Kierans, returned to inspect his residence at Magheramenagh Castle on Saturday 10 June. The Special Constabulary had evicted him on Saturday 27 May. The castle was occupied by British military from Thursday 8 June to Friday evening, 9 June, resulting in considerable damage to the interior as well as the destruction of many valuable books and documents. Fr O'Kierans found that many of the books had been burned and others thrown out of the building. Many important documents were also missing, including the vesting order of a farm, the title deeds of the site of Belleek Chapel and documents relating to school sites.[13]

Chapter 14

The Constitution of Saorstát Éireann and the 1922 Election

The Constitution of Saorstát Éireann was the final test for the Irish signatories to the Treaty with regard to the nature and meaning of the document. This would be the ultimate test for Michael Collins and Arthur Griffith who were the principal negotiators with the British cabinet. The Provisional Government had appointed the Constitutional Committee in January with instructions to have a draft version of the constitution ready before the end of February. According to Arthur Griffith, the only instructions given to the committee were printed copies of the Treaty and a request to prepare a draft constitution for Ireland within the context of the Treaty. However, the draft document was written in the context of republican principles with strong emphasis on Irish sovereignty and no references to the British monarch or the British Privy Council in the legislative appeals process. The republican version of the constitution or the desire for a document at variance with the guiding document, the Treaty, was at best wishful thinking.[1]

The British government had directed the Irish delegation to draft the document using the Constitution of Canada as the guiding document. When the draft was presented for consideration on Saturday 27 May, the British Prime Minister, Lloyd George, convened a meeting of the cabinet the following Monday, 29 May. At the conclusion of this meeting, a memorandum was issued criticising the draft document on behalf of the British government, which was subsequently handed to the Irish representatives. At a later meeting, held on Thursday 1 June, Lloyd George's opening comments were 'a serious situation had arisen with respect to Ireland, which called for an immediate decision ... The draft Constitution ... was purely Republican in character and but thinly veiled. It did not comply with the Treaty in substance or in form.'

Lloyd George also stated that the constitution submitted by the Irish representatives was not based on the monarchical principle and did not bring Ireland inside the British Empire. The king was not part of the legislature: he would not appoint the ministers, nor would he summon or dissolve parliament. Austen Chamberlain, the Lord Privy Seal, asked why the draft constitution had not been made public, to which Lloyd George replied that the British had considered this document as a negation of the Treaty and that to circulate or publish it would put the Irish representatives in a precarious position in that they had travelled to London with one document and would be returning to Ireland with a very different version. Lloyd George highlighted four points in which the draft constitution conflicted with the Treaty. They were that the position of the crown was repudiated; power was vested in the Irish government; the judicial committee of the Privy Council was rejected as the final court of appeal; and the oath of allegiance was not included in the document. In Lloyd George's opinion, 'Thus the Irish were challenging the most fundamental points of the Treaty.'[2]

The result of that cabinet meeting was a list of six questions, which were handed to the Irish delegation at 6 p.m. on Thursday 1 June, with a request that they should meet the British signatories at 6.30 p.m. Michael Collins and Arthur Griffith held a meeting with Lloyd George and requested more time, complaining that the time-frame was not adequate and the questions had raised a number of difficulties. The main areas of concern for the Irish delegation were the oath to the British monarch, appeals to the judicial committee of the Privy Council and more particularly the make-up of that committee. The three justices appointed to the committee, Lord Carson, Lord Sumner and Lord Cave, had in the past been publicly hostile towards Ireland.

Lloyd George concluded the meeting with Collins and Griffith, impressing upon them that they now had the best chance any leaders had ever had of securing real liberty for Ireland. Lloyd George also pointed out that 'if they failed to stand by the signatures they had appended to the Treaty they would be dishonoured and such conduct would be a departure from the high reputation for good faith, which Irish leaders had enjoyed in the past'.

It was then agreed that the Irish delegation would meet with Lloyd George the following day (Friday 2 June), with answers to the list of questions. Before the reply was received, the British cabinet convened a meeting on Friday morning to discuss the possible outcome of the answers to the questions and other related issues. In a reply to a query at that meeting on whether the Irish leaders realised that the time had come for them to choose between Éamon de Valera and the Treaty, Lloyd George said 'he did not think they quite realised the issue ... that Arthur Griffith did, but he thought Michael Collins appeared to think that he could carry the others [republicans] along with him'. Winston Churchill addressed the meeting saying, 'The more the fear of renewed warfare was present to the minds of the electors the more likely were they to go to the polls and support the Treaty.' The British government had anticipated a negative response to the questions and had planned their own amendments to the draft document.

The answers to the six questions were received by the British that evening and another cabinet meeting was convened at 8.15 p.m. to consider them. The British cabinet expressed general satisfaction with the terms of the reply. While some issues required further clarification, i.e. the position of the crown in Ireland and the appeal to the Privy Council, it was agreed that 'there was nothing in the letter to warrant breaking off negotiations at the present stage'.[3]

It was likely that the British had prepared themselves for this outcome and were merely orchestrating a situation whereby Michael Collins and others would be pitted against republican leaders. This would have the desired effect of the Irish fighting against each other as opposed to fighting the British or elements of the Belfast government. The prospects of a republican constitution were very slim, when measured against the

Treaty document. It was during this period that the British government's mistrust of Collins rose to the surface, with Lloyd George describing him as a 'wild animal – a mustang'. Lionel Curtis of the British colonial office described negotiating with Collins as writing on water and Lloyd George added, 'shallow and agitated water'.[4]

In the days leading up to Ireland's June election, the eagerly anticipated republican constitution was being heavily amended to the extent that it was reproduced as a colonial document corresponding with the terms of the Treaty. There was great anticipation among the electorate about the document before polling day, but because of delays caused by consultations with British and unionist MPs the document was not published until polling day. The result was that many went to the polls on Friday 16 June to vote for the panel candidates of the Collins/de Valera pact with the belief of a republican constitution at the forefront of their minds.[5]

The Constitution of Saorstát Éireann was in some respects similar to the original aim of the Sinn Féin policy laid down by Arthur Griffith in 1899, which gave recognition to the British Empire and was based on the principles of dual monarchy. Ireland was to be a dominion within the British Empire and its partition through the Government of Ireland Act 1920 would continue to exist through the Treaty Agreement and the Constitution of Saorstát Éireann. The immediate similarities of Saorstát Éireann and the Government of Ireland Act were the division of Ireland into twenty-six southern counties and six northern counties, each jurisdiction having its own parliament with limited powers in matters of defence, foreign affairs and fiscal matters.

Article 1 of the Constitution referred to Ireland's place of equal membership in the British Commonwealth of Nations, thereby giving Ireland dominion status within that commonwealth. Article 2 provided:

> All powers of government and all authority, legislative, executive and judicial in Ireland are derived from the people of Ireland and the same shall be exercised in the Irish Free State (Saorstát Éireann) through the organisations established by or under and in accord with this Constitution.

However, in section 2 it also said:

> ... the Constitution shall be construed with reference to the treaty ... And if any provision of the said Constitution or any amendment thereof or of any law made thereunder is in any respect repugnant to any provision of the scheduled treaty, it shall, to the extent of such repugnancy, be absolutely void and inoperable.

Although the 1922 Constitution recognised the people as the supreme law-giver, it also contained a dualism repugnant to republican ideology, in that the British monarch was to have a major influence in the legislative process under Article 12:

> A legislature is hereby created, to be known as the Oireachtas, it shall consist of the King and the two Houses ... the Chamber of Deputies otherwise called and herein generally referred to as 'Dáil Éireann' and the Senate otherwise known as 'Seanad Éireann'.

Article 17 contained the formula for the oath to be taken by members of the Oireachtas, which was to be taken in the presence of the king or someone nominated by him:

> I ... do solemnly swear true faith and allegiance to the Constitution of the Irish Free State (Saorstát Éireann) as by law established ... and that I will be faithful to H.M. King George V, his heirs and successors by law in virtue of the common law citizenship of Ireland and Great Britain and her adherence to and membership of the groups of nations forming the British Commonwealth of Nations.[6]

The 1922 election campaign faced a number of issues. The first was the promise of a republican constitution that did not materialise, which possibly led to the electorate unknowingly voting in favour of Ireland's union with Britain under the terms of the Constitution and the Free State Act 1922. The second was that there were seven uncontested constituencies with all sitting elected representatives being returned unopposed: Donegal; Clare; East Limerick and borough of Limerick; Kerry and West Limerick; Mayo North and West; Mayo South and Roscommon South; and Leitrim and Roscommon North. The third important issue was that the poll of electors was based on that of the 1918 general election register and had not been updated in the four years since then. This prevented thousands of young men and women in their late teens and early twenties from casting their votes which could have given a very different outcome to the election.

The election did not impede the activities of the IRA operating in Donegal and the boycott campaign continued when the midday trains for Letterkenny and Carndonagh were held up at Burnfoot on Saturday 17 June. A wagon of timber was detached at Toolan. The goods train, which was cleared of all merchandise on Friday, was brought back to Derry and repacked on Saturday. It was sent out again at 2.30 p.m., but was held up again and a considerable quantity of goods removed. The raids were increasing the pressure on the British military based in Derry who were considering invading Donegal to create a neutral zone in the Carrigans–St Johnston area in an effort to prevent further raids.[7]

The railway line passing through Carrigans and St Johnston *en route* to Derry from Omagh was the focus of most of the train hijackings. The rumours of a British invasion of Donegal were not to be taken lightly, as a few days earlier a British military officer, carrying a white flag, delivered a note to the OC at the St Johnston and Carrigans posts, which stated that unless the Belfast boycott ceased, these posts would be attacked and Specials put into occupation. The IRA's vice-commandant in Donegal, Charlie Daly, thought this would offer an opportunity where both the IRA Executive and Dáil forces could join together and engage with the British and avoid civil war in Donegal. The Dáil forces' garrison based in Lifford was composed of men from the 2nd Northern Division, Tyrone, under the command of Major Tom Morris. Daly went to Lifford and had a meeting with Morris, who was assured by him that the forces under his command would remain neutral and would not interfere with any actions of the republican forces against the British military or Special Constabulary. Daly explained his own position to Morris and regretted that he was unable to cooperate with him. He informed Morris that a republican garrison stationed nearby would give all assistance in the event of an assault on the 'border'.[8]

Despite recent developments, the northern offensive remained high on the agenda in some quarters, including Dublin. Liam Mellows summoned Sighle Bean Uí Dhonnchadha (Sheila Humphreys) to Donnybrook and outlined to her how both republican and Free State forces hoped to sink their differences through united action on the Six Counties. Cumann na mBan members were requested to set up a field hospital in County Donegal and Liam Mellows asked Sheila Humphreys to select a number of experienced members of the organisation to assist her in setting up the centre. All the arrangements were made and they were to be escorted to Donegal by Frank O'Donnell from Dungloe.[9]

Chapter 15

The Wilson Assassination – A Catalyst for Civil War

The assassination of Field Marshal Sir Henry Wilson, on 22 June 1922 in London, was the spark that ignited the fuse of the Irish Civil War. Wilson was MP for North County Down and security advisor to the Belfast government, and his ancestors could be traced to the plantation of Ulster and had taken part in the siege of Derry in 1689. His assassins were members of the London IRA: Joseph O'Sullivan and Reginald Dunne. O'Sullivan had previously served in the British army and had been employed in the British Ministry of Labour. At the time of the assassination, O'Sullivan was working at the Ministry of Munitions and was at work on the morning of Thursday 22 June, being relieved from his post at 1 p.m. O'Sullivan and Dunne shadowed Wilson for most of that afternoon, taking their opportunity as he walked from a taxi to his front door. Two police constables were also shot and the assassins initially escaped, but both men were captured a short time later. Michael Collins had issued the order to assassinate Wilson before the Truce and confirmed it during the Treaty negotiations. However, the British government believed the origins of the assassination lay with the IRA at the Four Courts in Dublin.

The British cabinet met that afternoon at 5 p.m. to discuss the day's events. The meeting was busy and matters relating to the arrest of suspected persons were high on the agenda. Those present considered their primary objective was to discover the circumstances surrounding the Wilson killing and that the police should 'search the premises of suspected and dangerous persons'. The documents found on Dunne and O'Sullivan, along with the revolvers used, were brought to the meeting by Colonel Carter of Scotland Yard.

Following inspection it was surmised that the various documents provided '*prima facie* evidence of the probability of a conspiracy in London which would justify the arrest of the suspected persons'. During discussion about the various documents, the focus of the meeting turned to the situation at the Four Courts in Dublin from where the British believed the plot to assassinate Wilson had emanated. There was a consensus that the Provisional Government should be 'pressed' to address the occupation of the Four Courts by the IRA Executive. The Commander-in-Chief of British forces in Ireland, General Macready, was immediately summoned to London. However, a communication was later received stating that he was at that time visiting Belleek to investigate the circumstances of the battle there earlier that month.[1]

The British government's initial response was an ultimatum to Michael Collins to take immediate action against the IRA Executive at the Four Courts or the British army would be redeployed to attack the IRA GHQ. At the conclusion of the cabinet meeting in London it was agreed that a letter would be drafted and sent to Collins that evening. The letter was written by Winston Churchill and signed by David Lloyd George:

> I am desired by ... Government to inform you that documents have been found upon the murderers of Field Marshal Sir Henry Wilson which clearly connect the assassins with the Irish Republican Army, and which further reveal the existence of a definite conspiracy against peace and order of this country.
>
> Other information ... showing that active preparations are on foot among the irregular elements of the IRA to resume attacks upon the lives and property of British subjects both in England and in Ulster ... The ambiguous position of the Irish Republican Army can no longer be ignored by the British Government. Still less can Mr. Rory O'Connor be permitted to remain with his followers and his arsenal in open rebellion in the heart of Dublin in possession of the Courts

of Justice, organising and sending out from this centre enterprises of murder not only in the area of your Government but also in the Six Northern Counties and in Great Britain. His Majesty's Government cannot consent to a continuance of this state of things and they feel entitled to ask you formally to bring it to an end forthwith ...[2]

The letter was signed about 8 p.m. that evening and was dispatched by special messenger to Dublin soon after. By the time the correspondence was received in Dublin the following day, Michael Collins had been summoned to Cork on urgent business. In his absence Diarmuid O'Hegarty, Secretary of the Provisional Government, replied to Lloyd George's letter:

My Government have been profoundly shocked by the tragic and untimely death of Sir Henry Wilson and they hasten to place on record their condemnation of the assassination by whomever it was perpetrated ... The Government (Provisional) was however satisfied that these forces contained within themselves elements of disruption which given time would accomplish their complete disintegration and relieve the Government of the necessity of employing methods of suppression ...[3]

However, O'Hegarty exercised a certain amount of caution and requested the presentation of the alleged evidence implicating the IRA to be passed to the Provisional Government:

The Provisional Government has no intention of tolerating such a condition of things and therefore requests your Government to assist them in dealing with the situation by placing at their disposal the information to which you refer.[4]

The documents found on Reginald Dunne related to matters of the IRB in Britain and made reference to the 'Big Fellow – arranging for an election'. The mention of the 'Big Fellow' raised further suspicions about Collins' intentions regarding the Treaty and other matters. The British government was becoming more frustrated and was by now very wary of Collins.[5]

Reginald Dunne and Joseph O'Sullivan were imprisoned in Wandsworth Prison where they received a severe beating on arrival, and later at their trial on Tuesday 18 July were convicted by a jury who took only two minutes to return a guilty verdict.[6] The death sentence was then handed down by the judge. In the interim, Michael Collins had arranged for the escape or rescue of Dunne and O'Sullivan from either Wandsworth Prison or from the prison van transporting them from the prison to the court. Joe Dolan, intelligence department, GHQ of the pro-Treaty IRA under the Provisional Government, was sent to London to discuss the matter with Sam Maguire and was put in contact with Seán Golden. The two men set about exploring possible ways to rescue Dunne and O'Sullivan. However, the outbreak of the Civil War in late June side-tracked the plan to rescue the two men. John Ellis, the English hangman, subsequently hanged Dunne and O'Sullivan on Thursday 10 August.[7] Their burials took place in the grounds of Wandsworth Prison.[8]

The British cabinet convened another meeting in the days following the assassination of Henry Wilson and was joined on that occasion by General Neville Macready, Commander-in-Chief of British troops in Ireland. Macready was in command of several thousand British military based in Dublin. The purpose of the meeting was to decide what to do with the IRA in the Four Courts. The decision was taken that a policy of retaliation would commence within days and that Macready would lead the British troops in an attack on the Four Courts using tanks, howitzer shells and even aeroplanes. The potential loss of life among the civilian population was raised by Macready but did not serve as a deterrent and the focus of that meeting and a subsequent meeting was what the best day would be – Sunday or Monday? The order was later cancelled due to fears expressed by Macready that an attack could possibly rebound to the detriment of the British military and lead to a reunification in the ranks of the IRA and increased support from the public. The military also raised the issue of the evidence found on Reginald Dunne as not being sufficient to lay the blame solely on the IRA Executive based at the Four Courts. The plan to attack was withdrawn at the last hour and instead it was decided that a final ultimatum be sent to the Provisional Government to take action against the garrison at the Four Courts and end their occupation, since permitting the existence of another authority encroached upon the Treaty agreement.[9]

The movement of Dáil troops into County Donegal over that same weekend in June was a clear indication that the Provisional Government was preparing a response to the British threats and ultimatums. Large numbers of troops began arriving in the county to bolster the local brigades with over 100 troops from Beggars Bush, Dublin, arriving in Letterkenny and taking up quarters at the workhouse at Asylum Road (High Road). Over 150 Dáil troops were garrisoned at the coastguard station in Rathmullan and other areas were strengthened including Buncrana, Drumboe Castle and Ballybofey.

The Free State election results were declared on Saturday 24 June with fifty-eight pro-Treaty party candidates, thirty-six Republicans, seventeen Labour, seven Farmers' Party, six Independents and four Unionists elected. Any prospects of the pro-Treaty and republican candidates forming the Third Dáil were destroyed with the compulsory requirement that each member elected take the oath of allegiance to the king under the terms of the Constitution: something republicans were loath to recognise.[10]

Chapter 16

An Cogadh na gCarad – The War between Friends

An Cogadh na gCarad – The War between Friends or *Cogladh na mBrathar* – The War between Brothers, more commonly known as the Irish Civil War, began at 4.15 a.m. on Wednesday 28 June with the shelling of the Four Courts in Dublin. Some members of the Donegal IRA were in the city when it started and received orders from Peadar O'Donnell to get back to Donegal immediately.[1] The attack on the IRA Executive headquarters was in direct violation of the agreement between the two sides regarding the northern offensive and was provoked by an act not of their doing, the assassination of Wilson. Unlike the War of Independence, the Civil War was to be a much more bitter conflict as it was now a war of brother against brother, family, friends and neighbours, who had stood together during the terrible years against the British. It was one of the saddest chapters in Irish history as families throughout Donegal and Ireland were at odds, with some taking the republican side and others taking the Free State side. The Army Executive on behalf of the Irish Republican Army based at the Four Courts issued a proclamation on the same day:

> The fateful hour has come. At the direction of our hereditary enemy our rightful cause is being treacherously assailed by recreant Irishmen. The crash of arms and the boom of artillery reverberate in this supreme test of the nation's destiny. Gallant soldiers of the Irish Republic, stand rigorously firm in its defence, and worthily uphold their noblest traditions. The sacred spirits of the illustrious dead are with us in this

great struggle. Death before dishonour being an unchanging principle of our national faith as it was of theirs still inspires us to emulate their glorious efforts.

We therefore appeal to all citizens who have withstood unflinchingly the oppression of the enemy the past six years to rally to the support of the Republic and to recognise that the resistance now being offered is but the continuance of the struggle which was suspended by the truce with the British. We especially appeal to our former comrades of the Irish Republican Army (who have been seduced from their allegiance to the Republic) to return to that allegiance and thus guard the Nation's honour from the infamous stigma that her sons aided her foes in retaining a hateful dominance over her. Confident of victory and of maintaining Ireland's Independence, this appeal is issued by the Army Executive on behalf of the Irish Republican Army.[2]

Peadar O'Donnell was a member of the Executive at the Four Courts and a signatory to the statement. The other signatories were Liam Lynch, Rory O'Connor, Joseph McKelvey, Earnán Ó Maille, Seamus Robinson, Michael Moylan, Michael Kilroy, Frank Barrett, Thomas Derrig, Tom Barry, F. O'Faolain, J. O'Connor, Liam Deasy and P. Rutledge.[3]

Despite the shelling of the Four Courts, Sheila Humphreys was informed that the offensive on the north was to continue and at 1.30 p.m. on the same day she was accompanied by Una O'Connor, Mary (Peg) Cuddihy and Máire Comerford, escorted by Frank O'Donnell, as they left Dublin by train for Donegal. Each woman had a small calibre revolver and they brought first aid equipment as well as cases of revolvers, ammunition and explosives. The party arrived in Sligo later that day and stayed with the republican garrison in the town under the command of Brian MacNeill. Liam Pilkington, who was in command of the 3rd Western Division, was also there and arranged for them to be taken to Ballybofey where the field hospital was to be established. They stopped off at Finner Camp for the night before continuing their journey the following morning. On arriving at Ballybofey, they were told that the Cumann na mBan team was not needed.[4]

The forces under the command of the Provisional Government or the government of the Free State were from this point on referred to as Free State forces. Dáil Éireann was still in existence and no authority had derived from that institution to abide by or to recognise the Treaty. The authority of the Treaty and the attack on the Four Courts were viewed as undertakings at the behest of the British government and in full recognition of the Treaty and were considered by many as the final act of the agreement between the Provisional and British governments.

Such was the pace at which events moved that few areas outside of Dublin were aware of the new situation. General Seán MacEoin of the Free State forces was in County Donegal on his honeymoon at that time and, following a minor accident, sent a telegram to Joe Sweeney for assistance. MacEoin's car was recovered and he was taken to Letterkenny where a civic reception was held in honour of the newlyweds. It was there that a dispatch rider approached Sweeney with the message that the Four Courts had been attacked that morning. Sweeney made immediate arrangements to have MacEoin escorted out of the area as it would be better in the situation for him to be in his own area.[5] As Sheila Humphreys and the others were returning to Finner Camp from Ballybofey, they were passed on the road by the escort party accompanying Seán MacEoin out of the county. When Frank O'Donnell and the Cumann na mBan party returned to Finner Camp, they pleaded with the small garrison to abandon the camp as they considered it too open to defend with such an inadequate party. But the camp commander, James Connolly, was of the opinion that there were no hostilities between the two sides in Donegal and that Finner would be safe. The Cumann na mBan women went as far as Bundoran with Frank O'Donnell and it was there in the early hours of the following morning that they received word of an attack on Finner Camp. They left Bundoran later that morning and stopped off at the IRA barracks in Sligo on their return to Dublin.[6]

Shortly after the announcement of the outbreak of the Civil War, the Free State forces stationed in Letterkenny at the former RIC barracks in Lower Main Street and the old workhouse on the High Road received orders to attack the IRA garrison occupying Ballymacool House and another large house (Rockhill House) across the river, the residence of a landlord family called Stewart, which the IRA had commandeered in late February. On Thursday 29 June, at 5 a.m., Free State forces under the command of Lieutenant James McMonagle launched the attack on Ballymacool House. They surrounded the house, which was then the property of the Boyd family. The mansion had been commandeered three weeks earlier by republican forces who evicted the tenants, Major Brett and his wife. Early on Friday morning the occupants were ordered to surrender and were given an hour to do so. However, this deadline was ignored and fifteen minutes after its expiration the Free State forces, equipped with bombs, rifles and machine guns, opened fire. There was a brisk exchange of gunfire but the resistance of the IRA was not long sustained, with two being injured by splinters, so the entire party of twenty soon surrendered. A small number managed to escape through the woods at the back of the house. Those arrested were removed to the No. 2 barracks in the town.

At the same time, on the other side of the valley, Eddie McMonagle led the attack on Rockhill House from the Oldtown through Crieve, approaching the house from the high ground. The IRA garrison had neglected to post sentries around the building, giving the Free State forces the advantage. They opened fire on the house, but the IRA forces quickly responded. Lieutenant Daniel Harkin was caught in the open of the front lawn and was wounded. He was removed to Lifford Hospital where he died of his wounds. The republican forces held out until the following day when a detachment of reinforcements arrived from Drumboe Castle. Another short battle ensued before the republicans abandoned the place through the rear of the building and escaped through the woods.[7]

Attention was then focused on Finner Camp in south Donegal. The Free State GOC, Joe Sweeney, gave the order to offer the garrison at Finner Camp an opportunity to surrender. A large party of Free State forces under Commandant Henry McGowan travelled to Finner Camp on the Thursday night and gave the order to surrender, but the small garrison ignored the ultimatum and later that night the attack began on the camp. A gun battle ensued for two hours but, having realised their resistance was hopeless, the camp was surrendered. The Finner Camp garrison suffered a number of casualties, including Volunteers Melly and O'Hagan, and one fatality, Captain James Connolly from Kinlough.[8]

The funeral of Captain James Connolly took place at Kinlough the following Sunday, 2 July. The atmosphere was described as sympathetic, as the young man was well known for his brave and selfless virtues and his death touched all hearts. Pity was expressed to his mother who had already buried her husband in September 1920 when a party of Black and Tans murdered him. Captain Connolly's coffin, draped in a Tricolour, was borne on the shoulders of his comrades and accompanied by a guard of honour made up of men from the 3rd Western Division. Following a volley of shots fired over his grave the oration was delivered by Brigadier Devins of the No. 1 Brigade, 3rd Western Division. During a moving oration Devins said, 'Captain Connolly would not wish to harbour thoughts of revenge or indulge in ill-feeling … Captain Connolly would have forgiven those who shot him had he had time for expressing forgiveness.'[9]

The speed with which the new conflict commenced and the immediate capture of three posts held by the IRA Executive prompted an immediate reaction from the divisional command of the IRA Executive 1st Northern Division. Under the temporary charge of Charlie Daly, the garrisons at Lifford and Castlefinn were ordered to relocate to Raphoe with a view to later moving to Glenveagh Castle in the mountains of west Donegal. The IRA's weak positions, under the command of the OC Derry City Brigade, were identified as Skeog, St Johnston and Carrigans, and all were directed to withdraw from those garrisons and move to Inch Fort on Saturday 24 June. The garrison at Skeog House remained in position, and the St Johnston and Carrigans posts were occupied by Free State forces from Drumboe and Letterkenny. The IRA garrisons relocating from St Johnston and Carrigans to Inch Fort were instructed to remain there until further orders were received.[10]

The attack on the Four Courts in Dublin was raised at Westminster on Friday 29 June. Colonel Ashley, by private notice, asked whether an account could be given to the House of the happenings in Dublin over the previous twenty-four hours. In his reply Winston Churchill denied any actions or threats from him were responsible for the opening of hostilities between opposing sides in Ireland:

> This morning at dawn the forces of the Provisional Government attacked the insurgent bands occupying the Four Courts in Dublin. This decision in no way arose out of the debate in this House, nor in consequence of the declaration of His Majesty's government to Parliament. It rose as the result of further aggressive anarchic action by Mr Rory O'Connor's insurgents ... I can add little to the information which has already been published by the press on the course of the fighting. The Provisional Government are solely responsible for the operations and they have so far made me no communication on the subject. They have declined all assistance from the Imperial forces, except so far as equipment is concerned ...[11]

The British government moved quickly to suppress any suggestion that the Provisional Government had acted under duress and Winston Churchill, then Secretary of State for the Colonies, raised the issue at a meeting of the British cabinet on Friday 30 June. The minutes of the meeting recorded:

> The Secretary of State appealed to any of his colleagues who were making speeches to dwell on the fact that they should avoid any suggestions that the Free State Government was acting on British inspiration, and to lay stress on the fact that they have undertaken the task on their own initiative.[12]

The opening of hostilities between the Free State forces and the IRA caught the republican forces in County Donegal unawares. They had not been prepared for a civil war as their attention and activities had been focused chiefly on attacking the Special Constabulary and British military along the border. To complicate matters further, all the 1st Northern Division officers, with the exception of one or two assistant officers, were either in Dublin or other parts of the country and some had not yet returned from the IRA Convention held in Dublin on 18 June. Many of the latter were arrested in Dublin or on the return journey, while others took several days to return. Seán Lehane, the division OC, did not return until mid-July.

Following analysis of the new situation and forced reorganisation of the division, the officers of the 1st Northern Division, under Charlie Daly, travelled from Glenveagh to Raphoe on the morning of Friday 29 June. They stopped at Letterkenny to attend mass in St Eunan's Cathedral and remained near the door, attracting the attention of the congregation. They then paid a visit to McCarry's Hotel for some refreshments, remaining vigilant at all times as they were unsure what measures were to be adopted by the Free State command in the county. Arriving at Raphoe later that evening they found the republican forces there in a similar state of confusion, not knowing what to do or what to expect. Charlie Daly, accompanied by Mick O'Donoghue, walked into Raphoe that night to meet with Willie Holmes, commander of the Free State forces there. Holmes stated that he had not received any instructions to engage with the republican garrison in the town and if he did, he would not act on them. The two men left assuring Holmes that they would not break the peace between the two forces in the town.

However, the following morning the men awoke to the news that the Free State forces had taken Raphoe. Sentries were posted, with machine guns positioned in the tower of the Protestant church. Willie Holmes had broken his word. The IRA officers surveyed the situation and a decision was taken to evacuate the town immediately with a small number of men remaining to monitor events.[13]

A party of Free State forces raided houses in the Churchill area on Thursday in search of IRA forces. A small party of republicans was discovered and a short battle ensued, with the IRA men retreating to the hills when they ran out of ammunition.[14] The IRA forces in the county were at a distinct disadvantage with certain officers being absent and many of those operating in the county not being native to the area. The arrests following the capture of bases in Letterkenny and Finner Camp were a heavy blow to the IRA. The strength of the Free State forces was greatly superior to those of the republican forces in the county. There are no accurate or official figures of IRA forces in Donegal, but the estimate was put at between 300 and 400 at the beginning of the Civil War. The breakdown of Free State forces in the county was as follows:

Stations	Strengths
No. 1 Brigade	
Dungloe	200
Doochary	40
Falcarragh	50
Dunfanaghy	60
Glenveagh	50
	400
No. 2 Brigade	
Letterkenny	200
Buncrana	200
Raphoe	80
Moville	50
Milford	50
Ramelton	50
Lifford	75
Carndonagh	40
Malin	25
Fahan	25
	795
No. 3 Brigade	
Glenties	150
Mountcharles	80
Killybegs	50
Dunkineely	40
Laghey Bar	80
Ballintra	50
	450

No. 4 Brigade

Drumboe Castle	170
Ballybofey	45
Stranorlar	30
Donegal	70
	315

Area of 2nd Northern Division

Greencastle	**200**

Area of 3rd Western Division

Finner Camp	300
Bundoran	80
Ballyshannon	160
	540

Total strength in barracks

No. 1 Brigade	400
No. 2 Brigade	795
No. 3 Brigade	450
No. 4 Brigade	315
2nd Northern Division	200
3rd Western Division	540
Total	**2,700**[15]

On Friday 30 June the focus of attention switched to Inishowen and the Free State forces at Buncrana took elaborate precautions to capture a group of republicans who had commandeered a large house called Ard Caen ten days earlier. In the early morning a detachment of Free State troops were on the roads leading to the town, while others occupied the train station and suspended the train service. Another party took possession of the telephone and telegraph station in the town, effectively controlling all communications. At 7 a.m. the republican forces were given fifteen minutes to surrender, which they did without a fight. After the round-up in Buncrana a detachment of Free State troops under Brigadier McLaughlin commandeered a train and proceeded to Carndonagh to capture republican forces billeted there. Strengthened by troops from Moville they reached Carndonagh at 11 a.m. and a message was sent to the republican garrison at the old police barracks, but after fruitless parleying with the assistance of two priests, a heavy bombardment of the building commenced from four different positions. One of the republican leaders, Charles Zammit from Derry, was injured in the head by a splinter from one of the steel shutters covering the windows. After approximately half an hour of sustained gunfire directed at the building a white flag appeared from one of the second-storey windows and the ceasefire was sounded. The republican forces surrendered. The prisoners were later conveyed by special train to Buncrana. Free State forces also took the Ballyshannon and Bundoran Barracks, gaining a large number of prisoners along with large quantities of arms and ammunition.[16]

Meanwhile in west Donegal James Boyle, Neil 'Plunkett' O'Boyle and a number of other IRA men were on their way to join the garrison at Glenveagh Castle on Saturday 1 July when they were surrounded by a party of Free State military at Crolly. All were arrested and first taken to Dungloe before being transferred to Drumboe Castle by lorry. *En route* to Drumboe Castle, O'Boyle jumped from the lorry as they passed through Doochary and escaped into a wooded area nearby. He later made his way to Glenveagh Castle and joined the garrison there.[17]

On the morning of Saturday 1 July approximately forty members of the IRA forces moved out from Raphoe to Glenveagh Castle. Some travelled by van or car while many proceeded on foot. They halted at a farmhouse several miles from Raphoe and spent the night in a large barn. The following morning after breakfast Charlie Daly ordered all men to fall in. Standing on top of a large boulder he addressed them, stating that 'the Republic had been attacked in Dublin by Free State troops using British guns. It behoved every loyal republican soldier now to defend the Republic in arms.' He then put it to everyone present that was not ready and willing to fight against the new enemy of the Irish Republic to drop out and go home; but no one left the ranks. The column marched away and on reaching the outskirts of Letterkenny found that most of the roads were held by Free State forces so they decided to camp within a few miles of the town that night. They continued on their journey early the following morning and succeeded in getting through without being noticed, and eventually arrived at Glenveagh Castle on Monday 3 July.[18]

The officers of the 1st Northern Division held an immediate conference and because of the absence of Seán Lehane the command structures were temporarily reorganised and the command area was put on alert in anticipation of attacks by the Free State military. That weekend Glenveagh Castle was established as the principal IRA GHQ in Donegal, where they continued to organise the divisional area for assaults on British forces. With the threat of attacks on other areas and realising the weakness of their forces against the Free State forces, the republican command decided to withdraw the Lifford and Raphoe garrisons to Castlefinn. Charlie Daly instructed Captain Jim Cotter and Mick O'Donoghue, divisional engineer, to take a column of men to Castlefinn with directions to continue attacks on the Special Constabulary at points along the border.[19]

In the days following the outbreak of the Civil War, Commandant Daly sent a dispatch rider to Eithne Coyle in Falcarragh asking her to report for active service under his command. She immediately made her way to the IRA headquarters at Glenveagh Castle, arrived there late at night and was met by Daly, Bernard O'Donnell, Donncha MacNelis, John Staunton from Westport and others. Coyle was instructed to establish a Cumann na mBan headquarters at Glenveagh and to organise first aid posts along the border. She was also tasked with establishing a communication route between the 1st Northern Division in Donegal and the 3rd Western Division in Sligo.[20]

During the Truce period quite a lot of people had joined the IRA and some were credited with carrying out deplorable acts not befitting IRA soldiers. However, owing to the integrity of the officers in charge of the 1st Northern Division at Glenveagh Castle, there had been less looting in their area than in others. This pattern continued after the Civil War had broken out. On one occasion, a captain decided to commandeer a sheep as he passed a farm on his way to Glenveagh Castle. He arrived at the castle and was asked by Bernard O'Donnell where he had got it. When

O'Donnell discovered the animal had been taken from a small farmer at gunpoint, a loss the man could not afford, he ordered the captain to return it and accompanied him back up the mountainside to the farmer's home.[21]

On Friday evening a party of Free State forces left Donegal Town to take over the Hall House, Mountcharles, which had been occupied by republicans for some months. On their arrival, they discovered the building had been evacuated. Several cars were burned and there was evidence of attempts made to burn the house.

Meanwhile in the east of the county some of the republican forces evacuated Skeog House and made their way to Inch Fort, where preparations were being made to withstand attacks by Free State troops. A number of gun crews, armoured cars and other up-to-date appliances were drafted into the county by Free State forces. At the same time, republicans at Glenveagh fortified the castle, laying landmines and setting up sniping and machine-gun posts covering the road and other approaches. The scene was set for a bloody war.[22]

Chapter 17

Another Effort to Avert Civil War in Donegal

In the midst of this tense and dangerous time, a party of adventurers was holidaying in Donegal and travelling extensively throughout the county endeavouring to explore as much as their time would allow. One member of this party was Fr William Hackett, the Jesuit priest from County Kilkenny who had played a prominent role in the war years between 1916 and 1921 when he served as a courier for the IRA. He was friends with many prominent figures and was enjoying his last holiday in Ireland before taking up new religious duties in Australia. He visited the IRA garrison at Glenveagh Castle in late June and recorded the visit in his journal:

> At last we joined the road that comes down Muckish Gap and faced for Glenveagh ... The lake is superb ... the castle belonged to a Mrs Adair whose death took place a few months ago – famous for clearing the estate of humans and stocking it with deer. Mrs Adair's castle is now in the hands of the Executive forces ...

Fr Hackett and his party approached the castle by boat:

> They were just getting up when we arrived and all were scruffy and bedraggled. They did not quite know what to make of us, but they gave us a wretched tea, served in Mrs Adair's drawing-room while the mist swept over the mountains ...

Hackett returned to Glenveagh on Saturday 1 July and heard the confessions of the garrison there. He mentioned meeting Donncha MacNelis, whom he described 'as kindness itself'.[1]

The IRA forces at Glenveagh Castle continued acquiring provisions for the garrison based there – taking them from trains and lorries transporting goods from Derry and other areas. The early morning train arrived at the nearby Churchill Railway Station on Monday 3 July and was cleared of all provisions including tea, flour, sugar and other commodities.[2]

Meanwhile the IRA column relocating from Lifford and Raphoe, under the command of Captain Jim Cotter, arrived at Castlefinn just after midnight on Tuesday 4 June. They made their way to Donaghmore House where they billeted for the night. Mick O'Donoghue was awakened early the following morning by a loud noise and jumped out of bed to see two figures running out of the room. He took his rifle and gave chase. Outside he saw a number of Free State forces standing under a tree at the bottom of the garden. He marched up to them and demanded to know what they were doing in the house and they told him that Commandant Glennon had ordered them to occupy it not realising it was already occupied by republican forces. Jim Cotter then joined them in the garden and asked who had taken his watch. A red-faced soldier stepped forward and presented the watch to him. Cotter demanded to see Glennon, who was by that time walking up the avenue towards the house. Despite earlier assurances from Major Tom Morris that he or his men would remain neutral, they were all present with Glennon. After a short conversation, Glennon informed Cotter that Joe Sweeney was very anxious to meet with Charlie Daly. Cotter immediately sent a courier to Daly at Glenveagh Castle and arrangements were made to set up the meeting. Cotter then ordered the garrison to evacuate Donaghmore House and return to Glenveagh Castle, without waiting for eviction orders from Free State forces. O'Donoghue and Cotter remained at the house and waited for Glennon and Sweeney to return the following morning, Wednesday 5 July.

The four, accompanied by an escort party, then travelled to the arranged meeting at Wilkin's Hotel in Churchill where Daly and others were waiting. This was the second meeting between the senior officers of the two opposing sides. Sweeney and Daly did most of the talking, with the tone of the meeting being quite friendly. Joe Sweeney was insisting that the republican forces in Donegal should return to their homes and the men from the southern divisions should leave Donegal with their arms and transport, but Charlie Daly was having none of this because the IRA forces were sent to Donegal on the authority of Liam Lynch and Michael Collins to continue the war on the new order of British rule in Ireland. Daly also considered Sweeney's demands as a form of surrender by republican forces and a dereliction of duty. Daly did agree to refrain from engaging with Free State forces if Sweeney agreed the same and not to arrest any republican forces in the county whose duty was to fight the British in the Six Counties.

After a few hours of talking the two sides reached a stalemate, with Joe Sweeney declaring the issue was one of authority, with the Free State being the only authority in Donegal, but Charlie Daly asserting that the only authority they recognised was the Irish Republic. While the meeting was in progress, the IRA men strolled around outside, eagerly awaiting the outcome. Eventually Sweeney stood up and said they had to be going, ending the meeting without resolution. As Sweeney and Glennon were getting ready to leave, Jim Lane motioned Mick O'Donoghue over to the door and said a volunteer named Jordan and some of the northern fellows outside were threatening to ambush Sweeney and plug him on the way back. This would have been disastrous as Sweeney and Glennon had been given a pledge of safe conduct. Daly ordered that none of the men were allowed to leave the village until Sweeney and Glennon had left and that two men should stand beside Jordan to prevent any attempt by him to carry out his threat. He then re-joined the others to bid goodbye to Sweeney and Glennon as they were entering the car.[3]

Also during that week IRA men from Crolly, Kincasslagh and Gweedore were instructed to report to Glenveagh Castle and many travelled to Churchill by train, but some were arrested at Crolly Station by Free State forces. A party of IRA men had taken possession of the schoolhouse, the old RIC barracks and a number of private houses at

Knockbrack, near Letterkenny in early June. They remained there until Tuesday 4 July when they also made their way to Glenveagh Castle. On Thursday, morning 6 July, a large party of Free State troops moved out from Buncrana and occupied the railway stations at Inch, Fahan and other positions. They effectively took control of the road leading to Inch Island.[4]

That afternoon the party of Jesuit priests, including Fr William Hackett, landed at Fahan after crossing from Rathmullan and were making their way by road to Inch Island. The Free State forces endeavoured to stop them but the priests insisted that they be allowed to continue to the island. Hackett recorded the visit to the island in his diary:

> … as we rode along the edge of the sea till we came to Rathmullan. This straggling village is on the lough opposite Fahan. Buncrana stands higher up on the lough, well in view on the Fahan side. Inch Island lay on the Fahan side and was about a mile and a half from Rathmullan … we had to hire a boat at six shillings for the round trip. The sail across was quite wonderful … I wanted to visit Inch but the boatmen were afraid they might be fired on. So was my companion, but I felt there was no ground for alarm and so we made for the fort. However, when a shot rang out we were half a mile from the fort the situation was unpleasant [*sic*] … we continued towards the fort. All was well. The men were delighted to receive us. Confessions were soon in full swing. When the simple lads emerged they knelt down on the grass and said their penance. Simple faith.[5]

Also on Thursday the Free State forces based at Stranorlar arrested John Quinn who was described as a senior officer of the IRA. He was subsequently taken to Drumboe Castle and held there. As a precautionary measure the Free State forces stationed at Stranorlar and at Ballybofey Barracks strengthened their defences by blocking roads with carts and wire entanglements in anticipation of a rescue attempt.

A few days later, on Sunday evening, 9 July, two young Derry men (Owen McCormack, a chemist, and James McCloskey) were arrested in Letterkenny. They were travelling in a car on the Port Road when they were stopped by Free State troops, taken to one of the local barracks and their car confiscated. Both men were held at Letterkenny for a short time before being transferred to Buncrana, which was the departure point for all prisoners to Newbridge Internment Camp in County Kildare. Meanwhile on Tuesday 11 July republican forces were busy disrupting movement along the main roads from Letterkenny to Ramelton and Letterkenny to Milford, which were blocked by large felled trees across both roads.[6]

In the days following the failed talks at Churchill, the IRA in Donegal carried out another reorganisation due to the absence of senior officers. Intelligence officers were sent to Derry and Tyrone to ascertain the positions of the commanders there. Dan McKenna, OC Derry, decided to join with the Free State forces while Brigadier Curran of Tyrone was remaining neutral. Brigadier Seán Larkin of south Derry had not yet returned from Dublin and Seán Lehane had not yet returned from the south. Peadar O'Donnell was among those captured following the surrender of the Four Courts and was held for several months at Mountjoy before being transferred to the Curragh Internment Camp.[7]

The IRA garrison at Glenveagh continued procuring supplies of foodstuffs and targeting merchants travelling on the roads in the Churchill area. John Gallagher, Church Lane, Letterkenny, was stopped when driving to Churchill on Wednesday night, 12 July. The IRA commandeered his car and removed various provisions to Glenveagh Castle. A lorry, the property of Joseph Burns, a merchant in Letterkenny, was delivering goods at Trentagh when it was stopped and confiscated by a party of IRA men. On the same day a number of republican forces were discovered at Newtowncunningham by Free State forces and arrested. During a follow-up search a large number of bombs were discovered and removed to Letterkenny Barracks with the prisoners.[8]

Another Cumann na mBan member, Roisín O'Doherty, joined the Glenveagh Castle garrison and worked with Eithne Coyle in the dispatch and intelligence department. The two women were also responsible for the transport of arms and equipment as there was less risk of their being searched because of the absence of female searchers among the ranks of the Free State forces. On one occasion, Charlie Daly sent them both with various instructions and messages to be delivered throughout the county and warned them that two bridges near Glenties were closely guarded night and day by Free State troops. They had instructions to go to Glenties and Dungloe, and then to Falcarragh, and to make contact with a man in Glenties who would guide them safely through a back road avoiding the patrols at the bridges. As soon as they left Glenveagh it began to rain very heavily, but they pressed on and there were a number of minor accidents along the way. They eventually arrived at Glenties about 4 a.m. and were given a warm welcome and tea. They explained their mission and handed over a dispatch. The contact then told them that he had just been released after three days interrogation and did not wish to be caught again. The two women explained that Charlie Daly told them they would be escorted out of Glenties. He guided them for a short distance when he suddenly stopped and said he did not know which bridge was guarded. He then just left them there.

The women decided to continue their journey through the fields and had to carry their bicycles on their backs through the swampy ground, with the heavy rain pouring down. They eventually arrived at a small bridge, crossed safely to the other side, continued on their journey by road and arrived to a very warm welcome at the home of Frank and Peadar O'Donnell at Meenmore. They received a hot meal and were able to wash and dry their clothes. Having rested for several hours, they left the O'Donnells, pressing on to near Falcarragh to pick up a stencil machine for the *War News Bulletin* and then back to Glenveagh. On their return to Glenveagh, they discovered that Kathleen McLaughlin had joined the ranks as a typist for the *Tirconaill War Bulletin*.[9]

About the same time a request was made by the Free State forces in Donegal to their GHQ in Dublin for extra men and equipment to counter the threat of the republican forces. A dispatch was sent to Dublin outlining the situation:

> Conditions in this division are not what they might be. The Executive forces have taken up three bases from which it will be very difficult to dislodge them with the number of men at our disposal ... our urgent

need at the moment is for ammunition and armoured cars and the sooner these are received the sooner will conditions settle down in this area.

The dispatch also reported a number of incidents involving attacks on Free State garrisons in the county:

> On Tuesday night a sentry at the Workhouse, Glenties was fired at and was wounded in the leg. A report has just come in that Lifford barracks in occupation of the 2nd Northern was attacked and Comdt Gen. Morris was wounded.[10]

Chapter 18

The Battles at Skeog

In the early hours of Friday 7 July, a party of IRA men was attempting to abandon the besieged fort at Inch Island to make its way to Glenveagh Castle. They were travelling in a car and crossed an embankment roadway from Inch Island to the mainland. Free State troops observed them and called on them to halt, which they ignored. The troops then opened fire on the car, causing it to crash into a bridge. The four IRA men, two of whom were injured, were arrested. The car was searched and four large bombs, five revolvers, two Mauser rifles and ammunition were found.[1]

The focus of the Free State troops' attention then turned to an area known as Skeog, on the boundary between Donegal and Derry. At approximately 4 p.m. on Friday large numbers of Free State troops arrived in the Skeog area from Buncrana and Newtowncunningham. Skeog House and a number of farmhouses nearby were surrounded. The officer in charge of the Free State forces sent a courier under a white flag with a note requesting the surrender of the IRA garrison, with a time limit before fire would be opened. The reply received from the IRA OC, George McCallion, was:

> In receipt of your demand to surrender barracks to your men. I wish to inform you that, as soldiers of Ireland and the Irish Republic, we will defend the barracks and the cause for which we stand till the last. Signed: George McCallion.

Shortly after this was received, the Free State officer gave the order to open fire, with the republicans responding; this continued throughout the evening. A party of IRA men at an outpost captured two Free State troops who had advanced to a point within 300 yards of Skeog. A Free State support party then stormed the post to which the two Free State troops had been taken. They used bombs and after a sharp exchange of gunfire succeeded in reaching the post where eight IRA men were captured and the two Free State men released. The attack, particularly from the front, was made over open country, in which the Free State troops were exposed to the fire from the garrison in occupation. People living in the area were terrified while the battle was in progress as bullets coming from Skeog whizzed through trees and farmers working in fields in the area were forced to take shelter. The passengers in the trains to and from Derry on the Lough Swilly Railway had a frightening experience when passing by the battle scene. Passengers were ordered to get down on the floor of the carriages. A Lewis gun in action was stopped to permit a train to get through in safety. It was said at the time that the Swilly train had never been seen travelling so fast between Bridge End and Burnfoot.

After several hours the Free State troops had tightened the cordon around Skeog House, and at some points come to within 100 yards of it. Shortly after 11 p.m. a white flag was displayed from a first floor window. At the same time, another was hoisted from an outpost at the gatehouse fifty yards from the main building. The ceasefire was then declared and the surrender of the republican garrison taken. Approximately fifty men marched out with hands raised and were approached by the leader of the Free State troops. They were subsequently removed in lorries to Letterkenny, arriving there in the early hours of Saturday morning and being placed in the courthouse. Among the prisoners was a woman who, on arrival in the town, was accommodated in McCarry's Hotel.

Shortly after arriving the prisoners began wrecking the interior of the courthouse. They smashed the front windows and then started throwing out portions of the gallery, judge's bench, solicitors' tables, books and records of the court. About a dozen cushioned chairs were also destroyed. During the morning the prisoners kept up a continuous uproar by hammering, breaking in the doors of the various rooms and smashing up everything they came across. They then set the interior on fire and smoke began billowing from the windows. Shortly afterwards the flames started to leap around the prisoners as they stood at the window facing the Free State troops lined up on the street below them. The men were waving the Tricolour, calling and cheering for an 'Irish Republic' and singing 'The Soldier's Song'. They were eventually removed from the building. The fire brigade was summoned and, after arduous work, extinguished the flames – but not before some damage was done to the interior. A number of the IRA men were wounded, but refused to be medically treated. The entire party was removed to the barracks adjacent to the courthouse.[2]

The damage caused to the Letterkenny courthouse was outlined in a letter to the Minister for Home Affairs, Kevin O'Higgins, from E. S. McKinney, the Register of Petty Sessions Clerk at the courthouse:

> I beg to report that the Courthouse has been wrecked by prisoners taken by the National troops and confined there on Friday the 7th July. All my old Order Books were cut and torn up and thrown out of the windows. The inside of the building is a complete wreck.
>
> I cannot get in to find out whether the Statutes are also torn up ... The prisoners then set fire to the building, but the fire was extinguished before it had done much harm.[3]

As the battle of Skeog was taking place, twenty-five fully armed men were successfully withdrawn from Inch Fort by motorboat. However, on their arrival at Ramelton they heard of the battle taking place at Skeog and, ignoring orders to continue to Glenveagh Castle, returned to Inch Island in anticipation of an attack there.

A member of the IRA, Hugh Morrison from Creggan Road, Derry, who had been seriously wounded during the battle at Skeog, died the following week at the County Hospital, Lifford. Morrison had been part of the IRA garrison in occupation at Skeog House and was handling a bomb when it exploded.[4]

Chapter 19

The Drumkeen Ambush

On Monday night, 3 July, an IRA column under the command of Charlie Daly and Jim Cotter moved out from Glenveagh Castle and made their way to the Rosses, marching down through Glendowan. They arrived at Doochary and rested there by the side of a mountain. Early the next morning the column moved through Doochary and on to Dungloe where, in a chance encounter, they held up a number of Free State soldiers who were disarmed and relieved of all useful items before being released. On entering Dungloe, they found the place deserted of all Free State troops and they remained there for the day before returning to Glenveagh Castle.

The IRA garrison based at Glenveagh Castle made preparations for a long stay and on Saturday morning, 8 July, a party of volunteers travelled to nearby Churchill and Termon to recruit female labour to do cooking and domestic work at the castle. Up to eleven young women returned to Glenveagh with the volunteers. On the same morning at Churchill a large party of IRA arrived in two cars from Glenveagh Castle and carried out a raid on a train from Derry, seizing a quantity of groceries, flour, sugar, etc., before returning to the castle. Another party was busy raiding shops in Creeslough for various foodstuffs.[1]

The garrison at Glenveagh Castle lived on food stores acquired through raids on trains, focusing on products from unionist firms based on the policy of the Belfast boycott. They had good supplies of flour, meal, sugar, tea and tinned, preserved and dried foodstuffs. Apart from some supplies of bacon, meat was scarce and they solved this problem by shooting deer in the mountains. On one occasion, four men went out to shoot deer and after a couple of hours came across a few of the animals quietly grazing. One of the men took aim and fired, hitting one, which dropped to the ground. As they approached their prize, it started to kick and Con Crowley pulled out his revolver, putting it to the deer's head, and fired a shot. With that the deer jumped up, sending Crowley flying into the air, and ran off for a short distance. The other three men were paralysed with laughter, accusing Crowley of giving the deer an injection of life instead of a bullet. They found the deer a little later and on inspection of the bullet hole to the head surmised that the bullet had ricocheted around the thick bone without penetrating the skull. The deer was taken back to the Castle and there was enough meat for the entire garrison for a few days.

The focus of the Glenveagh-based IRA switched from the northern offensive to engagements with the forces of the Provisional Government in Donegal because of the aggressive tactics of the Free State forces towards the IRA following the outbreak of the Civil War. On Monday 10 July Charlie Daly led a column of up to eighteen men from Glenveagh Castle and proceeded to Drumkeen village, on the main Stranorlar to Letterkenny road. They had learned, through their intelligence officer, that armed convoys travelled from Drumboe Castle, Stranorlar to Letterkenny every morning. The IRA column arrived in the village in the early hours of the following morning after a ten-mile cross-country night march and established their headquarters at a large farmhouse about 500 yards from the village. As soon as they arrived in the area they warned residents of the impending attack and put a guard on the houses of occupants who were either unionist or sympathetic to the Free State troops. Charlie Daly and the other officers discussed the proposed ambush and decided to use an electronically detonated landmine to disable any vehicles. This was to be placed on the Stranorlar side of the village and the IRA men were put into various positions along each side of the road.

That Tuesday morning started as a beautiful clear day with the sun shining brightly. There was very little activity along the road until approximately 2 p.m. when the sound of approaching motors was heard. A large touring car carrying a party of five Free State troops could be seen nearing the village. As it passed through the settlement the command to 'halt' was given but the car increased speed. No order was given to open fire, but four or five members of the ambush party started shooting, hitting the driver and causing the car to crash. When the vehicle came to a stop the other occupants jumped out, taking cover at the opposite side of the road, but soon surrendered.

The IRA members ran to the car to discover Jack Sweeney fatally wounded, having been shot five times with one bullet striking him in the head. The driver, Charles McGinley, was seriously wounded by a shot in the right lung. Another soldier, Sammy Dickson, was also slightly injured, as was Willie Sweeney, from Ballyarr. The fifth man was Neil O'Donnell from Letterkenny. Suddenly the sound of the accompanying lorry could be heard: it had approximately twenty men on board who, having heard the shooting, were approaching very slowly. They turned off on a side road about fifty yards from the landmine and sped off along a narrow by-road. The column remained at the ambush position for a short time as they anticipated that the lorry would return. Meanwhile the injured were removed to a house owned by a local family called Bonner, where Martin Quille, a chemist from Listowel, County Kerry, administered first aid. A priest and medical help were sent for. Charlie Daly then ordered the column to withdraw from the village and return to Glenveagh with two of the Free State soldiers, Willie Sweeney and Neil O'Donnell, as prisoners. They removed all usable items from the car, including five rifles with bandoliers, ammunition and a few revolvers.

The other soldiers returned to the scene a short time later and Charlie McGinley was placed on the lorry and conveyed to Lifford Hospital. By that time Fr John O'Doherty and Dr J. P. McGinley had reached Drumkeen from Letterkenny. Free State military reinforcements arrived from Drumboe and began scouring the area for the ambush party, but failed to find any trace of them.

Later that evening news of the ambush reached Glenveagh Castle and the recently returned 1st Northern Division OC, Seán Lehane, selected a group of men to go out as a relief party. They left Glenveagh in a lorry to locate the ambush party for fear that Free State forces would pursue them. As the column marched through Glenswilly, they met up with Lehane and the support party and then moved on to Templedouglas, between New Mills and Churchill, where they rested for a few hours. The two prisoners were escorted to the local doctor, Moloney, a Tipperary man. The younger man was only nineteen and the doctor said to him as he treated his facial wounds: 'A young chicken like you has no business going out to fight these ferocious Munster men. Go back to your Mammy laddie.' The other prisoner, Willie Sweeney, had received a bullet below the left shoulder. He was a tough character – when the doctor probed the wound with a fine steel rod, he never even flinched, with the only signs of discomfort being beads of sweat running down his face. The doctor failed to locate the bullet and decided to dress the wound. After a few hours, the entire IRA column decided to continue their journey back to Glenveagh where they questioned the two captives. After a short time, they allowed them to leave, to the relief of the younger prisoner who had heard rumours of the wild men in the republican forces. Seán Lehane warned them that if they were ever caught again that things might be different. They made arrangements with a local farmer to have the two men taken to Letterkenny.[2]

The remains of Jack Sweeney were conveyed to the No. 2 barracks in Letterkenny that day. The following day hundreds of sympathisers visited the barracks prior to the removal of the remains. The cathedral bell tolled as the coffin, covered with a Tricolour, was removed from the barracks for burial at Milford. The cortège was accompanied by a large number of soldiers and officers.

Charles McGinley died at Lifford Hospital on Tuesday morning and his remains were released on Wednesday afternoon, 10 July. The cortège arrived in Letterkenny that evening, accompanied by a large military escort.[3] The deaths of the two young soldiers merely served to heighten an already volatile situation between the two sides in Donegal and weighed heavily on the minds of the members of the IRA there. This fact was recognised by the IRA officers and in the days following the Drumkeen ambush they put it to the local men that anyone not willing to continue with the fight could drop out and return home. A small group of men left Glenveagh Castle. The local media reported this as a mass resignation in the aftermath of the tragic ambush.[4]

Chapter 20

The Fall of Inch Fort

The Free State forces had established a military cordon around Inch Island on 6 July and effectively cut the island off from the mainland with all approach roads guarded by large numbers of military. This was part of the preparations to dislodge the republican garrison holding the fort and portions of the island. On Sunday evening, 9 July, and throughout the following morning explosions were heard at Inch Fort in what was believed to be the IRA garrison destroying their supply of bombs. Also on Sunday evening a party of IRA men attempting to cross the River Swilly by boat was fired at from the Free State positions at Rathmullan and forced to return to the island. At approximately 4 a.m. on Monday two IRA men were arrested as they crossed the embankment from Inch Island to the mainland and were later transferred to Buncrana Barracks.

The *Derry Journal* published an article on Monday 10 July stating that the officer in command of the IRA at Inch Fort had communicated his desire to arrange terms for surrender. The article went on to say that Free State command had refused the request. John Mullan, the IRA OC at Inch Fort, responded to the article by letter, which was published in the Wednesday edition of 12 July:

> A Chara – With reference to a paragraph which appeared in your issue of date stating that I sent a note to OC 'National Forces' with the object of arranging terms, I now wish to contradict this statement, which is entirely false. I admit a note was sent by me asking for an interview to protest against a cowardly act on the part of 'National

The Fall of Inch Fort

Forces' at Fahan and Ramelton when they opened fire on three unarmed men while crossing to Ramelton in a motorboat. I would like you to make it clearly understood in your issue of the 12th that I did not ask for any terms of surrender and when I am asked I shall then give my answer. Furthermore, I wish to state that I received no warning against the destruction of commandeered foodstuff and whenever I want any advice regarding same I shall apply to quarters which shall have no connection with the 'National Forces'. I hope you will have space in your next issue for the foregoing statement and so clear up a serious misunderstanding. Mise - Seán Ua Maolain – OC Executive Forces – Inch Fort.[1]

In the same week a party of Free State forces from Buncrana descended on the Muff district. They had received information on Tuesday 11 July that a group of men were active in the area; a party of IRA had raided Bridge End Railway Station for provisions the previous day and had taken up quarters at the gate lodge attached to a property a short distance from the border. When the information was received at Buncrana a large contingent of military was sent to the area to investigate. As the Free State forces approached Kilderry, the IRA party abandoned the house and scattered into the woods nearby. A number of Free State soldiers pursued the men and a short battle ensued leading to the capture of three IRA men. During the operation, a Free State captain, William Brown, was shot and later died of his wound. The three IRA men were taken to Buncrana, with the other members of the flying column escaping.

On Wednesday evening large parties of Free State troops from Letterkenny and Buncrana converged on Newtowncunningham and arrested nineteen young men who were suspected of being involved with IRA activities in the area. Some of the prisoners were taken from the old Petty Sessions House, which was also used as an Orange Hall, and all the prisoners were then conveyed to Buncrana where they arrived about 2 a.m.[2]

The preparations for the assault on Inch Fort were increased following the arrival in Buncrana of a steamer under the control of the Free State government on Friday 14 July. An 18-pounder field gun was unloaded at

Buncrana pier as well as a large quantity of war *matériel*. The steamer later returned to Dublin with forty of the recently arrested prisoners who were later interned in Newbridge Camp. Following the arrival of the additional war *matériel* the Free State forces began finalising the plans for the assault on republican forces at Inch Fort. At approximately 7 p.m. on Saturday 15 July the field gun was placed in position near Fahan Railway Station. When the shells screamed overhead the IRA garrison knew the Free State forces meant business. Under cover of the bombardment, the Free State forces moved across the island in the direction of the fort. They stopped a car attempting to leave the island and arrested three men. As they were being led away one of the men said they were 'only going out for bread'.

The soldiers then surrounded a house near the shore belonging to Lord Templemore, and captured another four men. Five more were arrested on the island during the evening. Unknown to the IRA garrison the 18-pounder gun went out of action and the Free State forces sought the assistance of a British officer based at Dunree Fort. He found the gun to be in bad condition and surmised that it was not properly maintained causing it to seize.[3] As darkness fell they had drawn a cordon across the island and remained in their positions overnight. Reinforcements were sent from Buncrana and the final assault on the fort commenced on Sunday morning. Rifle fire and heavy explosions could be heard throughout the day and intensified as the day progressed. A Lewis gun was brought into action. About 5 p.m. the Free State forces made their way to the outskirts of the fort and came under heavy fire from the 'portholes' of the building. The Free State troops retreated a safe distance and decided to bombard the stronghold from close range with the heavy-duty Lewis gun. Shortly afterwards a white flag was hoisted, ending the engagement. When the garrison OC John Mullan emerged from the fort carrying the white flag and followed by twenty-one IRA men, the surrender was accepted by Adjutant Doherty. The entire garrison was taken into custody. The officer in charge of the Free State forces directed Mullan and his men to lift the landmines around the fort.[4] The thirty-three prisoners from the two-day operation were later removed under heavy escort to Buncrana.

Chapter 21

Republican Column 'On the Run'

The use of heavy artillery greatly altered the landscape of the Civil War in Donegal. The addition of the 18-pounder field gun gave the Free State forces a considerable advantage over the IRA. The use of this gun in the shelling and capture of Inch Fort unnerved the IRA based at Glenveagh Castle and the commanding officer Seán Lehane decided that it was no longer prudent to remain there.[1] Charlie Daly's dispatch shortly after the evacuation of their former headquarters gave a detailed description of their plight from the beginning of the Civil War:

> I found things wholly disorganised when I got back and the men not much better when the war came on in earnest. Lehane and most of the responsible officers were in Dublin at the last Convention. A few of them got back a week later. Nearly all the Cork men are still away. Lehane got here a couple of days ago … he had to walk from Sligo to North Donegal … I had no intention of attacking the Staters and they knew it, but still they attacked us … when they thought they had the advantage over us … We held back from taking life as long as we could, although we got plenty of opportunity. So we started out a couple of days ago. All the Free State troops in Donegal have got the country covered … 'tis only a matter of time until this business is over.[2]

The IRA garrison evacuated the castle in mid-July and almost eighty men went out as one column making their way to Churchill and then on to

Glendowan. A number of men were left behind with a Cumann na mBan member to continue publishing the *Tirconaill War Bulletin*.

After a short time, the column found that it was almost impossible to move around without drawing attention, not to mention the problem of securing billets and feeding such a large number of men in the rural areas. It was subsequently divided into three smaller groups with two groups of approximately twenty men each going to areas covering west and north-east Donegal, while the remainder proceeded in the direction of south Donegal. It was not long before the south Donegal group was considered too large and was divided again with fifteen men proceeding to the No. 4 Brigade area of east Donegal.[3] The column under Lehane and Daly (approximately twenty-five men) moved around in two separate groups, but never strayed too far from each other. They moved in individual columns in the direction of Fintown and established a temporary base. This was a relatively poor area but the locals fed the IRA men with whatever food they had, including potatoes, porridge and eggs. The column officers decided to carry out a raid on the mail car, which travelled from Ballybofey to Fintown, in the hope that they could discover some intelligence on the activities of Free State forces or people loyal to them in the area. They planned to hold up the mail car the following day, Saturday 22 July. At approximately 6 a.m., they mobilised and set off from Fintown in the direction of Ballybofey. They made their way along the road until they reached a small bar and woke the proprietor. They then had a whip-round and went in for some refreshments and cigarettes. They set off again on the Ballybofey Road and on reaching a hairpin bend decided to take up ambush positions there. At about 9 a.m. the mail car, a horse and cart, came along the road and was held up. The driver, horse and cart were then taken back to the temporary base near Fintown, where the mail was opened. A large quantity of stamps consigned for the Fintown post office were confiscated as were any cigarettes and tobacco, but they failed to discover any useful information relating to the Free State forces. They released the mail driver that afternoon.

The following day the column divided into two sections and again moved in the direction of Ballybofey. The larger group crossed the River Finn and continued east, while the smaller one continued along the road, reaching the village of Cloghan early in the morning. As they were approaching the front door of McGlinchey's Hotel a sudden burst of gunfire came from one of the first-floor windows. The IRA men immediately ran back down the road taking cover behind a fence. Two were slightly wounded, with one having a narrow escape when a bullet cut the top of his ear and grazed the side of his head, while the other had a bullet hole through his cap. The larger section, led by Seán Lehane, on hearing the shooting hurried towards the scene and joined up with the other group. Lehane immediately ordered the surrounding of the premises and when everyone was in position he approached the door, gun in hand, calling on the occupants to open the door and to come out with their hands up or the place would be bombed in two minutes' time. The door was opened and several Free State officers and soldiers were marched out and searched, but no weapons were found on them. Seán Lehane, Charlie Daly, Jack Fitzgerald and others carried out a thorough search of the premises. The owners, who were very hostile and denied there were any weapons in the house, accompanied them. They searched the entire house and then arrived at a door which was locked. They ordered the owner to open the door but he refused, insisting that it was his daughter's room. He soon changed his mind when told the door would be smashed in. The door was opened and they found four Webley revolvers, two of which had been fired. After that the column decided to make a hasty retreat from the area, as they were only several miles from the Free State Army HQ at Stranorlar.

They decided to make their way to Glenfinn, taking their prisoners, who were released after dark, with the usual parting words that they should thank the IRA for their lives, but to expect a very different outcome should they be captured again.[4] While the republican column was adjusting to its new situation, a meeting had been held in Clonmel on Friday 21 July and, owing to the arrest of some of the Four Courts garrison, new members, including Seán Lehane, were elected to the IRA Executive Council.[5]

When the main body of the IRA garrison evacuated Glenveagh Castle, a small group remained to continue intelligence work and to produce the *Tirconaill War Bulletin*. There was little activity at the castle until Wednesday 26 July when one member of the garrison, an intelligence officer, perpetrated what was considered to be a very serious offence when he began shooting at sheep grazing in the nearby fields. The sheep were the property of local republicans. The man shot and killed a number of sheep and wounded another. The No. 1 Brigade column OC Seamus McCann was in the nearby hills and, on hearing the gunfire, his immediate thought was that Free State forces were attacking the castle garrison. He decided to make his way there with a small column. On arrival at the castle the garrison captain told McCann what had happened. The intelligence officer refused to surrender his rifle when confronted. McCann later reported the incident to Seán Lehane through a dispatch and emphasised the bad feeling in the area since the episode. Such activity was frowned upon as it reflected badly on the IRA whose members, for the most part, were exceptionally disciplined when stationed at Glenveagh Castle. However, with the IRA effectively on the run in Donegal, the divisional staff was in no position to have the undisciplined officer reprimanded for his actions.[6]

Communications between the Donegal IRA command and field headquarters, Northern and Eastern Command, began to suffer once the column had moved out from Glenveagh Castle, due to the lack of proper facilities and equipment. As a result of this, communications between the Donegal command and Ernie O'Malley at field headquarters, Northern and Eastern Command, were generally inaccurate. The problem was not that the information was deliberately erroneous, but by the time field headquarters received the reports, events had taken a very different turn and the IRA's situation had deteriorated. One example of this was the report received by GHQ from Ernie O'Malley written on the 25 July:

> 80 men under Lehane and Daly left Glenveagh and are operating as a column; each man has a rifle and most of them also have small arms. They are not too well supplied with ammunition. They have no cars or machine guns. They left six men behind in Glenveagh Castle. Apart from this there are no other positions or columns in Donegal. I understand that they are starving and are very much in need of money. I have sent on some and have tried to fix up a line of communications with them.[7]

The column moved about between Glenfinn and the surrounding areas, staying in various houses scattered throughout the mountains. One morning some IRA men discovered poitín stills and reported them to Charlie Daly. It was discovered that there were stills all over the valley and that even the children going to school were given a drop in their bottles of milk. This disgusted Daly and he ordered the immediate destruction of all stills located and all poitín poured out. Daly wanted to impress upon the local population the high morals of the IRA, but many locals were surprised as this was a means of income for some of the population.

The column moved out of the Glenfinn area the following day and made their way further south, passing along the Bluestack Mountain range towards Glenties. They stopped at an area called Croaghbarnes on Wednesday 26 July, with some of the column settling approximately two miles further on in the direction of Glenties. They were spread out in a number of houses and sentries were posted before the majority of the men retired for the night. Shortly after 10 p.m., two of the sentries met up for a chat to stem the boredom and suddenly noticed the silhouettes of men approaching in the dark from the direction of the main road. They challenged the strangers to halt and asked who they were. When the reply was 'Dáil troops', the two IRA men immediately opened fire and the Free State forces scattered and returned fire. On hearing the shooting, Charlie Daly and the others got up, took up their rifles and equipment and rushed outside where they immediately came under fire. They were forced to scatter but regrouped further up the glen. After a quick roll-call, they discovered three men were missing: Donncha MacNelis, Joe McGurk and another volunteer. McGurk and the other IRA man were trapped in a small isolated house and had been surrounded before they could escape. They fought back until they exhausted their ammunition and were forced to surrender. MacNelis, who was also separated from the main body, met a party of the Free State troops along the road and was called on to halt. Dressed in a long black coat and black waterproof leggings, he was accompanied by a red setter dog. He was ordered to advance towards the Free State forces, who mistook him for a priest, which put them a little at ease. MacNelis asked who they were and the reply was 'Dáil troops'.

MacNelis immediately pulled his gun from his coat and began shooting as he ran through the bog using turf stacks as cover. Two members of the Free State forces were killed: Alfred Devine and James Scallon. The local press later reported the appearance of a priest accompanied by a dog during the skirmish between the two forces. The remainder of the column under Seán Lehane was based further west, but having heard the shooting, took up defensive positions along the road. Scouts were sent up the road to investigate and met Charlie Daly and the other column moving towards them. The Free State troops had learned of their presence in the area and had planned to flank the column with one group moving from Glenties and the other approaching from Stranorlar. The Glenties group had been moving ahead of the others and were discovered by the sentries.[8]

The column considered it unsafe to remain in the area and decided to march through the night. They had been planning to cross the Bluestack Mountain range the following day, but felt that it was risky to wait until daylight and the decision was taken to cross that night. Crossing this mountain range at night was a dangerous manoeuvre and their guide, a local man, had only ever crossed it in daylight. This would test their courage and endurance as they had to carry all their equipment with them, having received instructions from Seán Lehane that no matter how exhausted they got they were not permitted to discard any items. With the aid of the full moon they set off at approximately 1 a.m. and after several hours trekking, climbing, falling, wading and sinking through bogland, they began to descend the southern slopes of the Bluestacks at daybreak. They stopped in houses in the valley where they rested and were given food by their hosts. The local population was very friendly and even allowed them to shoot a sheep so that they could enjoy a decent meal. They told the IRA men of a man they called the 'Master' who lived in a big house over the hill and that he was a republican and supportive of their efforts. Later that evening, as they were all relaxing and digesting their great meal, they heard a commotion outside – dogs barking and someone whistling. Every man reached for his rifle and rushed outside to investigate, and who should they see coming up the road, but Donncha MacNelis and his companion, the red setter.

The men soon realised that MacNelis was the 'priest' referred to in the local press, as they had not been able to make sense of the report when they read it. The dog had somehow befriended MacNelis and followed him everywhere despite his efforts to chase it away. It was now Friday 28 July and they decided to stay in the area for a while and get some well-earned rest. Next morning some of the officers decided to walk to the Master's house to pay him a visit. He was the principal of the local parish school and his cousin, a priest, was staying with him. They received a great welcome and all were given refreshments – some wine and later high tea was served by the women of the house. They spent hours in conversation with their host and were both amused and flattered to have received so much attention and admiration following such trying experiences over recent months. They discussed various topics including the Treaty, the Civil War and the future of the country. That night they returned to their billets feeling up-beat and jovial after a comfortable and interesting day. The visiting priest promised that he would visit the parish priest the next day to arrange confessions and mass for the column, which was greatly appreciated by the men. They attended the parish chapel for confessions and mass the following morning.[9]

When the IRA evacuated Glenveagh Castle a number of men who were suffering from various injuries and ailments were transferred to the Red Cross field hospital situated in the grounds of Lough Veagh House at Gartan Lake near Churchill village. On Friday 28 July six patients from the hospital were making their way to the village to attend the local doctor. The Churchill area had been the focus of much activity from the Free State forces following the sheep-shooting incident at Glenveagh Castle. The IRA patients had driven from the hospital at Lough Veagh House in a Red Cross car to attend the doctor at Churchill when a party of Free State forces in the village stopped them. The officer in charge informed them that they were being detained and all were arrested, including three Kerry men: Christie Broden, Patrick Clifford and Martin Quille. Quille asked the officer in charge if he was going to respect the Red Cross and the reply was that he should obey orders. There were approximately seventy soldiers in the village and the six IRA men were taken to Wilkin's Hotel and placed in rooms there. The officer refused to grant the men permission to attend the doctor and refused to summon the doctor to the hotel. Some of the men began to sing and a soldier rushed in shouting at them to stop. The soldier then put a bullet up the breach of his gun and threatened them, but an officer instructed him to use the butt of his rifle if he wished to discipline them. Both the officer and soldier were verbally aggressive to the men, calling them murderers, etc. The Red Cross hospital was subsequently raided and all patients were conveyed to Churchill and later taken to Letterkenny where they were placed in cells in the basement of the barracks on the Port road.

In the early hours of Sunday 30 July one of the men became violently ill and requested a doctor. The physician did not arrive that morning and the prisoners announced that they had commenced a hunger strike demanding to be treated as prisoners of war. The majority of the soldiers and officers at the barracks were verbally abusive, calling the prisoners murdering bastards, etc. Later that morning Brigadier Jim Dawson of the Free State forces visited the prisoners and asked them to call off their hunger strike. He admitted that the conditions were shocking, but apologised as he had no other place for them. By Monday morning most of the able-bodied prisoners had been taken to Buncrana from where they were to be conveyed to Newbridge Camp in County Kildare. The ill prisoners were transferred to Lifford Hospital for treatment.[10]

One of the small IRA columns that had been directed to go to the west of the county established a temporary base in the Brockagh area, near Ballybofey. The column was under the command of Seamus McCann and the men were staying at a number of safe houses in the area. Two members of the column were billeted at a small house in the hills and while one was cleaning his gun, it accidentally went off, hitting John O'Neill. The column OC, Seamus McCann, was a short distance away at McKelvey's, and on hearing the shot immediately made his way to the house to find O'Neill lying on the floor with a hole in his stomach. McCann sent the owner of the house to Dungloe for a priest and a doctor. He returned some time later accompanied by Phil Boyle with a Crossley tender and conveyed O'Neill to the hospital in Glenties. McCann accompanied them, but was recognised by some Free State soldiers and subsequently arrested. He was held in a cell in the basement of the courthouse where he met a number of Orangemen who were also prisoners. They became good friends, as Seamus McCann recalled in his diary:

> These cells were built during the Land League days to keep the wild Irish underground as you had to look up to see the light ... While a prisoner here I met a few Orangemen who were also prisoners ... We were all in the same boat and became good comrades in misfortune while prisoners we were all united in getting fair play for all ... when the Orangemen were released they all arrived at my home in Derry and were very thankful for all I had done for them as prisoners.

Seamus McCann was then taken to Drumboe Castle where he met some of his old comrades, now Free State soldiers:

> I was only there (Drumboe Castle) an hour when we were on our way to Newbridge, County Kildare via Buncrana. We arrive in Buncrana that night about 288 prisoners. We were put aboard a ship called the *Lady Wicklow*.
>
> We were then herded down below where the cattle were kept and we were on this boat for 8 days. She sure was a Lady of Wicklow. Any way we arrive in Newbridge Camp and we're glad to get there after the boat journey.[11]

Over the last weekend of July the main IRA column under the command of Seán Lehane and Charlie Daly had moved to an area between Frosses and Glenties. Seán Lehane, accompanied by a number of IRA men, travelled further along the coast to scout for a possible safe area. Meanwhile the remainder of the column lazed about in the Binbane area and relaxed in the summer sun as the area seemed safe – but sentries were posted as a precaution. The day was warm and the atmosphere was carefree and happy, with the men playing games with the local children, in neglect of their duties.

All of a sudden, there was a burst of rifle fire in the distance bringing them back to the reality of their situation. The men scrambled for cover as the children ran to the safety of their mothers. The shooting was directed at a house on the main road to Frosses from Glenties, where two IRA sentries had retired for tea and were trapped. The IRA men nearest to the shooting raced across the hillside intending to outflank the attacking party. They took up positions to survey the scene as the shooting continued. A short distance in front they could see a figure standing against a fence but were reluctant to open fire, as they were unsure if it was a soldier or the farmer previously working the now abandoned mowing machine with horses still harnessed in the nearby field. They were also reluctant to shoot at the unidentified figure, as this would give away their positions. Some of the men then decided to crawl up the embankment to a small rock for a better vantage point and as they did so a shot roared from their left forcing them to drop back into a drain as more shots were fired in their direction. Mick O'Donoghue crawled along the ditch and, using a rock on top of the bank as cover, carefully peered over to examine the terrain. As soon as he raised his head, a bullet struck the top of the rock and sent pieces of stone into the air. He quickly dropped back into the drain, but had discovered the location of the opposing party, which was behind a large boulder. Joe McElroy, from Inishowen, was carrying grenades and passed one to O'Donoghue. McElroy crawled back up the embankment to give cover as O'Donoghue prepared the grenade. With a steady volley of shots from McElroy, the grenade was thrown in the direction of the boulder and both men fell back into the drain for cover. A deafening explosion followed and then, for a moment, deadly silence. The two then crawled back up the drain and met Jim Cotter with three others.

Cotter reported that he had spotted a party of men approaching over the hillside about half a mile away. They first thought that this might be Charlie Daly and the remainder of the column coming to their aid, but suddenly a volley of bullets passed over their heads and shots were fired along the edge of the drain grazing one man on the calf of his left leg. They were now thinking they had run into a trap whether the other side knew this or not. They remained silent and did not reply to the shooting, thinking the grenade may have deterred the Free State forces from pressing forward and finishing them off. The shooting ceased again and Jim Cotter with three others crawled back along the drain as O'Donoghue and McElroy stayed on to scout the area. Failing to locate any troops advancing, they went up along the drain until they reached the others. They moved across a field full of standing corn and using this as a cover moved cautiously out of the area, assisting their wounded comrade. Charlie Daly was waiting with the remainder of the column and was relieved to see them return; but a quick roll-call found two men missing.

The column moved further up the valley, took up strong defensive positions, and waited for the Free State troops' next move. From their new position, they could see a large body of men – approximately 100 – marching towards Frosses. The main body was moving in extended formation along the road with a couple of flanking parties moving through the fields. There was another large group in close formation in the centre, escorting the two missing IRA men, Aloysius McHugh from Donegal Town and Con Leary from Cork. The column contemplated pursuing the Free State forces to liberate the prisoners but the odds were about five-to-one against them and common sense prevailed.

Seán Lehane arrived back in the area from his scouting mission and ordered the immediate evacuation of the area.[12] By the following week the large column was considering the possibility of dividing into two groups and moving to different parts of the county as it was obvious that many search patrols were now focused on the south of the county.[13]

Chapter 22

Raids, Arrests and Escapes

By the end of July 1922, the Free State forces had focused their attention on extensive raiding to round up IRA men and those suspected of membership. The system adopted was the deployment of large numbers of troops, several hundred at times, moving in large columns, with one taking the lowlands and two or three columns moving through the mountains and hills to locate an IRA column and push them in the direction of another Free State column. This would keep the republican columns on the move, pushing them to near exhaustion and making it almost impossible to exist as a fighting unit. This system forced many IRA men to surrender.[1] On Monday 31 July an IRA man walked up the avenue of Drumboe Castle with his hands raised and surrendered. Another IRA man, Harry McGrath, a native of Oldtown, Letterkenny, was arrested during a general round-up in the area, after he was found suffering from the effects of hunger and exhaustion in a house near Glenveagh, and was taken to Letterkenny. He was held in Drumboe Castle and released after he agreed to join the Free State Army. Around the same time up to forty prisoners being held at Letterkenny were removed, taken to the train station under a very heavy escort and sent to Buncrana. On Monday night they were put on board the *Lady Wicklow* at Buncrana pier and conveyed to Dublin before being transferred to Newbridge for internment.[2]

The outbreak of the Civil War had diverted attention from the northern policy and the focus was now firmly on the conflict in the Free State. This was confirmed in Dublin following a conference, convened by Michael

Collins, of officers from the Six Counties on Wednesday 2 August. The conference was held at Portobello Barracks where the following policy was adopted:

> ... that all IRA operations in the six counties would cease forthwith – that men who were unable to remain in the six counties would be bound over to Barrack at the Curragh Camp, where they would be trained under their own officers to such tactics as would be applicable to the nature of fighting in the six counties – that these men would not be asked to take any part in the activities outside the six counties – that N.V.R. Forms would be presented for the purpose of receiving an allowance for the men – that the organisation in the six counties would remain unchanged and be carried on in the same way as it was in Ireland previous to 1918.

The officers and men from the northern divisions were transferred to the Curragh in mid-August and in the months that followed many were recruited into the Free State Army. This later led to a split in the 2nd Northern Division based at the Curragh and the divisional staff who had established a base in County Donegal.[3]

As a means of curtailing the movement of the IRA by night the Free State military authority issued a curfew order affecting a number of towns in County Donegal including Buncrana, Carndonagh, Moville, Milford, Raphoe, Letterkenny and Lifford:

> ... every person living in or within half-a-mile of the following towns in Tirconaill ... is ordered to remain within doors between the hours of 11.30 o'clock p.m. and 5 o'clock a.m., unless provided with a Permit in writing from the Competent Military Authority for the Area, or some Person duly authorised by him. All Persons abroad between the hours mentioned in the foregoing Order when challenged by any Officer or Soldier on duty must immediately halt and obey the instructions given. Failure to do so will be at their own peril. This Order shall come into force at 11.30 o'clock p.m. on the

3rd day of August, 1922. Dated this 31st day of July, 1922. Signed: R. O'Doherty (Capt.) 3 R Brigade Adjutant.[4]

The Free State forces stationed at Letterkenny received information that an IRA column was billeting in an area near Drumkeen village and a large number of Free State troops left Letterkenny shortly after 2 a.m. on Wednesday 2 August. Approximately one hour later they came upon the men. Sentries stationed outside the houses spotted the Free State troops approaching and immediately opened fire. The other members, some of whom were in bed, got up and grabbed their rifles to join in. A running battle ensued and lasted for up to two hours in the area between Drumkeen and Cark Mountain. At the conclusion of the fighting, some of the IRA column were rounded up and arrested. One, a man called Fries from Churchill, received a bullet wound to the hip. Another of the captured men was John Quinn, who some weeks earlier had been arrested and released on giving an understanding that he would not take up arms against the Free State government. The column leader, Alfie McCallion from Derry City, was also captured, though several IRA men successfully evaded capture. A number of bombs, rifles and ammunition were discovered in the houses used by the column. The prisoners, who were suffering from fatigue, were removed by lorry to Letterkenny and placed in the barracks beside the courthouse.[5] Further raids and captures were made throughout the week, including the arrest of John O'Brien from Ramelton, who was a member of the flying column previously operating out of Glenveagh Castle.

A young man named O'Hare, a cashier in the Letterkenny branch of the Belfast Bank, was arrested in the Glenveagh area on Wednesday evening, 2 August. Seamus Ó Grianna, publicity agent and former Gaelic organiser for Dáil Éireann, was arrested at the Letterkenny Railway Station on Thursday morning, 3 August. Hugh Murragh, of Termon, previously charged in connection with a mail robbery, was also arrested and all were taken to Letterkenny. A number of arrests were made in Buncrana under the military curfew issued in July, with nine people being arrested and detained until morning.[6]

A column of Free State troops operating in the west of the county approached Glenveagh Castle at about 2 a.m. on Friday 4 August, from four different points and, meeting with no opposition, decided to enter the castle. They were also in possession of a Red Cross ambulance from the hospital at Gartan. There were only eight men and one woman present and they offered no resistance. The printing press that produced the *Tirconaill War Bulletin* was seized during the raid. No weapons were found in the building. One of the men found at the castle was called Donovan and was acting OC of the castle. Together with other items found at Glenveagh were important dispatches which contained valuable information as to the strength, disposition and intentions of the IRA in the county.

A small IRA column was passing over the hills at Meenirroy near Fintown on the main Letterkenny to Glenties road that Friday evening, when unknown to them they were spotted by a party of Free State military passing on the road in two lorries. The vehicles travelled a short distance along the road before stopping, at which point the soldiers dismounted and doubled back on the column through the hills. The men were taken completely by surprise, offered no resistance and surrendered, expressing great disappointment on being captured. They were taken to Letterkenny later that evening and subsequently conveyed to Drumboe Castle. Others, including Frank Shields from Derry, were arrested in a house on the outskirts of Letterkenny. They were also taken to Drumboe Castle.

Free State forces were conducting a relentless campaign to capture IRA columns and on Saturday 5 August another group of men was seized in the Glenfinn area. A party of Free State troops had been scouring the hills in that area when they came upon the column. The men were concealed behind turf banks and were taken by surprise when Free State troops opened fire on them. The IRA returned fire, which continued for about twenty minutes, until one of the IRA pulled off his shirt and hoisted it on a stick as the signal for surrender. Several men were arrested with rifles, a revolver, bombs and ammunition.[7]

A large number of IRA from the 3rd Western Division, covering parts of Sligo and south Donegal, descended on the town of Bundoran on Tuesday 15 August and engaged with Free State troops on the streets of the town. The battle was described as ferocious and a call was made to Drumboe for reinforcements. The shooting continued throughout the day and persisted until Thursday. IRA men in a Lancia car attempted to remove a barricade but were forced to retreat under heavy fire from Free State forces. Sniper posts were set up at the western end of the town and they periodically fired on Free State posts. The main body of IRA men left the town in the early hours of Thursday morning, due to the large number of Free State reinforcements arriving from Drumboe Castle. However, a number of IRA men remained on the outskirts of the town and continued sniping at the Free State troops throughout Friday, Saturday and Sunday. Each time Free State troops replied with heavy machine-gun fire, but by Monday night, 21 August, the IRA had abandoned the area and the town had returned to normal.[8]

The six prisoners captured in the Drumkeen area on 2 August escaped from the Letterkenny No. 1 Barracks in the early hours of Friday morning 18 August. They had been confined to a cell on the ground floor and during exercise one found a piece of steel from which they made a makeshift hacksaw. They succeeded in cutting one of the iron bars protecting the window of the cell and made an opening large enough for a man to pass through. Outside were barbed wire entanglements, which they covered with their blankets to gain access to the adjoining premises.[9]

Over the same weekend a group of republican prisoners being held at the Petty Sessions Courthouse in Stranorlar escaped. One of the guards discovered the escape on Monday morning, 21 August, when he went to call the prisoners for breakfast. The captives had made a hole in the gable wall of the building and moved into the neighbouring house on Sunday night, making good their escape from there. They had been working on the hole for some time and had stacked up records from the Petty Sessions to conceal it from the guards.[10]

On Monday 21 August Fr William Hackett, who had heard the confessions of the IRA garrisons at Inch Island and Glenveagh Castle, was in County Cork to meet with Michael Collins who was midway through a tour of his native county. Fr Hackett had been meeting with members of the IRA Executive Council the previous evening at Muscarigh, near Béal na mBláth, and was possibly arranging to meet with Collins to discuss a peace formula. Hackett left a message at the Imperial Hotel which Collins did not receive until later that evening. Collins replied with a note apologising for the mix-up: 'I received your note this evening but was engaged when it was handed to me. Mr Mehigan was to arrange for you to see me, but through some misunderstanding you were not informed. Am sorry I missed you.'[11]

The meeting of the IRA Executive Council at Muscarigh drew a large number of IRA men into the area to provide protection for the officers. Scouts and barricades were positioned on all roads in the immediate area. Early the following morning Michael Collins left the Imperial Hotel in Cork City and travelled with his convoy to Macroom where he met a group of neutral IRA officers. They left Macroom at approximately 8 a.m. for Bandon, travelling via Béal na mBláth, and so passed close to the temporary IRA headquarters. At the Béal na mBláth crossroads the convoy stopped to ask a man for directions to Bandon. This was strange as the convoy included a Cork native, Michael Collins, as well as others who were familiar with the area. However, the man was an IRA scout, and it has been suggested that Collins wanted to let it be known that he was in the area in the hope of meeting with IRA officers. It was also unusual that the members of the convoy did not search and question a man standing along a country road.

A barricade was set up to prevent a surprise attack by Free State forces during the IRA Executive meeting at Muscarigh. At the meeting's conclusion the men were dismissed, but a party of five was told to remain behind to dismantle the barricade and disarm a landmine, which was set beside the road. Between 8 p.m. and 9 p.m. the Collins convoy was returning from Bandon when a scout spotted it and fired a single shot to warn the two men disarming the mine. The shot was heard by the convoy, which stopped with the men immediately exiting their vehicles and taking up positions. Both sides began shooting and exchanged gunfire for up to thirty minutes during which Michael Collins sustained a wound to the head, killing him almost immediately. Ironically, Collins had in his possession a pass from the IRA for safe passage through his native county.[12]

Collins' death was disastrous because he was the only person who could have healed the divisions between the two sides and quite possibly opposed the future actions of the Free State government. Some of his notes and conversations around that time suggest that he was prepared to enter into negotiations and desired some form of agreement whereby republicans would lay down their arms while retaining their principles.

Meanwhile, hostilities between the two sides continued in Donegal with a party of IRA attacking Free State forces based at Mountcharles in the early hours of Wednesday 23 August. The IRA men were positioned on high ground around the village and used rifles and Lewis guns to fire at the Free State posts. The Free State troops replied with similar weapons until, after an hour, the IRA retreated.[13] The situation for the IRA in the county was becoming more desperate, as Seán Lehane communicated to Ernie O'Malley:

> It is exceedingly difficult existing at all. The population is for the most part hostile – it couldn't be much worse in the 'six counties' – and is so poor that supporting a column of any effective strength is out of the question. There is scarcely any local co-operation even in such a small matter as scouting … The capture of No. 1 and 2 Brigade columns was followed by wholesale raids and arrests in North Donegal. These had the effect of demoralising the few men left who regarded the game as practically up.[14]

The IRA's North Eastern Command OC, Ernie O'Malley was doing all he could to relieve the situation in Donegal and was making arrangements with Frank Aiken, OC 4th Northern Division, to establish an armaments dump on the Donegal/Derry border to ensure weapons and ammunition would be available to the IRA of the 1st Northern Division. Ernie O'Malley was also considering putting the 1st Northern Division under the command of the 3rd Western Division, which already covered part of south Donegal and the general Sligo area. O'Malley informed Lehane that he was in favour of withdrawing officers from Donegal:

I would certainly be in favour of your withdrawing from Donegal, tho' I can see objections to that course of action, but officers who are only acting, as far as I can see, as a flying column and who are fit for staff work could be of great utility to areas which have a certain amount of men but which are badly staffed.[15]

Seán Lehane was reluctant to abandon Donegal:

Well I think I didn't mention that we should leave, I just gave you the situation as near as I could. I don't like the idea of leaving Donegal myself and most of the fellows don't, but at the same time we are only a part of an army and in my opinion we are only faking fight here and stealing about from place to place like criminals. I suppose it is only a matter of time until we are rounded up or more probably put out of action and I fear we will have nothing gained for the cause after. For my part of it I don't mind, but I wish those others from the South were somewhere else. I honestly don't care to be responsible for their massacre some fine morning soon.

There is not a fighting chance, as the people are out of sympathy with us because we are strangers and they have friends they would help in the Barracks rather than us. My idea in staying here was not to leave down the local men, but the only bunch of local men here who will fight is a bunch of men near Castlefinn ... Well I think we have left no stone unturned in that direction [west Donegal] but the people don't want a Republic. They want money and ease ... We are trying to organise still but only those we have already will work ... the only other plan I can see if we could go in twos and threes and snipe the enemy, but our southern accents sell us ...[16]

Ernie O'Malley's subsequent correspondence with the Chief of Staff, Liam Lynch, on 24 August was bleak:

I heard from Lehane on yesterday. I sent him some money today. Of the 115 armed men belonging to the original columns about 25 are left. The country is rotten, even the young girls and boys carry information and the priests exhort the people to go out of their way to spy on us. He is evidently in touch with the 3rd Western; he is very short of ammunition – rifle and revolver; he sent down a special messenger to me for stuff but I could do nothing.[17]

On Sunday 27 August, the commander of the republican forces formerly based at Inch Fort, Captain John Mullan, escaped from Drumboe Castle along with two other officers. However, Mullan was apprehended again the following Tuesday morning near Inch Road Railway Station and taken to Buncrana.[18]

Despite the bleak reports sent by Seán Lehane, the small pockets of republican forces situated in different parts of the county increased their activities at the end of August and into September. There was a mix of activity targeting both the Special Constabulary and the Free State forces as well as disrupting the local infrastructure.

On Monday 28 August, a small party of IRA men crossed into Derry and was preparing to launch an attack on a Special Constabulary post on the Buncrana Road. They were spotted by Specials at the post and when challenged, began firing. The men then made their way back in the direction of Donegal with a party of Specials in hot pursuit, but arrived safely back to Burnfoot. Another republican column ambushed Free State forces near the village of Bruckless, south Donegal, in the early hours of Friday 1 September. The Free State forces were travelling in an armoured car, which broke down, and while they were investigating the problem the IRA opened fire from concealed positions. The driver was shot in the hand and the others replied vigorously to the attack, but the IRA retreated into the darkness and escaped. The following day Free State troops took over the residence of J. R. O'Donnell in Dunkineely, in response to the increased activities of republican forces in the area. Despite this, small pockets of IRA units remained active in this area, with the road between Mountcharles and Inver being blocked with felled trees. A bridge on the main road between Donegal Town and Mountcharles, which was previously damaged in an explosion, was again blown up and destroyed.

This was followed by further disruption when the telegraph wires between Inver and Dooran Road Railway Stations were cut.

A party of Free State troops conducted searches at the Isle of Doagh, Inishowen, for IRA prisoners who had escaped from custody. During the operation one of the weapons accidentally fired and the bullet struck another soldier in the head. The injured man was removed to Lifford Hospital for treatment. The remaining soldiers continued searching the area and recaptured several of the prisoners, who were taken into custody at Buncrana.[19] About the same time a number of republican prisoners from various parts of Donegal were taken to Buncrana before their transfer to Newbridge Internment Camp.

The main IRA column under the command of Seán Lehane and Charlie Daly was moving through the Mountcharles area where they met with Brian Monaghan, IRA brigadier in south Donegal. Monaghan informed them that the Free State forces had temporarily abandoned Mountcharles village and the commanding officers considered this a good opportunity for the men to buy much-needed provisions. The entire column descended on the village early on Monday morning, 4 September, and visited the local drapery shop where they were able to purchase heavy shirts, socks and underwear with money remaining from the bank raid at Buncrana in early May. The stamps commandeered from the mail car near Fintown in July were cashed in at the local post office and netted £5, enabling them to buy a good supply of cigarettes. The column remained in the village for most of that day and made their way back to their billets in the valley later that evening.

It rained heavily that night and all the men were soaked through to the skin by the time they reached their destination. Contrary to the rules of not entering their billets until daybreak, in their miserable and damp condition, they knocked up the inhabitants and entered. Four men went into one dwelling and having apologised for the intrusion stood around the turf fire to dry off. They raked the ashes and suddenly there was a tremendous explosion with red turf and ash flying into their faces. One of the men felt a sharp stinging sensation in his right shin and discovered a large burn when he lifted his trouser leg. They searched around the hearth and found an empty bullet case: a bullet had evidently fallen out of one of the bandoliers when someone bent over the fire to light a cigarette and no one had noticed. Luckily, the wound was only superficial and quickly healed.

A few days later the column under Lehane and Daly was split up once again. Charlie Daly took one contingent to west Donegal while Seán Lehane took the other to the east of the county focusing on the Castlefinn area.[20]

On Monday 4 September an IRA flying column was captured in the Glendowan area by Free State troops from Letterkenny, Dungloe and Glenveagh. The search and round-up operation began in the early hours of the morning and the IRA column was taken completely by surprise, with no shots being fired. Among the men captured were the five who had escaped from Letterkenny in August. They were later conveyed to Letterkenny, before being transferred to Carndonagh. They had been there for only a few days when eleven men, including James Boyle from Dungloe and Joe Toner from Killea near Derry, escaped. The group separated, with Boyle and Toner reaching the Inishowen Mountains, where they lost their way. Without realising it, the two men had crossed the border on the outskirts of Derry. They walked into a patrol of Special Constabulary who ordered them to walk a short distance over to their camp. Halfway between the patrol and the camp, they came to a crossroads and made a run for it, disappearing into the nearby woods. They continued walking until they reached the mound of Aileach, above the townland of Burt in County Donegal, where they rested for a while before going their separate ways. James Boyle made his way back to Churchill and had not been long in a house when it was raided. He escaped through a back window and made his way to Glendowan where he later met with Joe O'Donnell from Dungloe and Jack Shields from Monaghan. The three men then made their way towards Dungloe to try to make contact with the remaining men in that area.[21]

The Free State forces continued to search the Glendowan area that Monday and called at the house of IRA quartermaster John Mullan, where they found 8,000 rounds of rifle ammunition, 500 rounds of revolver ammunition, 50 bombs, 1,000 feet of fuse, a large quantity of rifles and a number of important documents. This capture was described as 'the largest yet made' by Free State forces.

Early on Monday morning, the road bridge at Drumbollogue which crosses the River Glasha between Letterkenny and Glendowan, was partly blown up and another bridge at Gartan was completely demolished. There was further activity in the north of the county, with eight republicans (four of whom were at a dance) being arrested in Buncrana on Monday night.

The following night four republican prisoners, Joseph Maguire, Matt Gilfedder, John Kane and Tom Doherty, escaped from Finner Camp. They removed boards from their hut and tunnelled out, making their way over sand dunes. Two of the escapees, Tom Doherty and Matt Gilfedder, were recaptured a short time later.[22]

A few weeks after his escape from Carndonagh James Boyle had a chance encounter with Joe Sweeney, Commandant General of the Free State forces in Donegal. On Tuesday 26 September, Sweeney was travelling by car from Burtonport to Dungloe with his father and two brothers. They stopped so that Sweeney's father could collect samples of local minerals in the nearby hills. Sweeney and one of his brothers remained on the road with the car while his father and other brother walked up the hill. James Boyle was making his way through Meenmore carrying a rifle when he noticed Sweeney standing on the road. Sweeney spotted him and called on him to halt. Boyle immediately took cover and fired. They exchanged shots for a considerable time before Boyle retreated and moved off under cover of the surrounding hills. That evening and for most of that week the Free State military converged on the area, carrying out extensive searches of the hills near Crovehy.[23]

The difficulties experienced by the IRA in Donegal were described in a report for the month of September from Ernie O'Malley to Liam Lynch:

> 1st Northern: I met messenger from Lehane – he is reduced to twenty armed men; the majority of the unarmed men there seem to be of very poor stuff; there is very big enemy force in the county and they are very active. I have sent him on some money ... the situation in this

area is bad. What has accounted for the armed strength having fallen very low.[24]

In another report Ernie O'Malley informed Liam Lynch, Chief of Staff, that conditions were deteriorating:

> 1st Northern: No organisation worth speaking of at least no local organisation to give assistance to the men there. There is a small flying column left in the West of the county and another small one of about five or six men round about Castlefinn area. I did not like, and do not still, to forward you a report received from the area, as it would not do if it fell into enemy hands – suffice to say that the local organisation left our men down there.

The report from O'Malley to Lynch contained an extract from Seán Lehane's letter:

> It is a pity nothing can be done in the 2nd Northern; it is impossible just now, as the Ulster Free Staters are co-operating with the Southern Free Staters here on the Donegal border. They have helped in trying to surround some of our men who are yet at liberty in that direction. They have lent Joe Sweeney munitions and guns.[25]

Charlie Daly also outlined the desperate position in a letter to his brother Thomas, then serving in the Kerry IRA. In the letter, dated 17 September 1922, Daly described their plight:

> I wonder could you do anything to awaken GHQ to a sense of its responsibilities to us here in Donegal. Here we are with one small column trying to hold our own against desperate odds. A month ago I never expected that one of us would be left by now. Neither would we only for the cowardice of the Staters. We wouldn't have existed for 24 hours were we in any other part of Ireland.

He described how the clergy and the local population were opposed to their presence in the county:

> A hostile civil population and a hostile clergy; nearly all the priests with the exception of one or two, are out against us. They condemn us as 'murderers', 'robbers', etc., and encourage the people not to harbour us and to report all our movements to the enemy. Without these things it is hard enough to exist, the people are so cursedly poor. The poor devils have hardly enough to feed themselves, let alone anybody else.

Daly was critical of Liam Lynch and said that they could easily leave Donegal, but were reluctant to do so:

> I don't know in the name of Goodness what is up with Liam Lynch. He sent us up here and then seems to have forgotten all about us. I think I can safely say that there isn't another column in the country that is up against so much odds or has endured more hardship than ours. There is a very easy way out of it, if we only wished.
>
> All we would have to do is to get across Donegal Bay into Sligo where we would be safe, and I think the fellows here would not regret our departure.
>
> But we won't do that. We will stick it out, no matter what comes … I am confident that if we can carry on for a little longer we will be all right, for the people are fast turning in favour and the faint-hearted among our own are picking up courage again. Even without Donegal, the fight will be won in the rest of the country anyway.[26]

Chapter 23

Eithne Coyle's War Ends

Eithne Coyle had for some time taken sole responsibility for the boycott campaign against the transport of unionist merchandise through County Donegal, as well as being involved in intelligence work and carrying dispatches. As part of this activity she had secured a safe route for transporting dispatches between the 1st Northern Division, Donegal and 3rd Western Division, Sligo, by contacting a friendly fisherman who ferried her between St John's Point in Donegal Bay and Mullaghmore on the north Sligo coast.

In September 1922 Coyle was sent to Dublin with dispatches to acquire arms, a typewriter and other equipment. To ensure the dispatch got to Dublin, Roisín O'Doherty was sent on the same mission and travelled through the Six Counties, while Coyle travelled via Sligo. Both women arrived safely and returned with several dispatches, taking the same precautions on the return journey. Coyle visited Seamus Devins at Sligo with dispatches before returning to Donegal. Devins was killed two days later in a battle with Free State forces under General Seán MacEoin.[1] Coyle was arrested on Monday 25 September 1922 near Donegal Town, while returning from the 3rd Western Division Sligo by boat, when a Free State patrol ordered the craft ashore. She had a number of documents on her person, including correspondence for Seán Lehane.

Coyle was first taken to the Rock Barracks at Ballyshannon, where she was held for six weeks in a room beside the guardroom; she was afforded little privacy. She made numerous requests for a transfer to more suitable accommodation and to be assigned a female attendant. Each request was refused and she eventually went on hunger strike. Her mother wrote to the parish priest at Ballyshannon asking him to intervene. However, his reply was not very heartening: he said that if half of what he had heard about her was true, his congregation was a lot better off without her. Coyle was a week into her hunger strike when she was moved first to Drumboe Castle and then on to Buncrana, where a female attendant was assigned to her, at which point she ended her protest. She was held at Buncrana for two weeks and then moved on to Dublin on the cattle boat *Lady Wicklow* as the authorities knew she had escaped before and were not prepared to risk transporting her by road or rail. She was imprisoned at Kilmainham Jail until her release in December 1923.[2]

Chapter 24

Emergency Powers

The Free State government introduced the Emergency Powers Resolution during a Dáil session on Wednesday 27 September, which provided for the establishment of military courts or committees. It provided powers for various punishments of offences against the Free State government and troops, including the penalty of death. This piece of legislation passed through the Dáil the following day.[1]

The British cabinet gave the introduction of the Emergency Powers Resolution a cautious welcome and in praising the measure said:

> Another indication of strong government was the approval in principle by the Dáil by 48 votes against 18 of the institution of military courts with powers to punish offenders with death; penal servitude, imprisonment and fines ... These strong measures ... are undoubtedly copies from those carried out by the Imperial authorities in 1920–21 ... whether these new courts will really be effective, or whether the whole policy is political bluff, remains to be seen.[2]

At the same time in Donegal the responsibility for law and order transferred from the Free State military to the new unarmed civic guard, to leave the military free to deal with the war. To facilitate the arrival of the new authority the Free State forces based in Letterkenny evacuated the No. 1 Barracks situated at Lower Main Street on Thursday 28 September making way for the arrival of fifty officers, who were expected in Letterkenny the following day. The civic guard was later officially established as An Garda Síochána through the Irish Free State Act in August 1923.[3]

Despite the curfew directive and the unrelenting pursuit by the Free State forces in Donegal, a number of small pockets of IRA columns remained active in the county. On Tuesday night, 3 October, a column of five men descended on the town of Lifford and walked into a Free State military curfew patrol who called on them to raise their hands: one did, but the others ran away in the direction of the remainder of the patrol. Both sides started shooting and soon the men garrisoned at Lifford Barracks joined in. The IRA column was greatly outnumbered and was forced to make a hasty retreat. At that time over fifty men occupied the Lifford Barracks.

There was further IRA activity the following week, on Monday 9 October, when shots were fired at the military barracks in the village of Ramelton. The Free State military occupying the barracks did not reply to the shooting, suspecting it was a ruse to conceal other activity in the area. Instead, the soldiers crept out the back door and searched the area, but failed to find anyone. A short time later they received information that a residence at Roughpark, Ballymaleel was being raided. The Ramelton-based military immediately went to Ballymaleel, but again failed to locate anyone. Later that day Free State forces operating in the Kilmacrennan area captured an IRA column, which had been operating in the area. Before being arrested, the eight men smashed their rifles.[4]

The Emergency Powers legislation passed into law and the Free State Proclamation was published on Tuesday 10 October outlining the offences and punishments to be imposed for any actions against the Free State military or the government. Depending on the nature and gravity of the offences the following punishments could be imposed: death, penal servitude, imprisonment, deportation, internment and fines. Members of the IRA arrested in possession of weapons or other armaments faced the death penalty.[5]

By October 1922 the Civil War in Donegal had been reduced to a game of cat and mouse and the primary objective of the republican forces in the county was to evade capture. In a report to Ernie O'Malley in mid-

October, Seán Lehane described how the unrelenting attention of the Free State forces was making their effort to even exist near impossible. With large Free State columns consisting of over 200 men moving in encircling formations, the IRA columns were constantly on the move:

> There were very few fights for month, owing to activity of enemy columns in large numbers and working in co-operation ... During the month the enemy has given his attention to wholesale raiding and rounding up ... This is a very effective means of tiring out our men because when you feel like resting your men you find that you are in some cases only more enveloped. On last occasion ... in South Donegal, only the coming of darkness saved us from running into a column of 200 men, after getting away from a column of forty men with two machine guns, with whom we had a small scrap. They guard their barracks, towns etc., by means of placing columns all round at about three or four miles distant and keeping only a maintenance party of five or six in the barracks itself ... We have now decided to do away with columns, and break up the div. staff and Southern men here into a few parties. We are therefore on the run and find it almost impossible to expose arms or travel by day ... The Deputy OC [Charlie Daly] is gone to West [Donegal] and we are gone to East Donegal.[6]

The extensive searches continued around the county and a search of the Churchill area on Tuesday night, 17 October, yielded a valuable discovery: a box of bombs and a complete wireless apparatus with dynamos, valued at thousands of pounds. They also discovered a box of bombs in a plantation adjoining the residence of Mrs Catherine Johnstone, Lough Veagh House. In a subsequent search, a revolver and ammunition were found at the residence of Hugh McKay, Churchill, who had two sons interned in Newbridge Internment Camp at the time. In a follow-up operation, the republican field hospital in the grounds of Lough Veagh House at Gartan Lake was raided and patients were removed from their beds in an aggressive manner, to the protests of the Cumann na mBan nursing staff. The nurses objected to the removal of some patients suffering from contagious diseases, who were being treated in isolation, but their complaints were ignored and all the patients were put on lorries, taken to Letterkenny and held in cells at the barracks there.[7]

Catherine Johnstone and her daughter Georgina, the occupants of Lough Veagh House, were arrested the following week and a sentry was placed at the lodge, with the troops continuing their searches of other areas in the Churchill district. Other items found in the area around Lough Veagh House were detonators, ammunition, wire for detonating landmines and a car. Shortly afterwards two men were seen approaching the house through the woods and the sentry three times called on them to halt. They failed to do so and the sentry fired, wounding one of them while the other escaped. The injured man, Patrick Fries, was from the area, and was conveyed to Lifford Hospital, but died the following evening. Catherine Johnstone and her daughter applied for a writ of habeas corpus, which was refused. On appeal the two women were released by order of the Dublin Court of Appeal on Monday 4 December.[8]

The introduction of the Emergency Powers legislation in September greatly altered an already desperate situation for republican forces in Donegal. By October 1922 the Emergency Powers Resolution awakened a sense of reality in many local republicans. The Free State military authority published notices on 10 October announcing the establishment of military courts or committees which outlined the charges and penalties for various offences, and offered an amnesty to those wishing to abandon the war. It stated that anyone wishing to avail themselves of the terms would need to hand over armaments to the local military barracks. Everyone who complied was permitted to return home and would receive a full pardon. The proposal obviously weighed heavily on the minds of some, as an intelligence report from the Free State Army's Donegal command in late October stated that fifteen locals had availed of the amnesty:

> ... in response to the proclamation the following surrendered; Bernard O'Donnell – Rannafast, Annagry; James O'Donnell – Rannafast, Annagry; Owen Bonner – Derryheeney, Doochary; Bernard Bonner – Derryheeney, Doochary; Charles Doran – Lettercloth, Doochary;

James Ward – Loughanure; Hugh Ferry – Drumnaraw, Creeslough; James MacBride – Drumnaraw, Creeslough; Hugh McCafferty – Drumnaraw, Creeslough; Edward Boyle – Drumnaraw, Creeslough; Pat Boyle – Termon; John McGreanra – Termon; James McGreanra – Termon; Pat Gallagher – Termon; James O'Donnell – Termon.[9]

The situation for the Donegal-based republican forces continued to deteriorate according to Seán Lehane in a report to the OC North Eastern Command, Ernie O'Malley. He asked for advice on what to do regarding their plight:

> What would you advise [on] re-organisation, etc.? ... we had just decided going on the run properly as we have to go six or seven miles by night to get a house to stay in. What does GHQ decide on for dealing with the priests etc.? I had a note from C[harlie] Daly who is in West Donegal during past fortnight, in which he states that the confessionals are used for getting information. Youngsters are scared into giving information to the clergy, etc. In East Donegal, where we are at present, the Protestants are by far our best friends, the reason being, I suppose, that they are free from Church Tyranny. Daly thinks West Donegal hopeless, and he has asked to leave it before it is too late; so I have written to him calling himself and his men off this way. Perhaps after a little ease here that it would be possible to organise local help, get us mines and electric apparatus, etc., and start again in the near future. The Staters may ease off and become less vigilant after a time.[10]

The reply from Ernie O'Malley gave little hope for the men in Donegal and the inference could be drawn that it was only a matter of time before those from the south would be ordered to abandon Donegal:

> I cannot issue any definite instructions on the question of re-organisation of the area but you should certainly leave some good local men in charge and make them responsible for organisation. Give

them what instructions you can; arrange for forwarding reports to the Head Quarters of the 3rd Western ... The most important work would be re-organisation and training of engineers and I doubt if you could leave officers behind who would be capable of this. We have no engineers here – in fact, we were depending on you for a few ... Re: Priests: it is very hard to issue any drastic instructions to deal with such. I'm afraid we will have to leave them severely alone.[11]

The Presbyterian community in East Donegal was sympathetic to the local IRA column operating under the command of Seán Lehane. They gave their support to the IRA because they believed republicans were fighting for a principle, while they saw the Free State forces as fighting for a wage.[12]

Chapter 25

Newbridge Internment Camp and the Escape

The Civil War began in late June 1922 and by early October over 100 republicans had been arrested in County Donegal following a relentless campaign by the Free State military. Depending on the nature of the arrest, the male prisoners were sent to Mountjoy Jail or interned at Newbridge Internment Camp in County Kildare and female prisoners were incarcerated in Kilmainham Jail.

All new arrivals at Newbridge Camp received a lecture from the camp governor, a man called Hayes. He welcomed them by saying, 'You will each get one knife, fork, spoon, mug and plate – three blankets and you better not try to escape and we have taken very good care that you won't so that's that.'

A camp council was formed and it was decided that it would be run along military lines, with a camp OC and staff, with two battalions. There were some 2,000 men interned at Newbridge Camp. Each block was to have an officer commanding and each room was to have a section leader. The prisoners could move freely around all day from 7 a.m. until 8 p.m. The compound was hemmed in with barbed wire about twelve feet high, with an armed sentry every forty yards who overlooked it. It was also floodlit at night and the sentries were often heard shouting, 'put out that light'. Anyone who had a light on after 9 p.m. had to be prepared to take cover as the hut would be fired at. When a group of Donegal men arrived in the camp, the other men who served in the county were very glad to meet them again, especially Frank O'Donnell, as the last they heard of him was that he was taken to Lifford Hospital having been wounded during an ambush by the Special Constabulary. They were all brought to V Block where they spent a long night talking about their ups and downs in Donegal and the few good families that had stood by them.

A short time later another group of men from Donegal arrived, including Joe O'Donnell, who had been captured after a fight in the hills near Brockagh. They wasted very little time and soon started exploring possible escape opportunities. It was decided to start digging tunnels, with G Block being the first to get going, followed by R and then V.[1] Neil Plunkett O'Boyle from Lackenagh, Burtonport, west Donegal was one of the main tunnel diggers in the R Block tunnel. The tunnel from G Block was not successful as a lorry drove over the roof of it and the front wheel collapsed into the tunnel.

The chief engineers in the R Block tunnel were Thomas McHenry of Kildare and a man from Cork called O'Donovan. Neil Plunkett O'Boyle had worked in the coal mines in Scotland and had previous experience of engineering having assisted his father who was a civil engineer. It was a tough job digging the tunnel in the darkness. At one point they came across a brick wall and it took five days to get through that.[2] They discovered they could dig a tunnel to an unused sewerage pipe (a 'V' shaped pipe approximately 2 feet high and 150 yards long), which ran under the football field and then under the road before coming out at the River Liffey. The tunnelling crew first came out through an old mill about ten yards from the Liffey, so they dug down again and successfully completed their task. The camp officers decided on the date for the escape: Sunday 22 October. On the Saturday night, the men of V and R Blocks said their goodbyes to each other, as some were going to Kerry, Kildare and Dublin, while others were going to the northern counties including Donegal.

Following this, the men in R Block decided to break out later that night rather than waiting until the following day. They would not be missed until Monday morning as there was no roll-call on Sundays.[3] Neil Plunkett O'Boyle was the first into the tunnel to begin the escape.[4] When Seamus McCann visited R Block on the morning of the designated date of the escape and discovered that the inmates had made an early exit, he immediately returned to V Block and held a meeting with the others. It was decided they should go as soon as possible as they would not get another chance until the following weekend. They resolved to get in touch with all the Block OCs and all the prisoners were called to parade for mass, which effectively disguised the absence of those from R Block. For the remainder of the day men were detailed to come and go from that block to give the impression it was still inhabited. Later that morning, Seamus McCann sent a scout out through the sewerage pipe, who succeeded in getting through to the opening at the River Liffey. They then held a meeting in G Block with all the Block OCs to arrange for different groups of men to get out that night.

The V Block batch left at 8 p.m. and included Frank O'Donnell, Donegal; John Quinn, Donegal; John O'Brien, Donegal; Dan McGee, Donegal; Seán McCool, Donegal; Alfie McCallion, Derry; Seamus McCann, Derry; Leo Burke, Mullingar; Anthony McDonnell, Tyrone; James McGurk, Tyrone; Charlie McGleenon, Armagh and Jim Spain, Dublin, who was their guide to his native city. There, he organised safe houses and contacts for all, but was shot dead a few days later by Free State troops as he entered his own house. Three of the tunnel escapees, McCann, O'Donnell and McCallion, were temporarily posted to the 1st Eastern Division by Ernie O'Malley.[5]

One of the men who escaped from R Block, Neil Plunkett O'Boyle, made his way to Dublin and was put up by Sheila Humphreys at her home in Ailesbury Road. He received a change of clothes and remained there until sometime later, when Pat Brennan brought him to Wicklow. He later formed a flying column in County Wicklow, but was fighting against very heavy odds. On Tuesday 15 May, while he was resting with his men at Valleymount in the Wicklow Mountains, they were surrounded by a party of Free State troops from Naas and ordered to surrender. Other members of the column included Daniel McGee from Falcarragh, and James McMorrow and Patrick Farrell from County Leitrim. O'Boyle asked the Free State troops to hold their fire until the occupants of the house, a mother and her daughter, could escape to safety. The appeal was refused and the Free State officer in charge threatened to throw grenades through the windows. O'Boyle said he was surrendering and shouted he was coming out. He walked out of the house with his arms raised and approached the Free State OC, McCorley, who was from Belfast. O'Boyle spoke a few words to him and McCorley raised his revolver and shot him first in the eye and then in the head.

At the inquest held the following day at Naas Military Barracks under Dr Cosgrave, coroner for North Kildare, a verdict was returned of death by a bullet wound inflicted by an officer in the execution of his duty. The coroner said he did not think an investigation necessary and had been asked to hold the inquest by the military themselves as they wished to make clear they had nothing to conceal. Neil Plunkett O'Boyle's body had been identified by Mary Lambert, who was a teacher at Lacken National School, Blessington, County Wicklow. O'Boyle had stayed with the Lamberts at their house on many occasions. Both Mary Lambert and her husband accompanied O'Boyle's remains back to Kincasslagh, County Donegal for burial.[6]

Chapter 26

Arrests and Executions

The long-drawn-out Civil War in County Donegal was nearing its conclusion. In late October 1922 Seán Lehane received the official order from Ernie O'Malley, instructing all officers and men from the southern counties to withdraw from Donegal. Lehane, who was at that time operating in the Castlefinn area of east Donegal, sent a dispatch to his deputy OC, Charlie Daly, who was in west Donegal. Daly received the dispatch from a Cumann na mBan member, Kitty McGee, while billeted in the Gweedore area:

> I have received an order from E. O'Malley authorising us to leave Donegal at once and withdraw our men. I believe our work here is impossible. We have to steal about here like criminals at night and it gets on one's nerves. In order that we may try and make arrangements, could you please bring your lads on towards Drumkeen and we will go that length to meet you. Send word to [James] Brown the OC as to when you are coming and we will know. We will be able to talk over things there ... Until I see you and the lads, Good Luck. Seán Ó Liathan.[1]

The column under Charlie Daly had existed under miserable conditions for some time, having to move through the hills and bogs of west Donegal to avoid the roads because they were generally heavily patrolled. They were based in the Gweedore area when they received Seán Lehane's dispatch, and they immediately set off to meet with the others at Drumkeen in east Donegal. They moved through the mountains in the direction of Dunlewy

Arrests and Executions

and after several hours arrived in the townland of Meenabul early on Thursday 2 November.

Two members of the column, Frank Ward and Daniel Coyle, were from the Falcarragh area and arranged billets in two houses located at the foot of Errigal Mountain. Every man was suffering from starvation and exhaustion, so none had the energy to stand sentry and all entered their billets for rest. Their hosts were friendly and generous, but unknown to them a visitor to one of the houses during the day was less sympathetic and requested permission to leave. He went to Falcarragh where he reported their presence to the local military barracks. At approximately 5 p.m. a large party of Free State military left Ballyconnell House in the direction of Dunlewy. They travelled most of the journey by road and, continuing on foot, arrived at the targeted houses shortly after 7 p.m. They surrounded the area before entering the first house where they found Timothy O'Sullivan, James Lane, Frank Ward and Daniel Coyle in the kitchen. Charlie Daly was in an adjoining room and walked out saying that he was responsible for all men and weapons in the house.[2] In the neighbouring house the other members of the column were discovered: Seán Larkin, Daniel Enright and James Donaghy. Some of the men were in bed and others were sitting by the fireside; they offered no resistance and all showed signs of having undergone great hardship. They were handcuffed and removed by lorry to Falcarragh Barracks that night and transferred to Drumboe Castle the following day. The Free State military regarded the capture of the column as significant, stating that they formed the nucleus of a body that had been operating very effectively in the area for a considerable time.[3]

Meanwhile Seán Lehane and the remainder of his column, including Tom Mullins, Jack Fitzgerald and Con Connolly, were at Drumkeen. They waited for a day before making their way to the Donegal Town area where they commandeered a boat to take them to the Sligo coast. There they were met by Liam Pilkington, OC 3rd Western Division, and brought to a camp in the Arigna Hills, County Leitrim, where approximately 100 men were based. Their evacuation proved fortunate as the dispatch sent to Daly by Lehane was discovered when Daly and the others were arrested.[4]

One of the men captured at Dunlewy – Frank Ward – was separated from the others and taken to Finner Camp. He had been only a short time at the camp when an escape plot was discovered during a search of the cell he shared with Joe O'Gorman: a bottle of 'doped' whiskey was found concealed under a pillow. The authorities failed to discover how the container was smuggled into the camp, but it was suspected that one of the soldiers had passed it on to the prisoners, unaware of its true content. The bottle was later sent to a pharmacist for analysis, which showed that the whiskey was drugged with a substance liable to render a person unconscious.[5] Because of this discovery Frank Ward was transferred to Drumboe Castle.

The Public Safety legislation enacted in September 1922 provided for extreme measures, which were used as reprisals for the ongoing activities of the IRA. The first executions took place at Kilmainham Jail, Dublin on Friday 17 November, with four men being put to death: James Fisher, Peter Cassidy, Richard Twohig and James Caffney. The IRA's immediate response was to target government TDs who had voted in favour of the legislation, adding to an already hostile and tense atmosphere.[6] There was no noticeable reaction to the executions in County Donegal, where small pockets of republican columns from the 3rd Western Division remained active in the south of the county.

On Sunday night, 26 November, an IRA column in Mountcharles village held up a party of Free State officers travelling by car from Donegal Town to Killybegs. They were stripped of their uniforms and weapons before their vehicle was burned. No other action was taken against them and they were released. A follow-up report from the Free State command in Donegal played this down:

> The situation is quite normal except for an incident in the neighbourhood of Mountcharles in which some officers were reported disarmed ... The fact of such an incident taking place does not reflect credit on the command, a matter which was utilised by the Belfast press for propagandist purposes.[7]

Meanwhile, in late November, three of the Newbridge Camp escapees, Seamus McCann, Frank O'Donnell and Alfie McCallion, had made their way back to Derry where they met Tom O'Hara and Pat Lafferty. They were eager to return to active service and after a short time decided to link up with Neil Blaney (in the Fanad area), who had sent on information of the possible capture of a barracks in the area. Another Derry republican, Dot O'Donnell, was sent to Fanad to get in touch with Blaney who had scouted the possibility of taking Milford Barracks, depending on the availability of suitable men and equipment. On Tuesday morning, 28 November, Frank O'Donnell arranged with O'Hara and Lafferty to organise arms and Bertie McGinley was sent off to Fanad with a carload of weapons and other equipment. McGinley arrived there with the arms and delivered them to Blaney. The following day the other men arranged to travel across Lough Swilly from Fahan to Rathmullan by boat en route to Fanad, but all was in vain. McGinley delivered the arms safely, but on his way back to Derry was held up at Letterkenny and arrested on suspicion of conveying weapons to Fanad and, with the discovery of the weapons the next day, it was obvious that there was a Free State agent in the Fanad area.[8] Neil Blaney was arrested a couple of days later at Rye near Rathmullan.[9]

Meanwhile, across the lough in Inishowen, a group of prisoners escaped from the workhouse at Carndonagh on Monday 4 December. Some of them had developed scabies, a serious skin disease which necessitated medical treatment. When the doctor arrived, he requested that all those affected be given access to a bath and put into isolation. Six men were removed to the second floor where bathing facilities were provided. Later that night the orderly sergeant and the sergeant of the guard carried out a routine check of the prisoners and discovered the six had escaped. A search party was immediately sent out, but there was no trace of them in the immediate area. Contact was made with the military barracks at Buncrana and Greencastle informing them of the situation. Search parties were organised from both barracks, but there was no trace of the escapees.[10]

There was further activity in the east of the county on Monday 4 December when a large party of Free State troops converged on the Castlefinn area. They raided the house of J. J. Kelly at Drumdoit near

Castlefinn, and discovered a large consignment of arms and armaments including one Lee-Enfield rifle, a Mauser rifle, a Winchester rifle, two shotguns, rounds of varied ammunition, bombs and detonators.[11]

Later that night a large party of Free State forces from the Kinlough post in south Donegal descended on the nearby Glenade area, acting on information that two IRA officers, John and Edward McGloin, were frequenting a house in the area. A dance was regularly held in a country house and, as the two men were said to be regular visitors, the premises were raided. Six men were identified as being members of the IRA Glenade Company and all were arrested, including the targets of the operation. No arms, ammunition or documents were found in the possession of those held, who were later removed to Kinlough Barracks.[12]

A large-scale search operation was mounted in Churchill and the surrounding area, starting on Tuesday 5 and continuing until Thursday 7 December. As part of this action, raids were carried out in the Churchill, Termon, Glenswilly and Kilmacrennan areas, but no arrests or seizures resulted.[13] On Thursday 7 December a party of Free State forces was also operating in the Clady area and arrested a prominent member of Cumann na mBan, Miss A. O'Flaherty, after documents were discovered in her pockets relating to the activities of the IRA. She was immediately transferred to Buncrana.[14]

A summation of the bitterness and tragedy of the Civil War was observed with the executions in the early hours of Friday 8 December of four IRA officers at Mountjoy Jail, Dublin. These executions were in reprisal for the killing of Seán Hales, TD, and the wounding of Pádraig Ó Máille the previous day. One of the condemned men was Rory O'Connor who, less than a year earlier, was best man at the wedding of his friend, Kevin O'Higgins. Then Minister for Home Affairs, O'Higgins was involved in ordering O'Connor's death. Liam Mellows, Richard Barrett and Joe McKelvey were executed on the same day. McKelvey was from Belfast and had Donegal connections through his father, who was originally from Doochary in the west of the county.

In Donegal, a tragedy occurred on the evening of Saturday 11 December during an attempted escape from Drumboe Castle. Sometime after 4 p.m.

the prisoners were out for their evening exercise when Patrick Jordan and Hugh Gallagher made a run for freedom. The guard called on them to halt several times but the two men kept going, climbing a wall and then running through the woods. The alarm was raised and a party of soldiers went out in pursuit. Some of the soldiers discovered the men a short time later in the woods, and they were arrested and put onto a Crossley lorry. As the vehicle was making its way back to the castle, the captives jumped out and ran; a number of shots were fired, hitting them both. Hugh Gallagher got up and was limping away when the soldier fired again and he fell to the ground. He received a bullet to the back of the leg and one to the abdomen. Patrick Jordan was also badly wounded. One of the doctors who attended Gallagher said that when he arrived, his intestines were protruding. Four doctors tended to the men's wounds and did all they could, but were not able to save Gallagher who died the following morning. He was twenty-one years old at the time of his death and his remains were later returned to Pennyburn, Derry.[15]

Chapter 27

1923 – Pettigo Reclaimed

The village of Pettigo on the Donegal/Fermanagh border was still under British military authority following the battles of May and June 1922. The Free State forces had established a garrison there in late April 1922 and within a month the Special Constabulary began sniping at it from the Fermanagh side. The Donegal command was under Commandant General Joe Sweeney, who gave strict instructions not to engage with British forces or the Special Constabulary operating from the Fermanagh side. The aggressive tactics of the Special Constabulary were possibly a reaction to the kidnappings of prominent unionists by the IRA in February 1922. Another explanation may have been the mere presence of the Provisional Government forces in a predominantly unionist district, as the local unionist population supported the activities of the Special Constabulary. As already mentioned, the Pettigo incident was raised at a meeting between Michael Collins, Arthur Griffith and members of the British government in late May 1922 to the embarrassment of both Collins and Griffith, neither of whom was aware of the situation at that time and they refuted any suggestion of Dáil forces involvement. However, their denial of the involvement of forces under their control led to the British invasion of the Pettigo and Belleek areas in June 1922 and the British military remained in control of Pettigo until January 1923 and Belleek until August 1924.

The British occupation of Pettigo ended on Tuesday 9 January, with the arrival of over 150 officers and men of the Free State forces under the command of Captain McNaughten. This event was tinged with irony as they had arrived by special train from Clones, County Monaghan, having been accompanied from Newtownbutler through the Six Counties to Pettigo by a large RUC escort under the command of Captain Moore. The Free State forces took over barracks, accommodation and posts from the British military under the command of Captain Horborn of the South Staffordshire Regiment.

On the eve of the British withdrawal, the atmosphere in the village of Pettigo was tense. Some of the hardline unionists added to the tension by suggesting they would be murdered in their beds when the British withdrew. (Their fears were possibly based on their own treatment of the nationalist population following the battle of Pettigo in May/June since before and during that period the hardline unionists had been openly aggressive towards the nationalist population through violence and looting of property, etc.) They attempted to resist the withdrawal of the British military by petitioning the Belfast and British governments, saying they were being taken over by 'a gang of hooligans'. Some petitioned Captain McNaughten of the Free State command for permission to carry firearms for protection, but this was refused. The Church of Ireland minister, Rev. McKeagney, refused to shake hands with the officers of the Free State command and later delivered a scathing attack on the Free State administration from the pulpit, saying the presence in the town of men wearing a new and strange uniform filled him with deep apprehension as to the future. His comments made some members of his congregation uncomfortable as some were serving in the military and civic guard. The unionist media aided in fanning the flames with propaganda, resulting in six unionist families moving from the area. However, the anxieties of the people were soon quelled and relations between the two communities improved.[1]

By the beginning of 1923 the activities of the IRA had all but ceased; the majority of IRA men were in prison or internment camps, had emigrated or were demoralised to the extent that they had abandoned their cause. There was, however, some IRA activity in south Donegal with the 3rd Western Division, covering the Sligo/Leitrim areas, making sporadic but small attacks in the south Donegal area. In early January the Donegal command of the Free State military reorganised its command structures, covering, in addition to Donegal, the area north of the Ox Mountains in County Sligo and Sligo town. As Donegal was almost free of IRA activity, they focused on the south of the county and the newly extended areas.[2]

A Donegal native, Harry McLaughlin, serving with the Free State Army in County Kerry, was killed in an ambush with republican forces on Friday 29 December. His remains were brought on the train, first from Kerry to Dublin and then conveyed to Buncrana on Monday 1 January. Another native of Donegal, Private O'Connor from Letterkenny, was also killed in early January while serving in the south of the country during another battle with republican forces in County Kerry.[3]

While Donegal was relatively quiet, other areas of the country remained at crisis point with the IRA targeting political figures loyal to the Free State administration. On Wednesday 10 January, at a meeting of the Irish County Councils Association in Dublin, a party of IRA interrupted the meeting and read out a list of names, which included a TD for South Donegal, P. J. Ward. Those listed were told to make their presence known, but none were present as they were at the time attending a meeting of the Dáil. The IRA did not state their intentions, but it has been suggested that the individuals named were to be executed, if present.[4]

On Saturday 13 January two members of An Garda Síochána based at Ballyshannon were subjected to a terrifying experience at the hands of a party of IRA from the 3rd Western Division. A sergeant and a guard escorted a prisoner named Kerrigan from Ballyshannon to Sligo Jail and were held up on their return journey to Donegal. The train stopped at Dromahair Station and was boarded by a party of IRA men, who ordered all passengers to alight. When the two gardaí were discovered they were subjected to verbal and physical abuse, with both men injured: one received a serious wound to the back of the head and the other damage to his ribs. The gardaí were also told they would be 'plugged' and were relieved of their overcoats and other items. One of the guards was then taken down a road to be shot, but a local man intervened and his life was saved. They were then asked to give an undertaking to leave An Garda Síochána, but they refused.[5] Both men were let go when the IRA left the area.

The village of Creeslough was at the centre of a controversy following the arrest of Alexander O'Brien by a group of soldiers at a birthday party in the village on Sunday night, 14 January. According to the *Derry Journal* the arrest was for singing a certain song: 'The Red Flag' or 'Labour's Call'. However, a military report of the incident said O'Brien was a republican who had been sought for some time. The incident was later raised during a Dáil debate when Cathal O'Shannon, Labour TD for Louth and Meath, asked Richard Mulcahy, Minister for Defence, whether the soldiers had been invited to the party or attended without invitation. In reply Mulcahy said the soldiers had been invited and attended.[6]

A military patrol was allegedly attacked in Letterkenny at 1.45 a.m. on Tuesday 16 January in the Market Square area. It was passing Hegarty's Hotel, located opposite the Market Square on the Main Street, when shots were said to have been fired from the direction of Southwell Terrace overlooking the Market Square. The patrol returned fire for about fifteen minutes and many bullets struck houses in the terrace, with one house being hit several times. The house of Patrick Dawson, surveyor, had a narrow escape when bullets struck the brick frontage some inches from the windows and near the woodwork of the front door. Dawson's son, Jim, was a senior officer in the Free State Army. No one was injured during the shooting, but residents in the area were greatly alarmed. There was no evidence of anyone shooting from the vicinity of Southwell Terrace at that time and residents said they did not hear any footsteps before or after the shooting. When the gunfire ceased, the military conducted a thorough search of the area, but failed to find anyone or any empty bullet cartridges. Later that morning people attending early mass at St Eunan's Cathedral were held up and searched.[7]

The focus of attention switched to Donegal Town in the early hours of Wednesday 17 January when republican forces from the 3rd Western Division attacked Free State forces stationed in the town. The garrison was billeted in a portion of the workhouse at the time. A number of soldiers on sentry duty replied to the gunfire, but the shooting stopped after a short period. There was large-scale military activity in the town and surrounding areas the following day.[8]

The following night two Free State soldiers were accidentally shot while on duty at Ballyshannon Barracks. Private McGilvey was removed from his post at 9.30 p.m. following complaints from the public that he had been verbally abusive to passers-by. It was discovered that he had been drinking when Privates Bonner and Muldoon arrested him and brought him to the barracks where they placed him in the guardroom. They failed to relieve him of his rifle and McGilvey accidentally discharged it with the bullet striking Muldoon and, passing through him, lodging in Bonners' abdomen. Doctors attended the two men, but Bonner died a short time later. The subsequent inquest found that certain failings by the commanding officer contributed to the tragic accident and if appropriate actions had been taken the incident might not have happened. The inquest heard that McGilvey had accidentally discharged his weapon and that he was not aware of his actions due to his intoxicated state. The foreman of the inquest jury expressed the opinion that the military should exercise more precautions with regard to soldiers using firearms inside the barracks.[9]

In the aftermath of the arrest of Charlie Daly and the evacuation of republican forces from the county by Seán Lehane and others in November 1922, the impression was that Donegal had effectively been abandoned. The most senior and experienced IRA officer in the county at that time was Donncha MacNelis, who was active in the south. Liam Lynch, the IRA Chief of Staff, looked to MacNelis to continue the war in Donegal and in January 1923 both men endeavoured to put Donegal back on a war footing. In a letter from MacNelis to Lynch a request was made for assistance:

> Can you please forward a covering address for H.Q. N&E Command (Eng. Dept). A little help from them now might be worth a good deal later on. There has been no operation to speak of for some time, as we still lack the item I have asked for so often to complete those mines.

Liam Lynch wrote to the OC Northern Command requesting explosives for Donncha MacNelis:

> He [Donncha MacNelis] is a very capable engineer and a very sincere soldier, so I hope you will get in touch with him at once ... He requires explosives ... He is generally in west Donegal area – some place round Glenties.[10]

The series of correspondence suggests that while there was little interest in ending the Civil War, there was also little hope of Donegal returning to full-scale activity with so many IRA either interned or having abandoned the war there. The Free State command in Donegal endeavoured to quell any attempts at a return to full-scale war and the military combed the countryside in search of IRA personnel and armaments. The threat of executions was also a deterrent.

Chapter 28

Courts Martial and Executions in Donegal

During the capture of the IRA column at Meenabul, Dunlewy, in early November 1922, eight men had been arrested – Charlie Daly, Seán Larkin, Daniel Coyle, Frank Ward, James Donaghy, Daniel Enright, Timothy O'Sullivan and James Lane – and they were held at Drumboe Castle near Stranorlar. They were tried before a military court at that location on Thursday 30 November 1922 and charged with being in possession on 2 November 1922 of rifles, revolvers, a quantity of ammunition and bombs without proper authority. The members of the military court panel were the Deputy Divisional Commandant Joe Seán McLaughlin, State Solicitor William McMenamin, Divisional Adjutant Tom Glennon and the prosecutor, Mr Cunningham. The accused were convicted and, at a subsequent hearing held on Thursday 18 January 1923, sentenced to death by firing squad.[1] Up to that date thirty-four executions had taken place at various locations throughout the country. The pressure was obviously weighing on the men and a letter written by Seán Larkin to his brother Tom gave some indication of their apprehension:

> We are sitting on the edge of a 'Volcano' from day to day, and waiting each day for the 'eruption' to come. It is widely rumoured that we are sentenced to death, but we have not been told anything officially yet … the suspense is awful, but we are prepared for the worst, and all of us resigned for what fate has in store for us.[2]

> He [Donncha MacNelis] is a very capable engineer and a very sincere soldier, so I hope you will get in touch with him at once ... He requires explosives ... He is generally in west Donegal area – some place round Glenties.[10]

The series of correspondence suggests that while there was little interest in ending the Civil War, there was also little hope of Donegal returning to full-scale activity with so many IRA either interned or having abandoned the war there. The Free State command in Donegal endeavoured to quell any attempts at a return to full-scale war and the military combed the countryside in search of IRA personnel and armaments. The threat of executions was also a deterrent.

Chapter 28

Courts Martial and Executions in Donegal

During the capture of the IRA column at Meenabul, Dunlewy, in early November 1922, eight men had been arrested – Charlie Daly, Seán Larkin, Daniel Coyle, Frank Ward, James Donaghy, Daniel Enright, Timothy O'Sullivan and James Lane – and they were held at Drumboe Castle near Stranorlar. They were tried before a military court at that location on Thursday 30 November 1922 and charged with being in possession on 2 November 1922 of rifles, revolvers, a quantity of ammunition and bombs without proper authority. The members of the military court panel were the Deputy Divisional Commandant Joe Seán McLaughlin, State Solicitor William McMenamin, Divisional Adjutant Tom Glennon and the prosecutor, Mr Cunningham. The accused were convicted and, at a subsequent hearing held on Thursday 18 January 1923, sentenced to death by firing squad.[1] Up to that date thirty-four executions had taken place at various locations throughout the country. The pressure was obviously weighing on the men and a letter written by Seán Larkin to his brother Tom gave some indication of their apprehension:

> We are sitting on the edge of a 'Volcano' from day to day, and waiting each day for the 'eruption' to come. It is widely rumoured that we are sentenced to death, but we have not been told anything officially yet … the suspense is awful, but we are prepared for the worst, and all of us resigned for what fate has in store for us.[2]

The pressures brought to bear by the ongoing arrests and executions contributed to efforts by senior figures in the IRA to end the war. The IRA's Deputy Chief of Staff, Liam Deasy, had been arrested near the Galtee Mountains in January 1923 and was later sentenced to death by a military court. Deasy had expressed a desire for peace before his arrest and following his sentence requested a meeting with Richard Mulcahy, Minister for Defence, to discuss proposals for ending hostilities. Deasy was brought to Dublin where the two men met on Sunday 21 January. Mulcahy gave Deasy permission to forward a communication to the Executive Council of the IRA:

> I have undertaken for the future of Ireland to accept and aid in an immediate and unconditional surrender of all arms and men and have signed the following statement; I accept and I will aid in the immediate and unconditional surrender of all arms and men as required by General Mulcahy.

Mulcahy responded to the statement by suspending all executions until 10 February to await developments.[3] A ten-day amnesty was ordered to give the IRA an opportunity to consider ending hostilities:

> Bearing in mind the acceptance by Liam Deasy of an immediate and unconditional surrender of all arms and men ... That acceptance must weigh also with many leaders and many of the rank and file who have found themselves led step by step into a destruction that they never intended, but which has been the equal of the line of policy adopted by those to whom they looked for leadership. Notice is hereby given that with a view to facilitating such a surrender the Government are prepared to offer Amnesty to all persons now in arms against the Government who on or before Sunday 18 February 1923 surrender ...[4]

The sentencing of the prisoners at Drumboe Castle in January was raised at a meeting of the Tirconaill County Council held on Tuesday 20 February. At the meeting Mr Black, the assistant secretary, read several telegrams calling attention to a report that a number of executions were to take place at Drumboe Castle and urged the members to convene a special meeting of the council with a view to having the executions cancelled. Black explained that the council was at that time without a chairman, and before a special meeting could be held it would be necessary to have a requisition from five members. James Clarke, who presided over the meeting, said, 'The Government have repudiated all these recommendations and are not paying the slightest attention to them at all.' The local government inspector, Mr O'Farrell, who was also present at the meeting said, 'There are no executions to take place. The whole thing is a fake.' Another member, H. J. O'Duffy, said he had received several telegrams, one of which came from Derry, stating that these prisoners were sentenced to death and while he did not want to place any obstacles in the way of the government, as he had been a consistent supporter of the Free State since it came into being, he did not think it would serve any useful purpose if the executions took place. He said he was glad to have Mr O'Farrell's assurance that there was no truth in the rumour.

The Dunfanaghy Rural District Council held a special meeting on the same day and the following resolution was unanimously adopted:

> Resolved that having heard that several prisoners now in Drumboe Castle are at present under sentence of death, we, the Dunfanaghy Rural District Council, while strongly professing our loyalty to the Free State Government, would earnestly request them to exercise the prerogative of mercy in those cases and not to inflict the extreme penalty for the following reasons:
> (a) The whole county is at present in a fairly peaceable condition.
> (b) The District Courts are functioning regularly and without disturbance.
> (c) We believe that in this matter the District Council are voicing the opinion of the vast majority of the people of the rural district.[5]

The pursuit of the IRA continued with the search of a house in Magheraboy, Pluck, on Wednesday 21 February. The target of the search by Free State forces was the premises of John McAuley, resulting in the arrest of one of his young employees. Later that day Hugh Meehan from nearby Aughlihard was also detained and both men were taken to Letterkenny.[6]

In early March 1923 events in County Kerry adversely impinged on the lives of some of the prisoners being held at Drumboe Castle in County Donegal. About that time the Civil War in County Kerry spiralled into its most vicious and sinister depths. The turn of events in Kerry began on Tuesday 6 March 1923 when six Free State soldiers were killed while clearing a barricade near the village of Knocknagoshel which had been booby-trapped with a mine by the IRA. The Free State military command in Kerry responded by issuing a directive that in future republican prisoners would clear all barricades. This was put into practice the following day when nine republican prisoners were taken from Ballymullen Barracks in Tralee town to an area near the village of Ballyseedy. They were tied hand and foot to the barricade, which was booby-trapped: the mine was detonated, killing eight instantly. Unknown to the military one of the prisoners, Stephen Fuller, was blown clear by the blast. Fuller survived, was able to make his way to a friendly house and was taken to the home of Charlie Daly in the Firies area. He was cared for by the Daly family and received medical attention. Such was the carnage that nine coffins were prepared and one bore the name of Stephen Fuller.

The Ballyseedy massacre was quickly followed with a similar atrocity at Countess Bridge near Killarney the following day. On that occasion four prisoners were killed in a similar exercise with one, Tadhg Coffey, surviving. It was alleged that following the second incident soldiers were instructed to shoot the prisoners in the legs to avoid anyone surviving or escaping. Another similar incident followed on Monday 12 March at Cahirciveen where five prisoners were killed. A military court of inquiry was held the following month and was chaired by Major General Paddy Daly. The inquiry cleared the Free State military from any wrongdoing. The mines used in the three massacres were alleged to have been constructed at Tralee Barracks under the supervision of two senior officers of the Dublin Guard.[7]

While the violence of the Civil War was escalating in the south of the country, an incident in County Donegal, resulting in the death of Captain Bernard Cannon an officer of the Free State Army, sealed the fate of four condemned prisoners being held at Drumboe Castle. According to evidence given by Sergeant Patrick Gallagher, who had returned to Creeslough Barracks at approximately 11 p.m. from a patrol of the village, the attack started at 11.15 p.m. on 10 March with heavy fire being directed at the barracks from the direction of a stone wall opposite the building. It was suggested that when the shooting started Cannon opened the front door of the barracks and was shot in the chest. However, another account claimed that he was killed when a bullet passed through the door. Sergeant Gallagher moved his injured comrade from the door and into the guardroom where he said an act of contrition, which Cannon repeated before he died. Also stationed at the barracks was Corporal Patrick McLaughlin, who was sleeping at the time of the attack. He was awakened by the sound of gunfire and rushed to the top of the stairs to see Cannon lying dead.

Dr Coll of Dunfanaghy received a message at 10 a.m. the following morning requesting him to attend at Creeslough Barracks. On arrival, he examined the body and found a small wound to the chest with a larger wound to the back where the bullet had exited. The inquest into the officer's death was held at Creeslough on Monday 12 March and was presided over by Dr J. P. McGinley acting as coroner. Patrick Cannon, father of the deceased, gave evidence of identification and said his son was twenty-four years old at the time of his death. Sergeant Gallagher said he was on patrol duty and returned to the barracks at 11 p.m. on Saturday night. Approximately fifteen minutes afterwards he heard shots being fired outside and had barely reached his post when he saw Captain Cannon fall. Only a few shots had been fired at that time. He drew the injured officer away from the door but he died about ten minutes later. Gallagher said that during this time the attack continued, with the garrison replying to the attack and it lasted for about one hour.[8]

On the face of it, this incident gave the appearance of an attack by the IRA on a Free State barracks. However, there were no independent witnesses to offer corroboration to the evidence given by the soldiers and there have been suggestions that no attack occurred, or if it did happen, the IRA was not involved. Joe Sweeney, general officer commanding the Free State military in Donegal, conducted an investigation into the shooting and concluded that the fatal shot had been fired through the skylight above the door, which was at variance to the evidence given at the inquest. There was also an unspoken rule during this time that the IRA did not engage with Free State forces in towns and villages during Fair days. Many years later Sweeney also discussed the shooting with Frank and Peadar O'Donnell and both men said that there was no IRA activity in the area at that time and no attack on the barracks that night.[9] The officer commanding Creeslough Barracks at this time was P. H. Doherty and, although he was not present on the night, he also disputed that there was an attack by the IRA.[10]

Whether or not there was an attack, Commandant General Joe Sweeney reported the incident to the Free State GHQ in Dublin and a telegram was received at Drumboe Castle with an order that four prisoners were to be executed: Charlie Daly, Seán Larkin, Timothy O'Sullivan and Daniel Enright. There was much speculation at the time that the selection of three Kerry men was influenced by the recent events in their native county and that, additionally, Charlie Daly and Seán Larkin were selected because they had both been prominent IRB men in their respective counties. Whatever the reasons, Sweeney was reluctant to execute Seán Larkin, a man from the Six Counties, and sent a telegram to Dublin requesting confirmation of Larkin's name. The reply confirmed that Larkin was to be executed. Sweeney was responsible for ordering the firing party for the execution but he found this very difficult as he and Charlie Daly had been friends. Sweeney was of the opinion that it was, 'an awful thing to kill a man in cold blood, if you're on level terms with him. Trading shots with a man in a battle is one thing, but an execution is something else altogether.'[11] The four condemned were then informed that they were to die at dawn on Wednesday 14 March and were told to write their final letters to family and friends and to make the necessary preparations.

When news of the impending executions reached Cardinal Patrick O'Donnell, Bishop of Raphoe and a native of Kilraine, Glenties, he immediately convened a meeting of the clergy on Tuesday 13 March. At the conclusion of this meeting, two telegrams were sent to the government pleading for clemency. However, Cardinal O'Donnell's efforts on the eve of the executions were not public knowledge and the irony is that he later indirectly become a target of reprisal by the IRA. O'Donnell was a relative of Sweeney and the two men had met to explore the possibility of preventing the executions taking place. But as Sweeney was acting on orders from his GHQ in Dublin he could not stop the executions.[12]

Shortly after 6 a.m. on Wednesday 14 March 1923, the four prisoners were removed from their cells and given an opportunity to prevent their deaths. They were presented with the Free State 'form of understanding':

> I promise that I will not use arms against the Parliament elected by the Irish people, or the Government for the time being responsible to that Parliament, and that I will not support in any way such action. Nor will I interfere with the property or person of others.

The four refused to sign, choosing to face the firing squad. They were then taken to an execution site situated in the woods a short distance from the castle and Commandant General Charlie Daly (26), Brigadier Commandant Seán Larkin (26), Lieutenant Daniel Enright (23) and Lieutenant Timothy O'Sullivan (23) were executed. Their bodies were then buried in plots in the grounds of Drumboe Castle where they remained until late August 1924 when they were disinterred and moved to Athlone Military Barracks. They were released to their families in October 1924 and returned to their native counties for burial. These were the only executions to take place in County Donegal and at that time they brought the number of official executions nationally to sixty-seven.[13]

Speculation at the time suggested that confirmation of the sentence of death was only sanctioned following the alleged attack on Creeslough Barracks on Saturday 10 March. The only apparent activity by the IRA at that time was confined to the south of the county under the 3rd Western Division, taking in the Ox Mountains including Sligo Town and parts of south Donegal. The truth of this chapter of local and national history may never be fully known, but 'off the record' comments by prominent figures on both sides in later years dispute IRA involvement.

Dr James McCloskey, Carrigart, who at the time was convalescing at a Derry nursing home, wrote a letter which appeared in the *Derry Journal* and illustrated the use of false information by the Free State military authority in County Donegal. McCloskey was recovering from injuries sustained following an incident involving Free State military at Milford on Saturday 10 March. He wrote to contradict a previous report in the local press that McCloskey was injured following a shooting incident involving republican forces. Published on 14 March, his letter stated:

> It would appear from the report in today's [Monday 12 March] newspaper that Republicans were responsible for firing on Fr McMenamin and myself at Milford on Saturday night. This report is quite incorrect as it was Free State troops who held us up and fired upon us while the car was at a standstill, wounding Fr McMenamin in the face and myself in the leg. My only desire to give this publicity in the matter is to correct the false impression which the report in this day's newspaper would convey.

It was understood that Fr McMenamin and Dr McCloskey were travelling home from Letterkenny when they were called upon to halt by Free State troops at Milford and did so, but did not advance immediately when requested. Shots were then fired at the car. Fr McMenamin was cut in the face by a piece of glass from the windscreen, which was smashed by a bullet and Dr McCloskey received a bullet to the leg. McCloskey felt compelled to write the letter after an earlier report stated that he had been shot when he 'came within the line of fire of Irregulars operating as a flying column in the East Donegal district'.[14]

IRA reprisals following the executions at Drumboe started in the early hours of Saturday 17 March. The house of Captain O'Boyle at Malinmore was set on fire. The property of W. M. H. Sinclair, a senior British civil servant, was also burned. Sinclair's caretaker, John Scott, was awakened at approximately 3 a.m. by knocking on the front door and when he answered, he was told to clear out of the house. The IRA told Scott that they had nothing against him but that they were burning the house in reprisal for the executions of the four men at Drumboe.

The local IRA felt that the clergy should have made representations on behalf of the four condemned men, and as they were not aware of Cardinal O'Donnell's intervention, his home at Kilraine, Glenties, was also targeted late on Saturday 17 March.[15] The IRA arrived at the house shortly after 11 p.m. and informed the occupants that it was being destroyed as a reprisal for the executions at Drumboe. At the time, the cardinal's brother Daniel and other family members were in occupation. Daniel O'Donnell had been ill for some time and had to be carried from the house. The house was then saturated with petrol and set on fire. Many locals endeavoured to save the building and some outhouses were saved. Daniel O'Donnell died on Monday 7 May.[16] Cardinal O'Donnell later wrote of the incident in correspondence to a friend at the Irish College in Rome:

> My native home and everything in it was burned down on the night of St Patrick's Day with considerable harshness or cruelty to the inmates as a reprisal for Drumboe on the score that the Bishops cared little how many were executed.

Despite the nature of the destruction of his home, Cardinal O'Donnell understood the IRA's reaction:

> I suppose the poor fellows little knew that when the news [of the imminence of the Drumboe executions] reached me late the evening before, I managed after hours to make telegraphic communication with Dublin, and I sent the most earnest representations against the executions.

The cardinal was opposed to the executions and made his feelings clear when replying to the Irish Governor General, T. M. Healy, who had written expressing sympathy on the destruction of his home. Cardinal O'Donnell stated: 'The burning of my native home is indeed a very bad business. In my opinion, the executions at Drumboe, for which it was a reprisal, should not, to say the very least, have taken place.'[17]

The upsurge in IRA activity in south Donegal following the Drumboe executions provoked a response from the Free State Donegal command. Major General Sweeney issued a statement on 16 March to the effect that if the burning of property and other crimes by republicans did not cease within a given time, further executions would take place at Drumboe: there were several prisoners with the sentence of death hanging over their heads. The statement was issued and set out the offences and the penalties including the death penalty which by order of the Army Council would be imposed:

> Certain persons in County Donegal have been tried for having committed said offences and have been found guilty of having committed one or more of said offences. Be it known, therefore, that the infliction of the penalty of death in those certain cases depends entirely on the conduct of the un-arrested associates of persons who have been so found guilty.[18]

The upsurge in republican activity continued and in the early hours of Monday 19 March a Free State military patrol was fired at while on patrol in Ballybofey. The patrol returned fire and attempted to outflank the attacking party, but they managed to escape. There were no casualties reported following the attack. The home of a Free State military officer was also targeted on the same night at Carrick in south Donegal. The house, owned by the father of J. Cunningham, OC 46th Battalion, was burned.[19]

Reprisals by the Free State forces soon followed and the house of Brian Monaghan, Mountcharles, was subsequently destroyed by the Free State military as a reprisal for burnings by the IRA. One report stated that the building was blown up in the early hours of Wednesday 21 March, while another report stated it was burned. Monaghan's son Barney was an officer in the IRA at the time and the suspicion was that he was involved in activities in the area and that was the reason why his father's house was targeted.

On Wednesday night, 21 March, members of Cumann na mBan were arrested: Cissie O'Doherty, Mary MacBride and Rose O'Donnell. All three were later transferred to Buncrana Barracks.[20] In some instances the women held there were subjected to harsh treatment. They were confined in a disused portion of the building where the cells were damp and cold, and the blankets supplied were deliberately soaked in water. They were often verbally abused and some were subjected to physical abuse: Cissie O'Doherty from Dungloe was unmercifully kicked while in custody and had to be transferred to Lifford Hospital where she underwent surgery for her injuries. The other female prisoners held at Buncrana Barracks were Teresa McGeehan and Marian Blake.[21]

An IRA column from the 3rd Western Division attacked Dunkineely Military Barracks on Thursday morning, 22 March. The battle lasted for almost an hour and a number of bombs were used, as well as revolvers and rifles. During a lull, a number of Free State troops left the barracks and pursued the flying column, which made a hasty retreat. One of the troops was slightly wounded after being struck by a ricochet bullet.[22]

Chapter 29

Peadar O'Donnell – Held to Ransom

The executions at Drumboe on 14 March were meant to serve as a warning for the IRA to desist from further actions against the Free State forces. However, with the upsurge in IRA activity in the immediate aftermath the Free State command endeavoured to prevent any further actions and requested the transfer of Peadar O'Donnell from the Curragh Camp in County Kildare to Finner Camp in south Donegal. This was a clear indication that O'Donnell would be the next person to be executed in reprisal for any future activity. He was effectively being held to ransom as a deterrent to the IRA. Commandant Tom Glennon was the officer in command at Finner Camp and O'Donnell was immediately put into solitary confinement with no access to reading material, etc. His cell was subjected to daily searches, but there were some friendly guards in the camp and on his second day a small package from Kate McCarry, Letterkenny, was passed through his cell window. It contained a pair of rosary beads with a prayer for a happy death.

Peadar O'Donnell's fears were soon realised following a conversation with a soldier on sentry duty. The soldier said, 'I suppose you know what's said?'

'What's said?' asked O'Donnell.

'You're to be shot if anybody is shot outside; that's what said, anyway.'

On another occasion, O'Donnell was taking a bite out of a sandwich when he discovered a letter inside from Lile O'Donel confirming that he was a hostage and would be executed in reprisal for any further actions by the IRA.[1]

In a further move to stem the activities of the IRA, the Free State authorities put pressure on four prisoners under sentence of death to sign a statement calling on their comrades to desist. The following was published through the Free State government's publicity department on Friday 23 March:

> Drumboe Castle, 17 March 1923
> We, the undersigned, looking at the turn of events in Donegal in the clear light of reasoning deem it advisable to address those who are responsible for outrages and attacks, which have taken place recently in this area:
>
> (1) We believe the cause of our country could be best served by pursuing or opening some avenue towards a peace understanding.
>
> (2) As we are well aware the organisation was broken up prior to our arrests.
>
> (3) When arrested the late Charles Daly and his comrades were on their way to evacuate the county under official orders from HQ.
>
> (4) Therefore we can't see what is to be gained by such acts, unless jeopardise [sic] the lives of the men held under sentence of death, as we believe those responsible for such acts brought about the execution of Daly and comrades.
>
> (5) We believe we are held as hostages for the peace of the country and it is not in a spirit of fear we act, but we think it not fair to us to be held responsible for the acts of those whom we disclaim any knowledge or association with.
>
> (6) We believe if those persons would cease such acts, and do their best towards bringing about peace, it would be beneficial to the country and to ourselves.
>
> (7) We believe we are expressing the wishes of our deceased comrades in this appeal.
>
> (8) Liam Deasy was as good a soldier as Ireland ever produced and undoubtedly understood the situation in the country as well as anyone,

as he was in a position to know. Therefore, in doing likewise in this appeal, we do nothing we are ashamed of.

(9) We honestly believe that such acts are being done by irresponsible persons who are only self-interested.

Signed:
James J. Donaghy
James Lane
Frank Ward
Daniel Coyle[2]

With the threat of death hanging over him, Peadar O'Donnell responded to his dilemma by compiling a list of prominent political figures to be executed should that be his fate. He had established good relations with a soldier in the camp and persuaded him to pass on to his brother Frank a note which began with the words: 'Shoot them if they shoot me.' Lile O'Donel, who later married Peadar, visited the head office of the Labour Party in Dublin and arranged a meeting with Tom Johnston, then Secretary of the Labour Party. Peadar O'Donnell had also been elected TD for Donegal in the 1923 general election.[3]

The conversation is reported as follows:

'I called to tell you, Mr Johnston that you will be shot if Peadar O'Donnell is murdered in Finner.'

'What can I do? What do you want me to do? Tell me what you want me to do?'

'I have no request to make, Mr Johnston; I just called to deliver a message; I have delivered it; you will be shot dead if Peadar O'Donnell is killed in Finner. Good evening.'[4]

O'Donnell was later returned to the Curragh Camp, where he remained until he escaped on Sunday 16 March 1924. He walked out the front gate of the camp wearing a military uniform given to him by a soldier from west Donegal.

The threats of further executions effectively subdued the activities of the IRA in the county and the change was reflected in reports of the Free State Army command in Donegal:

> The position in the Donegal county portion of this command is most satisfactory and has been normal for quite a long time past. It is never the less necessary to retain quite a number of posts all over the area in order to keep Irregulars from coming from other parts of Ireland particularly the six county area to concentrate in Donegal ... The people are most friendly towards our troops. Ninety per cent of the troops in this county are local men ... In the Southern portion of the command ... the position is not so satisfactory as in the Northern portion of the command. The Eastern portion of this area is of a most difficult nature and is one of the worst areas in Ireland to get under control ...[5]

The republican campaign suffered a major blow following the death of Liam Lynch, IRA Chief of Staff, in County Tipperary on Wednesday 11 April. Lynch was with other senior officers, being pursued by a party of Free State military through the Knockmealdown Mountains when he was shot. He died in Clonmel at approximately 8.45 p.m. that evening and his death was announced the following morning.[6]

Lynch's death was closely followed by the capture of Austin Stack, TD, on Saturday 14 April. Stack had in his possession a document which indicated that republican leaders were preparing to end the campaign:

> Realising the gravity of the situation of the Army of the Republic owing to the great odds now facing them and the losses lately sustained and being of opinion that further military efforts would be futile and would cause only injury to our country without obtaining an advantage and being convinced that the defensive war which has been waged by our Army during the past nine or ten months has made it impossible that the Irish people will ever accept less than their full national rights, and fearing it would cause too much summoning and holding of full meetings of the Army Council or Executive.

We the undersigned members of the Army Council and of the Executive and officers of the Army, do hereby call upon and authorise the President of the Republic to order an immediate cessation of hostilities. Volunteers are requested to hand in their arms to _____, pending the election of a Government of the Free choice of the people.[7]

Another report (15 April) from the Donegal command to Beggars Bush described a peaceful scenario, with the IRA in Donegal no longer active: 'In North and South Donegal the Irregulars are broken as a military force and beyond occasional predatory excursions by small armed bands of four or five there is no activity.'[8]

The Irish Republican Army Executive Council met on 20 April 1923 at Poulacapple, near Mullinahone in County Tipperary. A motion was passed that the republican government and Army Council should 'make peace with the Free State Government' on the basis that 'the Sovereignty of the Irish Nation and the integrity of its territory is inalienable'. Another resolution put forward by Tom Barry and Tom Crofts, that all armed resistance should be called off, was turned down.[9]

The Civil War in Donegal had run its course by the end of April 1923, with a Free State military report for that month declaring the complete defeat of the IRA:

The past week marks another stride towards the complete defeat of the Irregulars in this command in that it has been the first week since the beginning of hostilities during which there has not been a single case of sniping at or attacking of posts in the area. No single instance of irregular activity has been reported with the exception of the burning of a Customs Hut at Killtyclogher, and the cutting of some trees across the road in west Donegal. A dozen active Irregulars have been arrested throughout different parts of the command – unarmed in all cases. Some of the prisoners state that they have entirely given up the struggle and that their organisation has practically fallen asunder during the past few weeks.[10]

A subsequent report issued by the Donegal command described the area as being very quiet and noted that there was no activity from republican forces.[11] However, there was some sporadic activity as another report from the Donegal command stated: 'The burning of Carrigans Station in North Donegal has been the first sign of their presence in this county ... for a few months past.'[12]

The IRA Executive Council, realising the continuation of hostilities was a futile exercise, convened a meeting in late May to discuss measures for declaring an end to hostilities. At the conclusion of the meeting the new IRA Chief of Staff, Frank Aiken, was instructed to issue an order to dump arms, which he did on 24 May. He emphasised the need to develop Gaelic civilisation and for the IRA to join the Sinn Féin organisation. In the absence of terms – any terms – from the government, Aiken issued the order to cease fire (already in operation) and instructed IRA personnel to safely dump arms:

> Comrades – The arms with which we fought the enemies of our country are to be dumped. The foreign and domestic enemies of the Republic have for the moment prevailed. But our enemies have not won. Neither tortures nor firing squads, nor a slavish press can crush the desire for independence out of the hearts of those who fought for the Republic or out of the hearts of our people. Our enemies have demanded our arms. Our answer is, 'We took up arms to free our country, and we'll keep them until we see an honourable way of reaching our objective without arms'. There is a trying time ahead for the faithful soldiers of Ireland. But the willing sacrifices of our dead comrades will give us the courage to face it in the knowledge that these sacrifices have insured the ultimate victory of our cause. Their examples and their prayers will help us to be like them, faithful to our ideals unto death. Signed: Frank Aiken – chief of staff.

Accompanying the order from Frank Aiken was a message from Éamon de Valera:

Soldiers of the Republic, Legion of the Rearguard. The Republic can no longer be successfully defended by your arms. May God guard every one of you and give to our country in all times of need sons who will love her as dearly and devotedly as you …

The Free State government permitted the publication of both orders on 29 May 1923, officially ending the Irish Civil War.[13]

Despite these developments, raids by the Free State forces in Donegal continued and, in the Rossnakill area of Fanad, James Blaney, James Doherty, James Fullerton and Joseph McCarthy were arrested. Nelly Kelly, who had been a nurse at the Red Cross Hospital based at Gartan, and a Cumann na mBan dispatch carrier, was arrested in Letterkenny in the early hours of Tuesday 29 May.[14]

By early June the scene was very quiet in Donegal and was summed up in a report for that month, which described the people as having more confidence in the Free State Army: 'Generally speaking, the people are beginning to place more confidence in the troops, and a certain number of would-be Irregular supporters are beginning to change, whether it is for purposes of intelligence work or not, I cannot definitely say.'[15]

Conclusion

The Civil War in Ireland sliced through the very fabric of a society that was in the process of healing following the war against the British. During the War of Independence the Irish people were the mainstay behind Óglaigh na hÉireann and Cumann na mBan. These organisations enjoyed the support of the people in their military and political endeavours to abolish the influence of the British government in Irish affairs. However, the Irish people were forced to choose one side over the other in the Civil War, which meant that neither side had the full backing of the people, leading to difficulties, particularly for the anti-Treaty side who found it much harder during this war to find supplies and shelter.

The peace brought about by the Truce of July 1921 had been widely welcomed, but this was soon after shattered by the Treaty of agreement between the Irish and British negotiating teams. The Articles of Agreement, which were later formatted and became known as the Treaty, served as the chisel that split the foundations of the revolutionary and political movement in Ireland. The terms of the Treaty were published in early December 1921 and the divisions in the ranks of the IRA began almost immediately. There was overwhelming support for the Treaty from the majority of the IRA men in County Donegal, followed by the support of over 90 per cent of the Sinn Féin branches in the county. Following the Dáil ratification of the Treaty in January 1922, the two opposing sides began consolidating their positions. This created great confusion among the population as each laid claim to being the legitimate authority of the people, both militarily and politically. The argument was whether the authority of the pro-Treaty Provisional Government should supersede the existing authority of the Republic.

As a means of healing the rift between the two factions of the IRA, the senior officers of the pro- and anti-Treaty factions pledged a continuation of the war against the Belfast government in a northern offensive, with a military offensive and the continuation of the boycott of goods originating from unionist firms in the Six Counties, which would serve to damage that economy. However, the majority of the IRA officers tasked with directing the northern offensive were from the southern divisions of Cork and Kerry, supported by republicans from Donegal, Derry, Tyrone, Fermanagh and Monaghan. When the Civil War began, the unfamiliar Donegal terrain was alien to most of these men and this served to be their undoing.

The Constitution of Saorstát Éireann was the last great hope for drawing Ireland back from the brink of civil war, but the aspiration to a republican constitution seemed ill-conceived and shallow when read in the context of the Treaty document. The possibility of a republican constitution died at the hand of the British pen and the document that was eventually published in the press on 16 June 1922 followed the letter and spirit of the Treaty. The majority of the Irish electorate went to the polls on the same day to vote on the pretext of a republican constitution that failed to materialise. Another problem was that the electoral register had not been updated since the election of 1918 and republicans were of the opinion that neglecting to update the register was a deliberate ploy by the Provisional Government to prevent a large portion of the eligible population from voting. Following the election results events accelerated toward all-out war between the Provisional Government and the IRA Executive.

The Donegal-based anti-Treaty IRA Executive was chiefly non-native, which could lead to the suggestion that if the northern offensive had not been a factor, the county may not have experienced as much conflict as it did. The primary objective of the northern offensive was to undermine and eventually overthrow the Belfast administration. Michael Collins had been heavily involved in the northern offensive and played a dangerous game of running with the hare and hunting with the hound. To the British he was the statesman who was prepared to abide by the letter of the Treaty and be its guardian, while to the IRA he was the only one who could unite the army through the continuation of the war against the British in the Six Counties.

Michael Collins was the intelligence mastermind responsible for bringing the British to the negotiating table, yet he could also be held responsible for bringing about the means by which the British would dictate the outbreak of Ireland's Civil War. Collins held one man responsible for the ongoing sectarian violence against the nationalist population in the Six Counties and that was Field Marshal Henry Wilson MP, who was also military advisor to the Belfast government. Collins miscalculated the British response to the assassination of Wilson, which came by way of the ultimatum to attack the IRA GHQ at the Four Courts in Dublin. The attack on the Four Courts on Wednesday 28 June launched Ireland into Civil War and was possibly a test by the British to gauge the true intentions of Collins. Before this, the British had become very impatient with him and there was suspicion about his intentions towards the IRA Executive.

The Civil War started without any general order for Free State forces to strike against the IRA garrisons in Donegal, causing great confusion and uncertainty. Despite the outbreak of war the IRA Executive forces remained focused on the northern offensive and meetings were held to prevent further conflict. The presence in Donegal of seasoned officers and men from the southern counties worried the Free State command in the county. These were war-hardened men sent to Donegal to engage with the forces of the Belfast government and to some extent they became unwilling participants in the new situation.

The IRA men in the county were forced to conduct the war while living in the mountains. Their problems were further compounded by the fact that the personnel of the Free State Army knew many safe houses from the War of Independence. The IRA was forced to exist through the kindness and generosity of the people while the whole time being hunted by the Free State forces in greater numbers. Wholesale raids and arrests throughout the county soon followed, with those arrested being transferred to the internment camp at Newbridge, County Kildare. The successful escape from this camp by the IRA internees in October 1922 was one of the few IRA achievements.

All hopes of ending the hostilities vanished on Tuesday 22 August with the death of Michael Collins at Béal na mBláth in west Cork. The British

Conclusion

possibly gained more from Collins' demise than the IRA as they had suspicions about his true intentions and his involvement in the northern offensive and the assassination of Henry Wilson.

The official order for the IRA evacuation of County Donegal came in late October from Ernie O'Malley. The republican forces were literally being chased from one side of the county to the other. There were very few safe houses, forcing the main body of men to split and move to different parts of the county. It was obvious that the IRA had been virtually defeated by early August and remaining on in Donegal seemed a futile exercise, but the officers of the IRA believed the situation would change and decided to hold out.

One IRA column was in the process of evacuating the county when arrested in early November 1922. Four members of this column were subsequently executed in reprisal for an alleged attack on Creeslough Barracks in March 1922. This incident was shrouded in controversy and was one of the many open wounds left by the Civil War in Donegal. The operations and intelligence reports dealing with the period 1 to 26 March 1923 are missing from the collection held at the Bureau of Military History, Cathal Brugha Barracks, Dublin. The missing reports would have included information of incidents occurring before the Creeslough shooting, the incident itself and any subsequent investigations. These reports are extant before and after the missing dates and most likely the missing reports were removed to conceal certain information relating to this incident. It has also been suggested that there was no IRA presence in that area at that time and the selection of Daly, Enright and O'Sullivan for the execution was most likely connected to the happenings in County Kerry about that time. The identities of the person or persons involved in this incident remain a mystery.

The executions in County Donegal effectively ended the war in the county, although as a further deterrent the Free State forces requested the transfer of Peadar O'Donnell to Finner Camp from the Curragh Camp. In August 1924 the bodies of the men executed at Drumboe the previous year were disinterred, stirring up bitter memories. The disinterring of the bodies was for some the final act of the Civil War in Donegal.

The 'dump arms' order of 1923 officially ended the Irish Civil War, but did not extinguish the aspiration of a republic. The 1923 decision merely suspended the physical force agenda and this would be resurrected through numerous campaigns up to the present day. Perhaps the greatest sacrifice of the Treaty was the exclusion of the six north-eastern counties. This gave the nationalist population a sense of abandonment and they were to suffer under a unionist dominated political system, which survived until the latter part of the twentieth century.

Appendix

Internment Records of Donegal Internees[1]

FEMALES

Kilmainham Jail

1. Rita Boyle, Dungloe
2. Eithne Coyle, Falcarragh
3. Lizzie Doherty, Dungloe
4. Ellen (Nellie) Kelly, Templedouglas, Churchill
5. Rosanna Kelly, Creeslough
6. Mary McBride, Dungloe
7. Kitty McGee, Creeslough
8. Mary McGee, Creeslough
9. Sadie McGee, Creeslough
10. Teresa McGeehan, Fintown
11. Cissie O'Doherty, Dungloe
12. Lena O'Doherty, Bundoran
13. Roisin O'Doherty, Dungloe
14. Rose O'Donnell, Ballybofey
15. A. O'Flaherty, Clady
16. Annie Timoney, Barnesmore

MALES

C: Curragh Camp
D: Drumboe Castle
F: Finner Camp
MJ: Mountjoy Jail
NB: Newbridge Camp
S: Sligo Jail

1. Neil Blaney, Rosnakill, Fanad, S & C
2. John Bonner, Cruckmore, Burtonport, NB
3. Manus Bonner, Mollyroe, Doochary, NB
4. Michael Bonner, Brockagh, Cloghan, NB
5. Neil Bonner, Lackenagh, NB, escaped 15/10/22
6. Paddy Bonner, Meenmore, Dungloe, NB
7. Patrick Bonner, Drumkeen, Stranorlar, NB
8. Edward Boyle, Gweedore, NB
9. James Boyle, Coolbeg, Ballyshannon, NB
10. John Boyle, Drumkeen, Stranorlar, NB
11. John Boyle, Crackakeelan, NB
12. Neil Boyle, Burtonport, NB
13. Owen Boyle, Milltown, Burtonport, NB
14. Pat Boyle, Gweedore, NB
15. Daniel Bradley, Buncrana, NB
16. Bernard Brady, Bundoran, NB
17. James Breslin, Glenties, NB
18. Michael Brice, Lettercran, S & C
19. Alex Browne, Drumareslough, NB
20. James Buchannan, Castle Street, Ramelton, NB
21. Con Byrne, Boragh, Carrick, NB
22. Hugh Byrne, Blogagh, Malin, C
23. John Francis Byrne, Dunkineely, NB
24. Willie Byrne, Dunkineely, NB
25. Eamonn Carty, Westend, Bundoran, NB

Appendix

26. Pat Carty, Westend, Bundoran, NB
27. William Carty, Westend, Bundoran, NB
28. Philip Campbell, Westend Terrace, Buncrana, NB
29. Vincent Campbell, Eastport, Ballyshannon, NB
30. John Cannon, Shananagh, NB
31. Daniel Cassidy, Buncrana, NB
32. John Cleary, Coolbeg, Ballyshannon, NB
33. Patrick Cleary, Ballyshannon, NB
34. John Connaghan, Carrowdraina, NB
35. Geoffrey Coulter, Ramelton, S
36. Patrick Coyle, Mountcharles, NB
37. William Coyle, Derrybeg, NB
38. Pat Craig, Brockagh, Cloghan, NB
39. Edward Cunningham, N.J. Ballyconnelly, Rathmullan, NB
40. James Curran, Dromore, Letterkenny, NB
41. Pat Daly, Westrock, Ballyshannon, NB
42. Aodh De Blacam, Falcarragh, NB
43. Joe Doherty, Bundoran, NB
44. John J. Doody, Ardsmore, Gortahork, NB
45. Cormack Doogan, Loughanure, NB
46. Peter Doogan, Gortahork, NB
47. Edward Duffy, Carrigart, NB
48. John Duffy, Carrigart, NB
49. Joseph Duffy, Beylaught, NB
50. Thomas Ferguson, Lockoo, Archill, NB
51. James Ferris, Omagh and Donegal, F
52. John Finlay, Derrykirk, NB
53. John Flanaghan, Dunkineely, NB
54. Neil Fleming, Carrigart, NB
55. James Friel, Downings, NB
56. John Friel, Dunmore, NB
57. Bernard Gallagher, Rampart, Dungloe, NB
58. Brian Gallagher, Mullaghduff, Kincasslagh, NB
59. Charles Gallagher, Caravan, Dungloe, NB

60. Dan Gallagher, Magheraclough, NB
61. Frank Gallagher, Drumkeen, NB
62. Hugh Gallagher, Ramelton, NB
63. Jack Gallagher, Calhame, Annagry, NB
64. James Gallagher, Leitrim Bogey, NB
65. James Gallagher, Milltown, Gweedore, NB
66. James Gallagher, Calhame Post Office, NB
67. Joe Gallagher, Eastport, Ballyshannon, NB
68. John Gallagher, Meenagowan, Dromore, NB
69. Joseph Gallagher, Bunbeg, NB
70. Seamus Gallagher, Gallows, Letterbarrow, NB
71. William Gallagher, 85 Erin Street, Ballyshannon, NB
72. John Gibbons, Churchill, Letterkenny, NB
73. James Gildea, Erin Street, Ballyshannon, NB
74. Patrick Gildea, Dunkineely, NB
75. John James Gilfedder, Chapel Street, Ballyshannon, NB
76. Matt Gilfedder, Chapel Street, Ballyshannon, NB
77. James Gillespie, Inver, NB
78. James Gillespie, Doochary, NB
79. John Gillespie, Doochary, NB
80. Hugh Gilmartin, Eastend, Bundoran, NB
81. Michael Gilroy, Bundoran, NB
82. John Gilvary, Bundoran, NB
83. Michael Gilvary, Rock, Bundoran, NB
84. Joseph Grane, Ranafast, Annagry, NB
85. Dan Green, Ranafast, Annagry, NB
86. Hugh Green, Ranafast, Annagry, NB
87. Seamus Green, Annagry, NB
88. Charles Harkin, Mountcharles, NB
89. Frank Harkin, c/o Greens Hotel, Letterkenny, NB
90. John Harkin, Croagh, Dunkineely, NB
91. Joseph Harkin, Ramelton, NB
92. Pat Harkin, Lettershambo, Drumkeen, NB
93. Hugh Hegarty, Letterbarrow, NB

Appendix

94. Manus Hegarty, Trimragh, Letterkenny, NB
95. James Higgins, Dunkineely, NB
96. William Holland, Drumkeen, Stranorlar, NB
97. John Jordan, Castle Street, Ramelton, NB
98. Patrick Jordan, Castle Street, Ramelton, NB
99. Daniel Kane, Port Road, Ballyshannon, F
100. Edward Kelly, Rossnowlagh, Ballintra, NB
101. Edward Kelly, Churchill, NB
102. John Kelly, Knockbrack, Letterkenny, NB
103. Patrick Kelly, Mountcharles, NB
104. Hugh Kilmartin, Bundoran, C
105. Jack Lanaghan, Mountcharles, 2 Town Hall, Bundoran, NB
106. Michael Lanagan, Ballintra, NB
107. Pat Lanaghan, Mountcharles, NB
108. Phil Lanagan, Ballintra, NB
109. Michael Loughlin, The Ross, Bundoran, NB
110. Charles Magee, Carrick, Derrybeg, NB
111. Patrick Magee, Feymore, Creeslough, NB
112. Charles Maher, Carrick, Derrybeg, C (Tintown B)
113. Alex Maley, Magheranappen, Convoy, NB
114. Michael Malley, West End, Bundoran, NB
115. John Meehan, Kilcar, C (Tintown B)
116. Patrick Meehan, Mountcharles, NB
117. James Molloy, Meenacloy, Bruckless, NB
118. Fred Mullan, Churchill, NB
119. Henry Mullan, Glendowan, Churchill, NB
120. Hugh Mullan, Glendowan, Churchill, NB
121. John Mullan, Glendowan, Churchill, NB
122. Albert Munday, Ballyshannon, NB
123. John Murphy, Town Hall, Bundoran, NB
124. Jim Murphy, Town Hall, Bundoran, NB
125. Hugh Murray, Stragraddy, Donegal, NB
126. Michael McCallig, St John's Point, Dunkineely, NB
127. John McClafferty, Dunmore, Falcarragh, NB

128. John McCole, Meenamullan, Gweedore, C (Tintown B)
129. Edward McConigley, Fanad, NB
130. Daniel McConologue, Glencarin, Letterkenny, NB
131. Willie McConologue, Kelloge, Churchill, NB
132. Sean McCool, Stranorlar, NB, escaped 15/10/22
133. Frank McDaid, Churchill, NB
134. Philip McDaid, Buncrana, NB
135. Willie McDaid, Waterloo Place, Donegal Town, NB
136. Joseph McDavitt, Kilcar, Athlone Military Barracks
137. James McDevitt, Greenore, Glenties, NB
138. John McDevitt, Greenore, Glenties, NB
139. Neal McDevitt, Aughaygault, Drumkeen, NB
140. Barney McFadden, Feymore, Creelough, NB
141. Francis McFadden, Feymore, Creeslough, NB
142. James McFadden, Portlough, Bogay P.O., NB
143. Dan McGee, Killult, Falcarragh, NB, escaped 15/10/22
144. Daniel McGee, Upper Doe, Gweedore, C
145. Con McGeehin, Derryheeny, Doochary, NB
146. James McGettigan, Glencree, Carrigart, NB
147. Con McGinley, Derrybeg, NB
148. Hugh McGinley, Dunfanaghy, NB
149. Hugh McGovern, Bundoran, NB
150. Daniel McGrath, Listillion, Letterkenny, NB
151. Edward McGrath, Listillion, Letterkenny, NB
152. Aloysius McHugh, 9 Charles Street, Donegal Town, NB
153. Patrick McInaw, Letterbarrow, NB
154. George McKay, Churchill, NB
156. Hugh McKay, Churchill, NB
157. John McKelvey, Stralongford, Drumkeen, C (Tintown A)
158. Charles McLaughlin, West End, Buncrana, NB
159. Hugh McMenamin, Castlefin, NB, escaped 15/10/22
160. James McNulty, Fanaboy, Gortahork, NB
161. Michael Naughton, West End, Bundoran, NB
162. Neil 'Plunkett' O'Boyle, Lackenagh, Burtonport, NB, escaped 15/10/22

Appendix

163. John O'Brien, Ramelton, NB, escaped 15/10/22, recaptured
164. Michael O'Doherty, Carrigart, Limerick Jail
165. Anthony O'Donnell, Milltown, Burtonport, NB
166. Barney O'Donnell, Fintra, Killybegs, NB
167. Dan O'Donnell, Ranafast, Annagry, NB
168. Daniel O'Donnell, Currin, County Donegal, NB
169. Daniel O'Donnell, Gartan Gatehouse, Churchill, NB
170. Frank O'Donnell, Meenmore, Dungloe, NB, escaped 15/10/22
171. Hugh O'Donnell, Dungloe, NB
172. James O'Donnell, Doochary, NB
173. John O'Donnell, Burtonport, NB
174. Joseph O'Donnell, Glenaughty, Letterkenny, NB
175. Manus O'Donnell, Derrybeg, NB
176. Pat O'Donnell, Drumalough, Glenties, NB
177. Pat O'Donnell, Magheraclough, NB
178. Patrick Leo O'Donnell, 30 Townsend, Buncrana, NB
179. Peadar O'Donnell, Meenmore, Dungloe, MJ / C / F
180. Willie O'Donnell, Main Street, Buncrana, NB
181. Joe O'Gorman, Bundoran, NB
182. M.J. O'Hagan, Bridge End, Gormanstown Camp
183. James O'Kane, Ross, Castlefin, NB
184. Joe O'Kane, Ross, Castlefin, NB
185. John Peoples, Killynane, Convoy, NB
186. David Quigley, Malin, NB
187. Maurice Quigley, Dunkineely, NB
188. Con Quinn, Fintown, NB
189. James Quinn, Mountcharles, NB
190. John Quinn, Magheracurrant, NB
191. Joseph Rush, Altcastle, NB.
192. James Semple, Dromore, Letterkenny, NB
193. John Semple, Dromore, Letterkenny, NB
194. Hugh Sharkey, Milltown, Burtonport, NB
195. John Sheerin, Ballyshannon, NB
196. Dan Shields, Macmeensis, Convoy, NB

197. Edward Sharkey, Annagry, NB
198. John P. Slevin, Barnesmore, C, Harepark Camp
199. John Sweeney, Carrigart, NB
200. Patrick Sweeney, Middledore, Bunbeg, NB
201. Owen Sweeney, Carrick, Derrybeg, NB
202. Michael Toner, Crossage, Breenagh, Letterkenny, NB
203. James Trearty, Creeslough, NB
204. Charles Ward, Lacklee, Churchill, NB
205. Edward Ward, Munroe, Dunfanaghy, NB
206. James Ward, Dunfanaghy, NB
207. William Ward, Cloghan, NB
208. Cathal Weir, Carrigart, NB

SIX-COUNTY MEN OPERATING IN DONEGAL AT TIME OF ARREST:

1. Alfie McCallion, 11 Barry Street, Derry, arrested 2/8/22, escaped, rearrested 4/9/22, NB 7/9/22, escaped 15/10/22
2. Seamus McCann, 5 Waterloo Street, Derry, arrested 4/8/1922, NB 1/9/22, escaped 15/10/22
3. James McCloskey, Derry City, NB
4. Owen McCormack, Derry City, NB
5. Colum McGill, William Street, Derry, NB
6. Frank McGee, Castlederg, County Tyrone, NB
7. Bertie McGinley, 17 Rossville Street, Derry, NB
8. Hugh McGinn, Eskra, County Tyrone, NB
9. Michael McGuckin, Dungannon, County Tyrone, NB
10. James McGurk, Carrickmore, County Tyrone, NB
11. Joseph McGurk, Carrickmore, County Tyrone, NB
12. Edward O'Flaherty, Clady, Urney, County Tyrone, NB
13. Charles Zammitt, 3 Artillery Street, Derry, NB

Glossary

Cumann na mBan:	Irishwomen's Council – auxiliary to the Irish Volunteers
Dáil Forces:	Forces under the command of the Provisional Government
Feiseanna:	Irish cultural competition (Irish dancing, music, art, language, drama, etc.)
Fianna (Éireann):	Irish republican scouting organisation
Free State:	Twenty-six county state formed following Treaty of 1921
GHQ:	General Headquarters
G-Man:	Member of detective branch of Dublin Metropolitan Police
Head Centre:	Most senior person in the Irish Republican Brotherhood
IRA Executive Council:	Anti-Treaty IRA governing council
IRA:	Irish Republican Army (IRA) *see also Óglach na hÉireann*
IRB:	Irish Republican Brotherhood (secret, oath-bound organisation)
Land League:	Irish land movement for tenants' rights
OC:	Officer Commanding
Óglach na hÉireann:	Irish Volunteers
Orangemen:	Members of the Orange Order
Provisional Government:	Government of the Free State under the terms of the Treaty
RIC:	Royal Irish Constabulary
RUC:	Royal Ulster Constabulary

Special Constabulary:	Quasi-paramilitary police force
TD:	Teachta Dála: Deputy to the Dáil / Member of Parliament
The Treaty:	Anglo-Irish Treaty 1921

Notes

ABBREVIATIONS
BMH: Bureau of Military History
British NA: British National Archives
MA: Military Archives
NA Dublin: National Archives of Ireland
NLI: National Library of Ireland
UCD AD: University College Dublin, Archive Department
WS: Witness Statement

INTRODUCTION
1. Conversation with Conall Cunningham, Spiddal, County Galway, February 2009.

CHAPTER 1: A BRIEF REVIEW OF THE WAR OF INDEPENDENCE IN COUNTY DONEGAL
1. Liam Ó Duibhir, *The Donegal Awakening – Donegal and the War of Independence*.

CHAPTER 2: 1921 – THE TRUCE AND BREATHING SPACE
1. Bureau of Military History (BMH), Witness Statement (WS) 1448, Patrick Breslin, Military Archives (MA).
2. C. S. Andrews, *Dublin Made Me* (Lilliput press, 2001).
3. BMH, WS 879, Brian Monaghan, MA.
4. Seamus McCann Diary, Private Collection of Seamus McCann, Letterkenny, County Donegal.

255

5. Mulcahy Papers, P7/A/27, University College Dublin (UCD) Archives Department (AD).
6. *Derry Journal*, 21/10/1921.
7. *Ibid.*, 24/10/1921.

CHAPTER 3: EITHNE COYLE AND THE MOUNTJOY ESCAPE

1. P61/2 (2), Eithne Coyle O'Donnell collection, UCD AD.
2. P61/5 (2), Eithne Coyle O'Donnell collection, account of Mountjoy escape by Linda Kearns, UCD AD; Proinsias Ó Duigneáin, *Linda Kearns – A Revolutionary Woman*.

CHAPTER 4: THE IRA CIVIC POLICE

1. *Derry Journal*, 4/11/1921.
2. *Ibid.*, 9/11/1921.
3. *Ibid.*, 4/11/1921.
4. *Ibid.*, 11/11/1921.
5. *Ibid.*, 18/11/1921.
6. *Ibid.*, 21/11/1921.
7. *Ibid.*, 23/11/1921.
8. *Ibid.*, 28/11/1921.

CHAPTER 5: THE TREATY SIGNED, BUT NOT SEALED

1. Michael Ó Cunnegáin, *On the Arm of Time*, pp. 32–33.
2. *Ibid.*
3. Dorothy Macardle, *The Irish Republic*, p. 466.
4. BMH, WS 782, Thomas McShea, MA; BMH, WS 1004, Daniel Kelly, MA.
5. CAB 23/27, IR 0018, Minutes of cabinet meeting 7/12/21, British NA.
6. Kenneth Griffith & Timothy O'Grady, *Curious Journey – An Oral History of Ireland's Unfinished Revolution*, pp. 264–265.
7. *Derry Journal*, 14/12/1921.
8. *Ibid.*

9. Kenneth Griffith & Timothy O'Grady, *Curious Journey*, pp. 264–265.

CHAPTER 6: DONEGAL DEBATES THE TREATY
1. *Derry Journal*, 28/12/1921.
2. *Ibid.*, 30/12/1921.

CHAPTER 7: 1922 – THE TREATY DEBATES AND VOTE
1. BMH, WS 879, Brian Monaghan, MA.
2. Niall MacFhionnghaile, *Dr McGinley and His Times*, p. 47.
3. *Derry People and Tirconaill News*, 7/1/1922.
4. *Derry Journal*, 9/1/22.
5. Kenneth Griffith & Timothy O'Grady, *Curious Journey*, pp. 268–269.
6. Michael Hopkinson, 'Michael Collins and the North'.
7. Journals of Fr William Hackett, Jesuit Archives, Hawthorn, Victoria, Australia. I would like to thank Dr Brenda Niall, Victoria, Australia, for access to this information.
8. *Derry People and Tirconaill News*, 7/1/1922.
9. Florence O'Donoghue Collection, Ms. 31,421 (13), NLI; Brian P. Murphy, 'The Irish Civil War 1922–1923, An Anti-Treaty Perspective'.

CHAPTER 8: 1922 – THE RELEASED PRISONERS AND THE CONDEMNED PRISONERS
1. *Derry Journal*, 18/1/1922.
2. *Ibid.*, 27/1/1922.
3. BMH, WS 782, Thomas McShea, MA.
4. *Derry People and Tirconaill News*, 21/1/1922; Michael Hopkinson, *Green Against Green*, pp. 79–80.
5. Ernest Blythe Papers, P24/554, Memo on north-east Ulster, 1922–26, UCD AD; Anthony Begley, *Ballyshannon and Surrounding Areas – History, Heritage and Folklore*; John Tunney, 'From Ascendancy to Alienation – A Study of Donegal's Protestant Community, 1881–1932'.
6. *Derry People and Tirconaill News*, 28/1/1922.
7. *An t-Óglach*, January 1922, BMH.

8. *Ibid.*, 11/2/1922.
9. Ernest Blythe Papers, P24/554, Memo on north-east Ulster, 1922–26, UCD AD.
10. *Derry People and Tirconaill News*, 18/2/1922.
11. Michael Hopkinson, *Green Against Green*, p. 80; Michael Hopkinson, 'Michael Collins and the North'.
12. BMH, WS 922, James Cunningham, MA; BMH, WS 814, Patrick G. Daly, MA.
13. BMH, WS 872, Thomas McShea, MA.
14. *Derry Journal*, 17/2/1922–20/2/1922.
15. *Ibid.*
16. *Freeman's Journal*, 20/2/1922.
17. CAB 23/29, IR 0010, Minutes of cabinet meeting 16/2/22, British NA.
18. CAB 24/133, IR 0071, Minutes of cabinet meeting 18/2/22, British NA.
19. John B. Cunningham, 'The Struggle for the Belleek – Pettigo Salient 1922', *The Donegal Annual 1982*, p. 42.
20. BMH, LE 4/16 A/0663, Joe Sweeney to Richard Mulcahy 16/2/1922.
21. *Derry Journal*, 22/2/1922.
22. *Ibid.*
23. Seamus McCann Diary, Private Collection of Seamus McCann.
24. *Derry Journal*, 24/2/1922.
25. Jim Herlihy, *The Royal Irish Constabulary – A Short History and Genealogical Guide*, pp. 109, 111.
26. *Derry Journal*, 24/2/1922.
27. *Ibid.*, 27/2/1922.
28. *Ibid.*, 3/2/1922–24/2/1922; Michael Hopkinson, *Green Against Green*, p. 56.

CHAPTER 9: THE SPECIAL POWERS BILL AND THE SIX-COUNTY POLICY

1. Dorothy Macardle, *The Irish Republic*, pp. 680–681, 704.

2. P17b/98 O'Malley Notes; S. 1011, Department of the Taoiseach Papers, NA Dublin.
3. Original copy in private collection of Liam MacElhinney, Lifford, County Donegal.
4. Florence O'Donoghue Collection, Ms. 31340/Ms. 31323, NLI.
5. Michael Hopkinson, 'Michael Collins and the North'.
6. Kenneth Griffith & Timothy O'Grady, *Curious Journey*, pp. 275.
7. Florence O'Donoghue Collection, Ms. 31340 (9), NLI.
8. Michael Hopkinson, 'Michael Collins and the North'.
9. P17A/184, O'Malley Notes, UCD AD; BMH, LE 4/16, A/0664, Correspondence between Charlie Daly, Eoin O'Duffy and Richard Mulcahy.
10. BMH, WS 922, James Cunningham, MA; BMH, WS 814, Patrick G. Daly, MA.
11. *Derry People and Tirconaill News*, 25/3/1922; S. 1801, Department of the Taoiseach Papers, NA Dublin; *Irish News*, 4/10/1996.
12. P17b/98, O'Malley Notes, UCD AD.
13. Kathleen McKenna Napoli Papers, Letter from Maud Gonne MacBride Re: Distress in County Donegal, Ms. 22,761, NLI.

CHAPTER 10: THE IRA CONVENTION AND SPLIT

1. Dispatch to 1st Northern Division Re: IRA Convention, private collection of Liam MacElhinney.
2. Seamus McCann Diary, Private Collection of Seamus McCann.
3. *Derry Journal*, 29/3/1922.
4. *Ibid.*
5. BMH, WS 1741, Michael V. O'Donoghue, MA; Private Collection of Liam MacElhinney; Florence O'Donoghue Collection, Ms. 31340 (9), NLI.
6. Florence O'Donoghue Collection, Ms. 31340 (9) and (6), NLI.
7. John B. Cunningham, 'The Struggle for the Belleek – Pettigo Salient', *Donegal Annual* 1982, p. 43.

CHAPTER 11: CHANGING OF THE GUARD AND THE BELFAST BOYCOTT

1. *Derry Journal*, 29/3/1922.
2. *Ibid.*, 3/4/1922.
3. BMH, WS 1741, Mick O'Donoghue, MA; Seamus McCann Diary, Private Collection of Seamus McCann.
4. *Ibid.*; *Donegal Annual* 1982.
5. *Derry Journal*, 7/4/1922.
6. *Ibid.*
7. P61/2, Eithne Coyle Collection, UCD AD; *Derry Journal*, 7/4/1922.
8. *Derry Journal*, 10/4/1922.
9. *Ibid.*, 12/4/1922.
10. P61/2, Eithne Coyle Collection, UCD AD.
11. *An t-Óglach*, April 1922, MA.
12. S. 1801, A, Department of the Taoiseach Papers, NA Dublin.
13. *Ibid.*
14. *Ibid.*
15. Seamus McCann Diary, Private Collection of Seamus McCann.
16. Florence O'Donoghue Collection, Ms. 31421 (12), NLI; S. 1322, Department of the Taoiseach Papers, NA Dublin.
17. Seamus McCann Diary, Private Collection of Seamus McCann.
18. *Derry Journal*, 17/4/1922.
19. *Ibid.*, 17/4/1921 and 19/4/1922.
20. Uínseann MacEoin, 'James McElduff', *Survivors*, pp. 180–181; BMH, WS, 145, Seán Corr, p. 21, MA.
21. P61/2, Eithne Coyle Collection, UCD AD.
22. *Ibid.*
23. *Derry Journal*, 26/4/1922.
24. *Ibid.*, 5/5/1922; Florence O'Donoghue Collection, Ms. 31340 (9), NLI.
25. *Donegal Vindicator*, 5/5/1922.
26. BMH, WS 1741, Michael V. O'Donoghue, MA.
27. *Derry Journal*, 5/5/1922.
28. *Donegal Vindicator*, 5/5/1922.

CHAPTER 12: THE NORTHERN OFFENSIVE AND THE NEWTOWNCUNNINGHAM TRAGEDY

1. Ernest Blythe Papers, P24/554, UCD AD.
2. Ernie O'Malley Notes, P17b/108 and P17b/112, UCD AD; BMH, WS 1741, Michael V. O'Donoghue, MA.
3. *Derry Journal*, 5, 12 and 19 May 1922; Ernie O'Malley Notes, P17b/108, UCD AD; Niall MacFhionnghaile, *Dr McGinley and His Times*, pp. 80–81.
4. *Derry Journal* 8/5/1922 and 10/5/1922; Ernie O'Malley Notes, P17b/108, UCD AD.
5. *Derry Journal*, 19/5/1922.
6. *Derry People and Tirconaill News*, 6/5/1922; Ernie O'Malley Notes, P17b/108, UCD AD.
7. 'To Clear a Patriot's Name', *An Phoblacht*, March 1971, © Aine Casey, Kerry.
8. S. 1801 A, Department of the Taoiseach Papers, NA Dublin.
9. Paul McMahon, 'British Intelligence and the Anglo–Irish Truce, July–December 1921', p. 533.
10. *Derry Journal*, 29/5/1922.
11. *Ibid.*, 12/5/1922.
12. *Ibid.*, 19/5/1922.
13. *Ibid.*, 22/5/1922.
14. *Ibid.*, 19/5/1922.
15. *Ibid.*, 22/5/1922.
16. Florence O'Donoghue Collection, Ms. 31,421 (13), NLI; Mulcahy Papers, P7a/145 and P7/B/87, UCD AD.
17. Seamus McCann Diary, Private Collection of Seamus McCann; BMH, WS 1741, Michael V. O'Donoghue, MA; *Derry Journal*, 22/5/1922.
18. Roger McCorley, O'Malley Notebooks, P17b/98, UCD AD.
19. *Derry Journal*, 31/5/1922.
20. Dorothy Macardle, *The Irish Republic*, pp. 711–715.
21. Mick O'Donoghue statement, Private Collection of Liam McElhinney; *Derry Journal*, 22/5/1922.

22. *Derry Journal,* 31/5/1922; Seamus McCann Diary, Private Collection of Seamus McCann; *Derry People and Tirconaill News,* 3/6/1922.
23. *Derry Journal,* 31/5/1922; *Donegal Annual* 1982.
24. Uínseann MacEoin, 'James McElduff', *Survivors,* pp. 180–181.
25. *Derry Journal,* 2/6/1922; Seamus McCann Diary, Private Collection of Seamus McCann; BMH, WS 1741, Michael V. O'Donoghue, MA.

CHAPTER 13: THE BATTLES AT PETTIGO AND BELLEEK

1. S. 1235, Department of the Taoiseach Papers, NA Dublin.
2. Paul McMahon, *British Spies and Irish Rebels – British Intelligence and Ireland 1916–1945,* p. 144.
3. BMH, WS 711, John Travers, James Scallon, Nicholas Smyth, Denis Monaghan, Felix McCabe, MA; BMH, WS 721, Nicholas Smyth, MA; Ernest Blythe Papers, P24/554, Memo on north-east Ulster 1922–26, UCD AD; *Donegal Annual 1982*; S. 1235, Department of the Taoiseach Papers, NA Dublin.
4. S. 1235, Telegram from Michael Collins to Winston Churchill, June 1922, Department of the Taoiseach Papers, NA Dublin.
5. BMH, WS 711, John Travers, James Scollan, Nicholas Smyth, Denis Monaghan, Felix McCabe, MA; BMH, WS 721, Nicholas Smyth, MA; *Donegal Annual 1982*; *Derry Journal,* 9/6/1922 and 7/6/1922.
6. BMH, WS 721, Nicholas Smyth, pp. 25–26, MA; S. 1235, Statement of Lieutenant Martin Provisional Forces, Department of the Taoiseach Papers, NA Dublin.
7. BMH, WS 711, John Travers, James Scollan, Nicholas Smyth, Denis Monaghan, Felix McCabe, MA; BMH, WS 721, Nicholas Smyth, MA.
8. S. 1235, Statement of Fr Bernard Hackett, CC, Pettigo, 30 July 1922, Department of the Taoiseach Papers, NA Dublin.
9. Michael Hopkinson, *Green Against Green,* pp. 86–87.
10. Paul McMahon, *British Spies and Irish Rebels,* p. 144.
11. Michael Hopkinson, *Green Against Green,* pp. 84–85.

12. CAB 24/137, Report by General Macready to cabinet 10/6/22, British NA.
13. *Derry Journal*, 14/6/1922 and 5/2/1923.

CHAPTER 14: THE CONSTITUTION OF SAORSTÁT ÉIREANN AND THE 1922 ELECTION

1. British cabinet meetings, Thursday 1 and Friday 2 June 1922, CAB 23/30, IR 0011; CAB 23/30, IR 0009, British NA.
2. British cabinet meeting 01/06/1922, CAB 23/30, IR 0009, British NA.
3. British cabinet meeting 02/06/1922, CAB 23/30, IR 0010, British NA.
4. Michael Hopkinson, *Green Against Green*, pp. 105–106.
5. Dorothy Macardle, *The Irish Republic*, pp. 720–722.
6. Constitution of the Irish Free State (Saorstát Éireann) Act 1922, original copy, Private Collection of Liam MacElhinney.
7. *Derry Journal*, 19/6/1922.
8. P17A/63, O'Malley Papers, UCD AD, Correspondence between Seán Lehane OC 1st and 2nd Northern Divisions and Liam Lynch C/S 19/09/1922.
9. Uínseann MacEoin, 'Sighle Bean Uí Dhonnchadha' (Sheila Humphreys), *Survivors*, p. 342.

CHAPTER 15: THE WILSON ASSASSINATION – A CATALYST FOR CIVIL WAR

1. Niall MacFhionnghaile, *Donegal, Ireland & the 1st World War*, p. 391; CAB 23/39, Minutes of cabinet meeting 22/06/1922, British NA.
2. CAB 23/39, Minutes of cabinet meeting 22/06/1922, British NA.
3. S. 1322, Department of the Taoiseach Papers, NA Dublin.
4. *Ibid*.
5. Michael Hopkinson, *Green Against Green*, pp. 113, 115.
6. Dorothy Macardle, *The Irish Republic*, p. 723.
7. Michael Hopkinson, *Green Against Green*, pp. 113, 115–116; BMH, WS 900, Joe Dolan, MA.

8. Niall MacFhionnghaile, *Donegal, Ireland and the 1st World War.*
9. CAB 23/39, Minutes of cabinet meeting 22/06/1922, British NA.
10. *Derry Journal*, 3/7/1922; Dorothy Macardle, *The Irish Republic,* Chapter 72, p. 723.

CHAPTER 16: *AN COGADH NA gCARAD* – THE WAR BETWEEN FRIENDS

1. Seamus McCann Diary, Private Collection of Seamus McCann.
2. P69/179, UCD AD, handwritten draft of proclamation issued on the day of the Four Courts attack.
3. *Ibid.*
4. Uínseann MacEoin, 'Sighle Bean Uí Dhonnchadha', *Survivors*, pp. 342–343.
5. Kenneth Griffith & Timothy O'Grady, *Curious Journey,* p. 287.
6. Uínseann MacEoin, 'Sighle Bean Uí Dhonnchadha', *Survivors*, p. 344.
7. Declan O'Carroll, *Rockhill House – A History*, pp. 24–25.
8. Declan O'Carroll, *Finner Camp – A History*, pp. 48–49.
9. *Donegal Vindicator,* 7/7/1922.
10. P17A/63, O'Malley Papers, UCD AD, Report from Seán Lehane to Ernie O'Malley, 19/09/1922.
11. S. 1322, Extract from British Parliament Debates Cols 2052–2053, 12/06–30/06/1922, Department of the Taoiseach Papers, NA Dublin.
12. CAB 23/30, Minutes of cabinet meeting 30/06/1922, British NA.
13. BMH, WS 1741, Michael V. O'Donoghue, MA; Seamus McCann Diary, Private Collection of Seamus McCann.
14. *Derry People and Tirconaill News*, 1/7/1922.
15. P17A/63, O'Malley Papers, UCD AD.
16. *Derry Journal*, 3/7/1922.
17. Letter from James Boyle to Frank McKay, Private Collection of Liam MacElhinney.
18. BMH, WS 1741, Michael V. O'Donoghue, MA; P17A/63, O'Malley Papers, UCD AD.
19. BMH, WS 1741, Michael V. O'Donoghue, MA.

20. BMH, WS 750, Eithne (Coyle) O'Donnell, MA.
21. *Ibid.*
22. *Derry Journal*, 3/7/1922.

CHAPTER 17: ANOTHER EFFORT TO AVERT CIVIL WAR IN DONEGAL

1. W. P. Hackett, SJ, Journal 1922, Australian Jesuit Archives, Hawthorn, Victoria, Australia – thanks to Dr Brenda Niall, Victoria, Australia, for this source; see also Dr Brenda Niall, *The Riddle of Fr Hackett*.
2. *Derry Journal*, 5/7/1922–7/7/1922.
3. P176/136, O'Malley Notes, UCD AD; P17A/63, O'Malley Papers, UCD AD; BMH, WS 1741, Michael V. O'Donoghue, MA.
4. *Derry Journal*, 12/7/1922.
5. W. P. Hackett, SJ, Journal 1922, Australian Jesuit Archives.
6. *Derry Journal*, 12/7/1922.
7. P176/136, O'Malley Notebooks, UCD AD.
8. *Derry Journal*, 12/7/1922.
9. P61/2, Eithne Coyle Collection, UCD AD.
10. P17a/46, O'Malley Papers, UCD AD.

CHAPTER 18: THE BATTLES AT SKEOG

1. *Derry Journal*, 10/7/1922.
2. *Ibid.*
3. Department of Justice Files, J62/37, NA Dublin.
4. *Derry Journal*, 12/7/1922.

CHAPTER 19: THE DRUMKEEN AMBUSH

1. *Derry Journal*, 12/7/1922 and 14/7/1922.
2. BMH, WS 1741, Michael V. O'Donoghue, MA; Niall MacFhionnghaile, *Dr McGinley and His Times*.
3. *Derry Journal*, 14/7/1922.
4. BMH, WS 1741, Michael V. O'Donoghue, MA; *Derry Journal*, 21/7/1922.

CHAPTER 20: THE FALL OF INCH FORT

1. *Derry Journal*, 12/7/1922.
2. *Ibid.*, 12/7/1922 and 14/7/1922.
3. *Ibid.*; British cabinet papers, Report from General Macready to the British secretary of state for war – CAB/24/138, British NA.
4. *Derry Journal*, 17/7/1922.

CHAPTER 21: REPUBLICAN COLUMN 'ON THE RUN'

1. BMH, WS 1741, Michael V. O'Donoghue, MA.
2. P176/136, O'Malley Notes, UCD AD, handwritten dispatch from Charlie Daly to Ernie O'Malley.
3. P17A/63, O'Malley Notes, UCD AD, Seán Lehane to Ernie O'Malley, 19/09/1922.
4. BMH, WS 1741, Michael V. O'Donoghue, MA.
5. P80/763, O'Malley Papers, UCD AD, Con Moloney to Ernie O'Malley, 22/7/1922.
6. P7/B/36, Mulcahy Papers, UCD AD.
7. P69/38, O'Malley Papers, UCD AD, Ernie O'Malley to Liam Lynch, 25/07/1922.
8. *Derry Journal*, 28/7/1922; BMH, WS 1741, Michael V. O'Donoghue, MA.
9. *Ibid.*
10. P17a/41, O'Malley Papers, UCD AD, Letter written in Mountjoy Jail, Dublin by Martin Quille, 3/08/1922.
11. Seamus McCann Diary, Private Collection of Seamus McCann; the boat was the SS *Lady Wicklow*.
12. *Derry Journal*, 2/8/1922; BMH, WS 1741, Michael V. O'Donoghue, MA.
13. P69/40 and P17A/57, O'Malley Papers, UCD AD; BMH, WS 1741, Michael V. O'Donoghue, MA.

CHAPTER 22: RAID, ARRESTS AND ESCAPES

1. P17A/65, O'Malley Papers, UCD AD, Seán Lehane to Ernie O'Malley, 15/10/1922.

2. *Derry Journal*, 2/8/1922.
3. John P. Duggan, *A History of the Irish Army – Roots and Rebellion*, pp. 312–313.
4. *Derry Journal*, 4/8/1922.
5. *Ibid.*
6. *Ibid.*
7. *Ibid.*, 7/8/1922.
8. *Ibid.*, 16/8/1922 and 21/8/1922.
9. *Ibid.*, 21/8/1922.
10. *Ibid.*, 25/8/1922.
11. Brenda Niall, *The Riddle of Father Hackett*.
12. Ó Cuinneagain, *On the Arm of Time*, pp. 79–81.
13. *Derry Journal*, 25/8/1922.
14. P17A/63, O'Malley Papers, UCD AD.
15. P17A/57, O'Malley Papers, UCD AD.
16. BMH, Captured Documents Collection, Correspondence between 1st and 2nd Northern Division and IRA GHQ, MA.
17. P69/40, O'Malley Papers, UCD AD.
18. *Derry Journal*, 30/8/1922.
19. *Ibid.*, 4/9/1922.
20. BMH, WS 1741, Michael V. O'Donoghue, MA.
21. Letter from James Boyle to Frank McKay, Private Collection of Liam MacElhinney.
22. *Derry Journal*, 6/9/1922.
23. Letter from James Boyle, Private Collection of Liam MacElhinney.
24. P24/1019, Ernest Blythe Collection, UCD AD.
25. *Ibid.*
26. P69/40, O'Malley Papers, UCD AD.

CHAPTER 23: EITHNE COYLE'S WAR ENDS

1. BMH, WS 750, Eithne (Coyle) O'Donnell, MA.
2. P61/2, Eithne Coyle Collection, UCD AD.

CHAPTER 24: EMERGENCY POWERS

1. Michael Hopkinson, *Green Against Green*, p. 81.
2. British cabinet papers, Report from Colonel W. Maxwell Scott to the British secretary of state for war, CAB/24/139, British NA.
3. *Derry Journal*, 29/9/1922.
4. *Ibid.*, 11/10/1922.
5. *Ibid.*, 13/10/1922.
6. P17/A/ 65, O'Malley Papers, UCD AD.
7. *Derry Journal*, 20/10/1922.
8. *Ibid.*, 4/12/1922.
9. BMH, Intelligence Reports, October 1922, MA.
10. BMH, Captured Documents Collection, MA.
11. *Ibid.*
12. P17b/108, Jack Fitzgerald, O'Malley Notebooks, UCD AD.

CHAPTER 25: NEWBRIDGE INTERNMENT CAMP AND THE ESCAPE

1. Seamus McCann Diary, Private Collection of Seamus McCann.
2. Pádraig Ó Baoighill, *Óglach na Rossan – Niall Pluincéad Ó Baoighill*.
3. Seamus McCann Diary, Private Collection of Seamus McCann.
4. *Ibid.*; Pádraig Ó Baoighill, *Óglach na Rossan – Niall Pluincéad Ó Baoighill*.
5. Seamus McCann Diary, Private Collection of Seamus McCann.
6. Pádraig Ó Baoighill, *Óglach na Rossan – Niall Pluincéad Ó Baoighill*; *Derry People and Tirconaill News*, 19/5/1923.

CHAPTER 26: ARRESTS AND EXECUTIONS

1. P17a/76, O'Malley Papers, UCD AD.
2. P17A/46, O'Malley Papers, UCD AD.
3. *Derry Journal*, 6/11/1922.
4. P17b/108, O'Malley Notebooks, UCD AD.
5. BMH, Intelligence Reports 1922, MA; *An t-Óglach*, 30 December 1922, Vol. IV, No. 29, MA, p. 1.
6. Michael Hopkinson, *Green Against Green*, p. 189.

7. *Derry Journal*, 29/11/1922; P7/B/120, Mulcahy Papers, UCD AD.
8. Seamus McCann Diary, Private Collection of Seamus McCann; BMH, Operations Reports, December 1922, Box 6, MA.
9. *Ibid.*
10. BMH, Operations Reports, statement by Captain R.J. McCool, MA.
11. *Ibid.*
12. *Ibid.*
13. *Ibid.*
14. *Derry Journal*, 11/12/1922.
15. *Ibid.*, 13/12/1922; BMH, Intelligence Reports, MA.

CHAPTER 27: 1923 – PETTIGO RECLAIMED

1. Report by Captain McNaughten, 9/04/1923, Department of the Taoiseach Papers, NA Dublin.
2. Michael Farry, *The Aftermath of Revolution – Sligo 1921–1923*, p. 90.
3. *Derry Journal*, 3/1/1923; *Derry People and Tirconaill News*, 6/1/1923.
4. *Donegal Democrat*, 12/1/1923.
5. *Ibid.*, 19/1/1923.
6. *Derry Journal*, 9/2/1923.
7. *Derry People and Tirconaill News*, 20/1/1923.
8. *Derry Journal*, 19/1/1923.
9. *Ibid.*, 24/1/1923.
10. P69/35 (268–270), UCD AD.

CHAPTER 28: COURTS MARTIAL AND EXECUTIONS IN DONEGAL

1. P17A/46, O'Malley Papers, UCD AD.
2. HA/32/1/92, Public Records Office, Belfast.
3. *Derry Journal*, 26/1/1923.
4. *Donegal Democrat*, 9/2/1923.
5. *Derry People and Tirconaill News*, 24/2/1923.
6. *Derry Journal*, 23/2/1923.
7. Harrington, Niall C., *Kerry Landing*, p. 149; Uínseann MacEoin, *Survivors*, p. 367.

8. *Derry Journal*, 14/3/1923.
9. Conversation between Peadar O'Donnell, Joe Sweeney and Ernie O'Malley, Bewley's, Dublin, 3/06/1949, O'Malley Notebooks, P17b/97, p. 40, UCD AD.
10. P. H. Doherty, in conversation with Patrick Dawson, Carndonagh, 1960, stated that there had been no such attack and that the shooting was the result of an incident not associated with the IRA.
11. Joe Sweeney, P17b/97, O'Malley Papers, UCD AD; Kenneth Griffith & Timothy O'Grady, *Curious Journey*, pp. 305–306.
12. Fr Pádraig S. Ó Baoighill, *Cardinal Patrick O'Donnell, 1856–1927*, pp. 162–164.
13. *Derry Journal*, 14/3/1923–16/3/1923; *Donegal Democrat*, 21/3/1924.
14. Fr Pádraig S. Ó Baoighill, *Cardinal Patrick O'Donnell, 1856–1927*, p. 164.
15. *Derry Journal*, 23/3/1923; *Derry People and Tirconaill News* 17/3/1923 and 12/5/1923.
16. Fr Pádraig S. Ó Baoighill, *Cardinal Patrick O'Donnell, 1856–1927*, p. 164.
17. *Derry People and Tirconaill News*, 17/3/1923.
18. P7/B/130, Mulcahy Papers, Radio reports from Donegal command, UCD AD.
19. *Derry Journal*, 21/3/1923.
20. P7/B/130, Mulcahy Papers, Radio reports from Donegal command, UCD AD.
21. *Derry Journal*, 8/10/1924.
22. *Donegal Democrat*, 23/3/1923.

CHAPTER 29: PEADAR O'DONNELL – HELD TO RANSOM

1. Peadar O'Donnell, *The Gates Flew Open*.
2. *Derry Journal*, 26/3/1923.
3. Dónal O Drisceoil, *Peadar O'Donnell*, p. 36.
4. Peadar O'Donnell, *The Gates Flew Open*.
5. P7/B/139 (6), Mulcahy Papers, UCD AD.
6. *Derry People and Tirconaill News*, 14/4/1923.

7. *Derry Journal*, 16/4/1923.
8. P7/B/139 (6), Mulcahy Papers, UCD AD.
9. Michael Hopkinson, *Green Against Green*, p. 256.
10. BMH, Intelligence Reports 1923, MA.
11. S. 1369/10 Department of the Taoiseach Collection, NA Dublin.
12. BMH, Intelligence Reports 1923, MA.
13. *Derry People and Tirconaill News*, 2/7/1923.
14. *Ibid.*
15. BMH, Intelligence Reports, Portabello Barracks, Dublin 19/6/23, MA.

APPENDIX
1. BMH, Internment Records, MA.

Bibliography

Andrews, C. S., *Dublin Made Me* (Lilliput Press Ltd, 2008)

Begley, Anthony, *Ballyshannon and Surrounding Areas – History, Heritage and Folklore* (Carrickboy Publishing, 2009)

Constitution of the Irish Free State (Saorstát Éireann) Act 1922 and Treaty, 1921

Donegal Annual (Donegal Historical Society, 1982, 2008)

Duggan, John P., *A History of the Irish Army* (Gill & Macmillan, 1991)

Farry, Michael, *The Aftermath of Revolution – Sligo 1921–1923* (University College Dublin Press, 2000)

Griffith, Kenneth & O'Grady, Timothy, *Curious Journey – An Oral History of Ireland's Unfinished Revolution* (Mercier Press, 1988)

Harrington, Niall, *Kerry Landing* (Anvil Books Ltd, 1992)

Herlihy, Jim, *The Royal Irish Constabulary – A Short History and Genealogical Guide* (Four Courts Press, 1997)

Hopkinson, Michael, *Green Against Green* (Gill & Macmillan, 2004)

Hopkinson, Michael, 'Michael Collins and the North', Lecture (Dublin Castle, August 2007)

Lawlor, Pearse, *The Burnings 1920* (Mercier Press, 2009)

Macardle, Dorothy, *The Irish Republic* (Wolfhound Press, 1999)

MacEoin, Uínseann, *Survivors* (Argenta Publications, 1980)

MacFhionnghaile, Niall, *Donegal, Ireland and the 1st World War* (2nd Edition) (An Crann, 2005)

MacFhionnghaile, Niall, *Dr McGinley and His Times* (An Crann, 1985)

McMahon, Paul, 'British Intelligence and the Anglo-Irish Truce, July–December 1921', *Irish Historical Studies* XXXV: 140 (November 2007)

McMahon, Paul, *British Spies and Irish Rebels – British Intelligence and Ireland 1916–1945* (Boydell Press, 2008)

Murphy, Brian, P., 'The Irish Civil War 1922–1923, An Anti-Treaty Perspective', *The Irish Sword* (Military History Society of Ireland, 1997)

Niall, Brenda, *The Riddle of Father Hackett* (National Library of Australia, 2009)

Ó Baoighill, Fr Pádraig S., *Cardinal Patrick O'Donnell, 1865–1927* (Faoilseacháin, 2008)

Ó Baoighill, Pádraig, *Óglach na Rossan – Niall Pluincéad Ó Baoighill* (Coiseim, 1996)

O'Carroll, Declan, *Rockhill House – A History* (Defence Forces Printing Press, 1998)

O'Carroll, Declan, *Finner Camp – A History* (Defence Forces Printing Press, 2007)

Ó Cuinneagáin, Michael, *On the Arm of Time* (Ronan Press, 1992)

O'Donnell, Peadar, *The Gates Flew Open* (Mercier Press, 1965)

Ó Drisceoil, Dónal, *Peadar O'Donnell* (Cork University Press, 2001)

Ó Duibhir, Liam, *The Donegal Awakening – Donegal and the War of Independence* (Mercier Press, 2009)

Ó Duigneáin, Proinsias, *Linda Kearns – A Revolutionary Woman* (Drumlin Publications, 2002)

Taylor, Rex, *Assassination – The Death of Sir Henry Wilson and the Tragedy of Ireland* (Hutchinson & Co (Publishers) Ltd, 1961)

Tunney, John, 'From Ascendancy to Alienation – A Study of Donegal's Protestant Community, 1881–1932', Dissertation (University College Galway, May 1985)

NEWSPAPERS

Derry Journal, 1921–1924
Derry People and Tirconaill News, 1922–1923
Donegal Democrat, 1924
Donegal Vindicator, 1922
Freeman's Journal
Irish Independent
Irish News
Manchester Guardian
Sentinel

UNIVERSITY COLLEGE DUBLIN ARCHIVES DEPARTMENT
Mulcahy Papers
Eithne Coyle Collection
Ernest Blythe Papers
Ernie O'Malley Notebooks and Papers

BUREAU OF MILITARY HISTORY
Captured Documents Collection
Intelligence and Operations Reports
Internment Records
The Irish Sword, 1997
Witness Statements 1913–1921

NATIONAL LIBRARY OF IRELAND
Florence O'Donoghue Collection
Kathleen McKenna Napoli Papers

NATIONAL ARCHIVES OF IRELAND (DUBLIN)
Department of Justice Files
Department of the Taoiseach Papers

AUSTRALIAN JESUIT ARCHIVES, HAWTHORN, VICTORIA, AUSTRALIA
Journal of W. P. Hackett, SJ, 1922

PRIVATE COLLECTIONS
Declan O'Carroll
Liam MacElhinney
Patrick Dawson
Seamus McCann

Index

1st Northern Division 23, 26, 28, 38, 42, 45, 58, 67, 75, 83, 87, 88, 91, 107, 108, 117, 118, 148, 149, 150, 154, 168, 190, 195, 196, 198
1st Southern Division 94
1st Ulster Division 23
2nd Northern Division 73, 75, 76, 77, 96, 114, 137, 152, 162, 185, 196
3rd Northern Division 113
3rd Western Division 96, 145, 148, 152, 154, 187, 190, 192, 198, 205, 211, 212, 217, 218, 219, 228, 232
4th Howitzer Battery 126
4th Northern Division 56, 114, 190
5th Northern Division 60, 61, 91
18th Infantry Brigade 126
46th Battalion 231
165th Infantry Brigade 118

A

Aiken, Frank 56, 57, 61, 112, 190, 238
Andrews, C.S. 'Todd' 28, 29, 30
Annagry 203
Anti-Treaty 16, 17, 56, 73, 74, 79, 81, 83, 84, 86, 90, 94, 98, 100, 114, 127, 240, 241
An t-Óglach 62
Antrim 42, 43, 79, 114
Ardara 43, 105
Ardsbeg 105
Armagh 33, 42, 56, 112, 130, 208
Army Convention 56, 57, 81
Army Council 56, 89, 231, 236, 237
Army Executive 144, 145, 237
Articles of Agreement 16, 42, 44, 45, 51, 54, 55, 240
Ashley, Colonel 148
Athlone 33, 228
Atkinson, T.J. 61
Aughlihard 225
Auxiliaries 16, 24

B

Ballindrait 112
Ballintine, Head Constable Joseph 115
Ballintra 61, 127, 151
Ballyarr 168
Ballybay 43
Ballybofey 39, 43, 70, 91, 93, 98, 116, 143, 145, 146, 152, 159, 174, 180, 231
Ballyconnell 16, 211
Ballykinlar 24
Ballylar 55
Ballymacool House 146, 147
Ballymaleel 201
Ballyseedy 225
Ballyshannon 61, 66, 87, 93, 95, 152, 153, 198, 199, 218, 220
Banbridge 17, 72, 100
Barrett, Frank 145
Barrett, Richard 214
Barry, Patrick 91
Barry, Tom 75, 117, 145, 237
Barton, Robert 41
Béal na mBláth 188, 189, 242
Beggars Bush 75, 76, 109, 143, 237
Belfast 17, 18, 42, 44, 54, 58, 59, 60, 64, 65, 72, 73, 79, 80, 84, 86, 87, 89, 90, 91, 92, 93, 96, 97, 100, 108, 114, 120, 128, 129, 131, 134, 137, 139, 166, 209, 212, 214, 217, 241, 242
Belfast Bank 95, 102, 106, 126, 186
Belleek 23, 61, 68, 85, 86, 119, 120, 121, 122, 124, 130, 131, 140, 216
Best, Richard 59
Billary Hill 127, 128
Birkenhead, Lord 41
Birmingham 64, 77, 78
Black and Tans 16, 24, 33, 68, 113, 148
Blake, Marian 232
Blaney, James 239
Blaney, Neil 58, 213
Bluestack Mountains 177, 178
Boa Island 121, 122, 123, 124, 125
Bonner, Bernard 203

275

Bonner, Owen 203
Bonner, Private 220
Boycott 81, 84, 86, 87, 89, 90, 91, 96, 97, 116, 137, 166, 198, 241
Boyle, Edward 204
Boyle, James 153, 194, 195
Boyle, Pat 204
Boyle, Phil 180
Bracen, Lt 25
Bradley, John 58
Breenagh 29, 30
Breen, Dan 21
Bridge End 164, 171
British Commonwealth 50, 135, 136
Britton, Hugh 66, 67
Brockagh 180, 207
Broden, Christie 85, 179
Brown, James 210
Brown, William 171
Broy, Ned 41
Brugha, Cathal 112, 130, 243
Bryson, Packy 105
Bunbeg 109
Buncrana 39, 48, 49, 58, 79, 80, 86, 91, 96, 102, 103, 104, 106, 107, 108, 109, 143, 151, 152, 153, 159, 160, 163, 170, 171, 172, 180, 181, 184, 185, 186, 192, 193, 195, 199, 213, 214, 218, 232
Bundoran 38, 87, 99, 146, 152, 153, 187
Burke, Leo 208
Burke, Mary (May) 34, 35, 36
Burke, Seamus 36
Burnfoot 101, 102, 137, 164, 192
Burns, Bill 102
Burns, Charles Herbert 71
Burns, Joseph 160
Burtonport 26, 43, 45, 87, 97, 105, 195, 207

C

Caffney, James 212
Cannon, Bernard 226
Carlow 36
Carndonagh 31, 39, 46, 48, 87, 96, 137, 151, 153, 185, 194, 195, 213
Carney, Frank 26
Carrick 16, 46, 64, 93, 231
Carrickmacross 59
Carrick-on-Shannon 87
Carrigans 118, 137, 148, 238
Carrigart 38, 89, 229

Carson, Lord 133
Cassidy, Peter 212
Castlederg 63, 113, 116, 117
Castlefinn 50, 111, 112, 116, 117, 148, 154, 157, 191, 194, 196, 210, 213, 214
Cavan 74
Cave, Lord 133
Chamberlain, Austen 41, 133
Chartres, John 41
Childers, Erskine 41
Churchill 89, 96, 150, 157, 158, 160, 166, 169, 173, 179, 180, 186, 194, 202, 203, 214
Churchill, Winston 41, 64, 80, 91, 120, 123, 124, 128, 130, 134, 140, 149, 160
Clady 63, 64, 68, 94, 112, 116, 214
Clarke, James 224
Clifford, Patrick 85, 179
Cloghan 50, 175
Clonelly House 68, 123
Clones 43, 92, 217
Clonmany 31, 38, 46, 48
Clonmel 175, 236
Coffey, Tadhg 225
Coll, Charles 93
Collins, John 94, 95
Collins, Michael 18, 36, 41, 47, 51, 52, 54, 55, 60, 61, 64, 65, 68, 71, 73, 74, 85, 91, 92, 108, 112, 114, 120, 123, 124, 129, 132, 133, 134, 135, 139, 140, 141, 142, 158, 185, 188, 189, 190, 216, 241, 242, 243
Comerford, Máire 145
Conlon, John 65
Connolly, Captain James 148
Connolly, Con 211
Connolly, Patrick 71
Constitution 17, 42, 55, 56, 57, 71, 84, 132, 133, 134, 135, 136, 143, 241
Constitutional Committee 55, 132
Convoy 39
Cork 18, 74, 75, 84, 94, 98, 100, 117, 141, 173, 183, 188, 189, 207, 241, 242
Cornershesk 58
Corr, C. 58
Cotter, Jim 154, 157, 166, 182, 183
Cotter, Seamus 84
Countess Bridge (Kerry) 225
Coyle, Daniel 211, 222, 235
Coyle, Eithne 32, 33, 34, 35, 36, 90, 96, 97, 116, 154, 160, 198, 199
Craig, James 60, 64, 67, 68, 91, 92, 120,

Index

129, 130
Creaney, James 58
Creeslough 43, 90, 91, 166, 204, 219, 226, 227, 228, 243
Crieve 147
Croaghbarnes 177
Crolly 25, 153, 158
Crovehy 195
Crowe, Tadhg 21
Crowley, Con 167
Crumlin Road Jail 59
Cuddihy, Mary (Peg) 145
Culdaff 37, 46, 48
Cumann na mBan 15, 32, 33, 34, 36, 46, 63, 67, 97, 138, 145, 146, 154, 160, 174, 202, 210, 214, 232, 239, 240
Cunningham, Edward 16
Cunningham, James 64, 77, 78, 231
Cunningham, Joseph 16
Curragh Internment Camp 160, 185, 233, 235, 243
Curtis, Lionel 135

D

Dáil courts 23
Dáil Éireann (An Dáil) 15, 16, 17, 21, 23, 41, 44, 45, 49, 50, 51, 53, 54, 61, 71, 79, 81, 84, 85, 86, 87, 91, 92, 95, 96, 97, 98, 99, 102, 103, 104, 105, 106, 107, 109, 110, 112, 114, 115, 116, 117, 119, 120, 121, 122, 126, 129, 136, 137, 143, 146, 177, 186, 200, 216, 218, 219, 240
Dalton, Emmet 27, 28, 30, 41
Daly, Charlie 75, 76, 77, 83, 84, 88, 96, 98, 99, 101, 103, 104, 107, 108, 117, 137, 148, 150, 153, 154, 157, 158, 160, 161, 166, 167, 168, 169, 173, 174, 175, 176, 177, 178, 181, 182, 183, 193, 194, 196, 197, 202, 204, 210, 211, 220, 222, 225, 227, 228, 234, 243
Daly, Patrick 64, 65, 78, 79, 225
Daly, Thomas 196
Dawson, Jim 105, 180, 219
Dawson, Patrick 219
Deasy, Liam 145, 223, 234
Derrig, Thomas 145
Derry 18, 25, 33, 37, 38, 42, 43, 58, 59, 60, 65, 66, 68, 79, 85, 86, 87, 88, 89, 90, 91, 92, 93, 96, 98, 99, 101, 103, 104, 105, 106, 109, 111, 113, 117, 118, 120, 121, 137, 139, 148, 153, 157, 159, 160, 163, 164, 165, 166, 181, 186, 187, 190, 192, 194, 208, 213, 215, 224, 229, 241
Derryheeney 203
Desertegny 48, 79, 81
Desertmartin 113
de Valera, Éamonn 26, 49, 52, 53, 54, 71, 112, 114, 129, 134, 135, 238
Devenny, John 105
Devine, Alfred 178
Devins, Brig. 148
Devins, Seamus 198
Dickson, Sammy 168
Doagh, Isle of 193
Doherty, Adjutant 172
Doherty, Jack (Buncrana) 102, 103
Doherty, James (Fanad) 102, 239
Doherty, John 58
Doherty, Malachy 66
Doherty, P.H. 227
Doherty, Tom 195
Doherty, William 49
Dolan, Joe 142
Donaghmore House 157
Donaghy, James 211, 222, 235
Donegal Town 46, 66, 67, 71, 95, 116, 127, 155, 183, 192, 198, 211, 212, 219
Donegan, Moss 84, 88
Doochary 151, 153, 166, 203, 214
Doran, Charles 203
Doughlas, Blacker 61
Down 24, 42, 130, 139
Downey, Mary 80
Drimarone 29
Dromahair 218
Dromore 60, 68, 100, 128
Drumboe 16, 61, 67, 96, 98, 103, 104, 106, 107, 111, 143, 147, 148, 152, 153, 159, 167, 168, 181, 184, 187, 188, 192, 199, 211, 212, 214, 222, 223, 224, 225, 226, 227, 228, 229, 230, 231, 233, 234, 243
Drumbollogue 195
Drumdoit 213
Drumhariff Hill 127
Drumkeen 166, 167, 168, 169, 186, 188, 210, 211
Drumnaraw 204
Drumoghill 50
Drumquinn 23, 127
Dublin 18, 21, 22, 24, 26, 28, 29, 33, 41, 45, 47, 48, 51, 57, 61, 63, 64, 65, 70,

277

71, 73, 76, 77, 83, 85, 87, 93, 94, 99,
100, 106, 107, 111, 112, 114, 115,
116, 117, 120, 124, 138, 139, 140,
141, 142, 143, 144, 145, 146, 148,
149, 150, 153, 160, 161, 172, 173,
184, 198, 199, 203, 207, 208, 212,
214, 218, 223, 227, 228, 230, 235,
242, 243
Dublin Guard 225
Duffy, George Gavin 41
Duffy, Joseph 69, 70
Duggan, Éamonn 41
Dump arms order 15, 238, 244
Dundalk 77
Dunfanaghy 151, 224, 226
Dungannon 32, 96
Dungloe 22, 25, 27, 28, 29, 30, 82, 90, 93,
138, 151, 153, 161, 166, 180, 194,
195, 232
Dunkineely 46, 151, 192, 232
Dunlewy 210, 211, 212, 222
Dunne, Reginald 139, 140, 141, 142
Dunree Fort 172
Dwyer, Paddy 21

E

Elections 17, 21, 22, 23, 32, 49, 52, 53, 56,
62, 71, 91, 114, 132, 135, 136, 137,
141, 143, 235, 237, 241
Ellis, John 64, 65, 142
Ellis, William Knox 112
Emergency Powers legislation 200, 201,
203
England 21, 24, 33, 34, 46, 52, 60, 64, 75,
77, 79, 81, 130, 140
Enniskillen 63, 85, 86, 122, 124, 128, 131
Enright, Daniel 85, 211, 222, 227, 228,
243
Erne, Lough 120, 121, 123
Errigal 211
Executions 18, 20, 59, 60, 64, 65, 212, 214,
221, 222, 223, 224, 227, 228, 229,
230, 231, 233, 234, 235, 243
Executive Council (IRA) 84, 93, 95, 98,
99, 120, 175, 188, 189, 223, 237, 238

F

Fahan 48, 109, 151, 159, 171, 172, 213
Falcarragh 38, 151, 154, 161, 208, 211
Fanad 23, 49, 55, 58, 213, 239
Farrell, Patrick 208

Fermanagh 18, 23, 38, 42, 43, 62, 63, 68,
75, 85, 88, 92, 93, 96, 98, 115, 119,
120, 121, 122, 123, 125, 216, 241
Ferry, Hugh 204
Finnegan, Michael 42, 43, 44, 58, 59
Finner Camp 66, 86, 87, 98, 145, 146, 147,
148, 150, 152, 195, 212, 233, 235, 243
Fintown 174, 187, 193
First Dáil 21
Fisher, James 212
Fitzgerald, Jack 84, 88, 107, 117, 175, 211
Fitzgerald, Seán 84
Fitzpatrick, James J. 43, 59
Fletcher, Esther 103
Flood, Patrick 127, 128, 129
Flying column 25, 26, 64, 171, 186, 191,
194, 196, 208, 229, 232
Four Courts 18, 79, 85, 93, 94, 107, 117,
139, 140, 142, 143, 144, 145, 146,
148, 149, 160, 175, 242
Foxhall 96, 97
Foyle, Lough 109
Free State 16, 18, 42, 55, 83, 107, 124,
129, 135, 136, 138, 143, 144, 146,
147, 148, 149, 150, 151, 152, 153,
154, 155, 157, 158, 159, 160, 161,
162, 163, 164, 165, 166, 167, 168,
170, 171, 172, 173, 174, 175, 176,
177, 178, 179, 180, 181, 183, 184,
185, 186, 187, 188, 189, 190, 192,
193, 194, 195, 198, 200, 201, 202,
203, 205, 206, 208, 209, 211, 212,
213, 214, 216, 217, 218, 219, 220,
221, 224, 225, 226, 227, 228, 229,
231, 232, 233, 234, 236, 237, 239,
242, 243
Fries, Patrick 203
Frongoch 20
Frosses 181, 182, 183
Fullerton, James 239

G

Gallagher, Danny 119, 123
Gallagher, Eddie (Burtonport) 105
Gallagher, Edward (Carrick) 93
Gallagher, Francis 43, 59
Gallagher, Hugh 67, 215
Gallagher, James 66, 67
Gallagher, John (Donegal Town) 66
Gallagher, John (Letterkenny) 160
Gallagher, Patrick (Donegal Town) 71,
226

Index

Gallagher, Pat (Termon) 204
Gallagher, Sgt Patrick (Creeslough) 226
Galvin, Denis 84, 88, 117
Garrison 68, 88
Gartan 187, 195, 239
Gartan Lake 179, 202
Geelan, DI 39
German Plot 21
Germany 21, 108, 109
Gilfedder, Matt 195
Gillen, Daniel 87
Gillespie, Neill 96
Glebe 58
Glenade 214
Glencolmcille 88
Glendowan 166, 174, 194, 195
Gleneely 37
Glenfinn 175, 177, 187
Glenmaquin 90
Glennon, Col Tom 87, 98, 103, 104, 106, 107, 108, 157, 158, 222, 233
Glenswilly 50, 168, 214
Glenties 29, 38, 92, 151, 161, 162, 177, 178, 180, 181, 182, 187, 221, 227, 230
Glenveagh 30, 88, 109, 148, 150, 151, 153, 154, 155, 156, 157, 158, 159, 160, 161, 163, 165, 166, 167, 168, 169, 173, 175, 176, 179, 184, 186, 187, 188, 194
Golden, Seán 142
Gorey 36
Gorman, Const. 43, 58, 59
Government of Ireland Act 17, 42, 54, 55, 100, 135
Grant, Johnny 105
Greencastle 74, 152, 213
Greenwood, Hamar 38, 41
Gretton, Col 38
Griffin, Albert 93
Griffith, Arthur 41, 49, 52, 55, 65, 71, 81, 82, 83, 96, 112, 123, 132, 133, 134, 135, 216
Gweedore 158, 210

H

Hackett, Fr Bernard 128
Hackett, Fr William 54, 156, 159, 188, 189
Hamilton, William 61
Harkin, Daniel 147
Haughey, Johnny 74, 75
Haughey, Susan 105

Healy, T. M. 230
Hegarty, Seán 88, 109
Hewart, Gordon 41
Higgins, John 113
Hodge, DI 38
Hogan, Daniel 60
Holmes, Willie 150
Home Rule 42
Horborn, Captain 217
Huddlestone, Leslie 69
Humphreys, Sheila 138, 145, 146, 208
Hutton, Jim 102

I

Inch 109, 148, 155, 159, 163, 165, 170, 171, 172, 173, 188, 192
Inishowen 31, 37, 38, 46, 48, 152, 182, 193, 194, 213
Inver 38, 91, 192, 193
IRB 47, 51, 79, 141, 227
Irish Parliamentary Party 21
Irish Self-Determination League 78, 79
Iskaheen 48

J

Johnstone, Catherine 202, 203
Johnston, Patrick 'Poppy' 43, 44, 58, 59, 61, 64, 65, 93
Johnston, Tom 235
Jordan, Michael 38
Jordan, Patrick 38, 215

K

Kane, John 195
Kavanagh, John 103
Kavanagh, Mary Ellen 103
Kearney, William 127
Kearns, Linda 33, 34, 35, 36
Kelly, Daniel 42, 43
Kelly, James 116
Kelly, J.J. 213
Kelly, Michael 37
Kelly, Nelly 239
Kelly, Tom 96
Kelly, Willie John 96
Keogh, Aileen 34, 35, 36
Kerry 18, 75, 84, 98, 107, 137, 168, 179, 196, 207, 218, 225, 227, 241, 243
Kerrykeel 39
Kesh 124, 126

279

Kidnappings 63, 64, 65, 67, 68, 92, 216
Kilcar 46, 93
Kilcullen 36
Kildare 36, 160, 180, 181, 206, 207, 209, 233, 242
Kilderry 171
Killea 194
Killtyclogher 237
Killybegs 46, 151, 212
Killygarvan 48
Killygordon 50, 58, 70
Kilmacrennan 71, 201, 214
Kilmainham Jail 199, 206, 212
Kilroy, Michael 145
Kincasslagh 93, 158, 209
Kindrum 49
King George V 46, 136
King, Richard 120
Kinlough 61, 89, 148, 214
Knockbrack 159
Knocknagoshel 225

L

Lafferty, Pat 213
Lagan 88, 89, 108
Laghey 67, 151
Lane, James (Jim) 84, 158, 211, 222, 235
Lanigan, James 47
Larkin, Seán 113, 160, 211, 222, 227, 228
Larkin, Tom 222
Laverty, Pat 112
Lawson, Ernest 67
Leary, Con 183
Lee, Pat 93
Lehane, Seán 75, 83, 84, 87, 88, 96, 98, 99, 101, 102, 103, 104, 106, 107, 108, 109, 110, 111, 112, 113, 117, 150, 154, 160, 168, 169, 173, 174, 175, 176, 178, 181, 183, 190, 191, 192, 193, 194, 195, 196, 198, 202, 204, 205, 210, 211, 220
Leitrim 61, 96, 137, 208, 211, 217
Leonard, Patrick 42, 44, 58, 59, 61, 64, 65
Letter 123, 124, 125, 127
Lettercloth 203
Lettercran 125
Letterkenny 22, 28, 29, 37, 45, 50, 58, 86, 87, 90, 96, 97, 98, 104, 106, 111, 116, 137, 143, 146, 148, 150, 151, 154, 159, 160, 164, 165, 167, 168, 169, 171, 180, 184, 185, 186, 187, 188, 194, 195, 200, 203, 213, 218, 219, 225, 229, 233, 239

Lifford 68, 69, 86, 94, 103, 111, 112, 116, 118, 137, 147, 148, 151, 154, 157, 162, 165, 168, 169, 180, 185, 193, 201, 203, 207, 232
Lincolnshire Regiment 85, 125, 126, 131
Lisburn 17, 72, 100
Lismullaghduff 50
Lisnaskea 63
Liverpool 33, 34, 64, 65, 78
Lloyd, George 42, 44
Lloyd George, David 26, 41, 55, 132, 133, 134, 135, 140, 141
London 16, 18, 41, 42, 44, 50, 52, 53, 65, 66, 70, 78, 120, 123, 124, 133, 139, 140, 142
Longford 32, 87
Loughanure 204
Lough Veagh House 179, 202, 203
Louth 56, 74, 219
Lowery 123, 124
Lynch, Liam 18, 56, 57, 61, 74, 81, 85, 93, 94, 99, 106, 112, 145, 158, 191, 195, 196, 197, 220, 236
Lyttle, Const. 43, 58, 59

M

MacBride, James 204
MacBride, Mary 232
MacBride, Maud Gonne 36, 81, 82
MacBride, Seán 41
MacEoin, Seán 61, 96, 99, 146, 198
MacLochlainn, Joseph (Seán) 102, 103
MacNeill, Brian 145
MacNeil, Susan 125
MacNelis, Donncha 88, 154, 157, 177, 178, 179, 220, 221
Macready, Neville 44, 93, 140, 142
Magheraban 58
Magheraboy 224
Magherafelt 113
Magheramenagh Castle 121, 122, 131
Maguire, Joseph 195
Maguire, Patrick 43, 59
Maguire, Sam 79, 142
Malin 31, 38, 46, 48, 151
Malinmore 229
Manchester 65, 78, 131
Manorcunningham 109
Mansion House 21, 55, 57, 71, 83, 112
Martin, Lt 126
McAteer, Patrick 43, 59, 93
McAuley, John 225

Index

McCafferty, Hugh 204
McCallion, Alfie 83, 87, 186, 208, 213
McCallion, George 163
McCann, Seamus 29, 69, 83, 88, 116, 176, 180, 181, 207, 208, 213
McCanny, Bernard 127
McCarroll, John 63
McCarry, Kate 233
McCarry's Hotel 87, 96, 98, 106, 150, 164
McCartan, Paddy 36
McCarthy, Joseph 239
McCloskey, Dr James 159, 229
McCool, Private 105
McCool, Seán 208
McCormack, Owen 159
McCormack, Patrick 21
McCranahan, Joe 58
McCusker, William 93
McDonnell, Anthony 208
McDonnell, Archie 96
McElduff, James 96, 116
McElligott, Michael 85
McElroy, Joe 182, 183
McElwee, Anthony 69
McGee, Daniel 208
McGee, Kitty 210
McGee, Paddy 42
McGeehan, Henry 113
McGeehan, Teresa 232
McGill, Daniel 105
McGilvey, Private 220
McGinley, Bertie 213
McGinley, Charles 168, 169
McGinley, Dr Joseph Patrick 49, 51, 91, 168, 226
McGinley, John 105
McGleenon, Charlie 208
McGlinchey, Pat 115
McGloin, Edward 214
McGloin, John 214
McGoldrick, P. J. 49, 67, 91
McGowan, Henry 147
McGowan, Peter 103
McGrath, Bridget 125
McGrath, Harry 184
McGrath, John 125
McGreanra, James 204
McGreanra, John 204
McGuinness, Charlie 108
McGuire, Pat 103
McGurk, James 208
McGurk, Joe 88, 103, 177
McHenry, Thomas 207

McHugh, Aloysius 183
McHugh, John 128
McKay, Hugh 202
McKeagney, Rev. 217
McKelvey, Joseph 85, 94, 145, 214
McKendrick, James 38
McKenna, Dan 75, 160
McKinney, Edward 79, 80, 81
McKinney, E.S. 165
McLaughlin, Brig. 153
McLaughlin, D. 58
McLaughlin, Harry 218
McLaughlin, Joe Seán 222
McLaughlin, John 91
McLaughlin, Joseph 86, 102, 106, 107
McLaughlin, Kathleen 161
McLaughlin, Pat 102
McLaughlin, Patrick 226
McLaverty, Dr 36
McMahon family massacre 79, 80, 81
McMahon, Francis 80
McMahon, Gerald 80
McMahon, John 80
McMahon, Michael 80
McMahon, Owen 80
McMahon, Patrick 80
McMenamin, Fr 229
McMenamin, William 222
McMonagle, Eddie 147
McMonagle, James 147
McMorrow, James 208
McNaughten, Captain 216, 217
McNulty, James 43, 59
McRory, Dan 58
McRory, M. 58
McShea, Thomas 43, 44, 58, 59, 61, 64, 65, 93
Meehan, Hugh 225
Meehan, Patrick 66
Meenabul 211, 222
Meenbanad 22, 25
Meenirroy 187
Meenmore 25, 161, 195
Melenon House 99, 103
Mellows, Liam 85, 99, 138, 214
Melly, Vol. 148
Milford 38, 48, 69, 70, 71, 89, 151, 160, 169, 185, 213, 229
Milltown 80
Minagh 58
Monaghan 18, 23, 43, 59, 60, 64, 74, 77, 92, 194, 217, 241
Monaghan, Barney 231

281

Monaghan, Brian 88, 193, 231
Moore, Captain 217
Moore, Major 61, 121
Morrison, Hugh 165
Morris, Tom 75, 77, 137, 138, 157, 162
Mountcharles 93, 109, 151, 155, 190, 192, 193, 212, 231
Mountjoy Jail 33, 34, 160, 206, 214
Moville 38, 48, 87, 151, 153, 185
Moylan, Michael 145
Moylan, Seán 99
Muff 38, 87, 109, 171
Mulcahy, Richard 18, 24, 61, 68, 73, 74, 77, 81, 83, 95, 112, 219, 223
Muldoon, Private 220
Mullan, John 29, 30, 170, 172, 192, 194
Mullins, Tom 84, 211
Murlog 50
Murphy, Johnnie 102
Murragh, Hugh 186
Murray, Edward 105
Murray, Joachim 93
Myles, Major J. S. 61

N

Newbridge Internment Camp 160, 172, 180, 181, 184, 193, 202, 206, 213, 242
Newcastle 78
Newry 112
Newtownbutler 43, 217
Newtowncunningham 79, 87, 102, 103, 104, 105, 106, 107, 108, 109, 110, 160, 163, 171
Newtownhamilton 112
Newtownstewart 43
No. 1 Brigade 27, 30, 148, 151, 152, 176, 190
No. 2 Brigade 26, 29, 45, 151, 152, 190
No. 3 Brigade 29, 121, 151, 152
No. 4 Brigade 43, 67, 152, 174
North Eastern Command 190, 204
Northern offensive 18, 85, 87, 100, 108, 113, 117, 130, 138, 144, 167, 241, 242, 243

O

O'Boyle, Neil Plunkett 153, 207, 208, 209
O'Brien, Alexander 219
O'Brien, Art 78
O'Brien, John 186, 208

O'Connor, Joe 145
O'Connor, Josie 34, 35
O'Connor, Private 218
O'Connor, Rory 56, 85, 93, 95, 102, 112, 140, 145, 149, 214
O'Connor, Una 145
O'Doherty, Cissie 232
O'Doherty, Fr John 168
O'Doherty, Hugh C. 65
O'Doherty, Joseph 21, 49, 53
O'Doherty, Roisín 160, 198
O'Donel, Lile 233, 235
O'Donnell, B. 55
O'Donnell, Bernard 154, 203
O'Donnell, Cardinal Patrick 227, 228, 230
O'Donnell, Daniel 230
O'Donnell, Dot 213
O'Donnell, Frank 22, 29, 83, 88, 107, 138, 145, 146, 161, 206, 208, 213, 235
O'Donnell, James (Rannafast) 203
O'Donnell, James (Termon) 204
O'Donnell, Joe 83, 107, 194, 207
O'Donnell, Neil 168
O'Donnell, Patrick 58
O'Donnell, Peadar 23, 25, 26, 28, 29, 30, 45, 54, 69, 83, 87, 88, 89, 94, 107, 116, 117, 144, 145, 160, 161, 227, 233, 235, 243
O'Donnell, Peadar 31
O'Donnell, Peter 43, 59
O'Donnell, Rose 232
O'Donoghue, Mick 84, 88, 107, 154, 157, 158, 182, 183
O'Donoghue, Mick 150
O'Donovan, James 56
O'Donovan, John 84
O'Duffy, Eoin 47, 60, 61, 74, 75, 76, 77, 99, 106, 112
O'Duffy, H. J. 224
O'Faolain, F. 145
O'Farrell, Commandant Michael 126
O'Farrell, Mr 224
O'Flaherty, A. 214
O'Flaherty, Edward 94
O'Flaherty, Molly 94
O'Flaherty, Samuel 49
O'Gorman, Joe 212
Ó Grianna, Seamus 186
O'Hagan, Vol. 148
O'Hara, Tom 213
O'Hegarty, Diarmuid 141
O'Higgins, Kevin 165, 214
O'Kierans, Fr L. 121, 131

Oldtown 147, 184
O'Leary, Denis 84
O'Loan, Henry 43, 59
Omagh 74, 112, 118, 137
Ó Máille, Pádraig 214
O'Malley, Dan 77
O'Malley, Ernie 56, 145, 176, 190, 191, 195, 196, 201, 204, 208, 210, 243
O'Neill, John 180
O'Reilly, Patrick 43, 59
O'Shannon, Cathal 219
O'Sullivan, Billy 84
O'Sullivan, Gearóid 99
O'Sullivan, Joseph 139, 140, 142
O'Sullivan, Timothy 85, 211, 222, 227, 228, 243

P

Partition 42, 55, 56, 72, 73, 74, 135
Pearse, Pádraig 28, 42
Peterhead Jail 66, 93
Pettigo 61, 68, 119, 120, 121, 122, 123, 124, 125, 126, 127, 128, 129, 130, 131, 216, 217
Pilkington, Billy 96
Pilkington, Liam 145, 211
Plumb, Const. 88
Poitín 31, 37, 177
Porter, John 49
Portobello Barracks 185
Portonode 124
Privy Council 132, 133, 134
Pro-Treaty 16, 17, 18, 54, 55, 56, 75, 79, 85, 86, 91, 100, 110, 114, 142, 143, 240
Provisional Government 18, 50, 55, 63, 64, 67, 68, 70, 73, 81, 89, 91, 95, 99, 108, 119, 123, 124, 128, 132, 140, 141, 142, 143, 146, 149, 167, 216, 240, 241

Q

Quille, Martin 85, 168, 179
Quinn, John 159, 186, 208

R

Ramelton 38, 50, 69, 89, 95, 151, 160, 165, 171, 186, 201
Rankin, Dr 105
Rannafast 203
Raphoe 50, 86, 88, 90, 99, 100, 106, 111, 112, 113, 115, 116, 117, 148, 150, 151, 153, 154, 157, 185, 227
Rathmullan 16, 143, 159, 170, 213
Red Cross 179, 180, 187, 239
Republican constitution 17, 56, 134, 135, 136, 241
Robinson, Seamus 21, 145
Rockhill House 147
Roscommon 32, 33, 137
Roscor 120
Rossnakill 58, 239
Royal Irish Constabulary (RIC) 17, 21, 22, 23, 24, 25, 27, 32, 33, 37, 38, 39, 43, 44, 68, 70, 71, 79, 80, 86, 87, 94, 100, 115, 146, 158
Royal Ulster Constabulary (RUC) 17, 115, 124, 217
Rutledge, P. 145
Ryan, Tim 35, 36

S

Saorstát Éireann 42, 55, 56, 71, 132, 135, 136, 241
Scallon, James 178
Scallon, Jim 125
Scotland 24, 66, 81, 92, 93, 207
Sharkey, Owen 93
Sharkey, Private 105
Sharkey, Willie 27
Sheils, Patrick 38, 86
Sheridan, Francis 43, 59
Sheskinarone 93
Shields, Frank 187
Shields, Jack 194
Sinn Féin 16, 17, 20, 21, 22, 23, 24, 26, 39, 40, 46, 47, 48, 51, 63, 70, 71, 96, 114, 135, 238, 240
Sion Mills 105
Six Counties 17, 18, 42, 55, 61, 64, 72, 73, 74, 75, 77, 79, 81, 84, 87, 90, 91, 92, 96, 98, 100, 102, 108, 112, 113, 115, 117, 128, 129, 130, 138, 158, 185, 190, 198, 217, 227, 241, 242
Skeog 109, 148, 155, 163, 164, 165
Sligo 33, 87, 96, 145, 146, 154, 173, 187, 190, 197, 198, 211, 217, 218, 228
Smyth, Col 100
Smyth, Nicholas 123, 125
Solly-Flood, Maj.-Gen. Arthur 129, 130
South Staffordshire regiment 126, 217
Spain, Jim 208
Special Constabulary 17, 44, 60, 61, 63, 68,

72, 79, 80, 85, 88, 91, 92, 94, 97, 98, 99, 100, 104, 108, 111, 113, 114, 115, 116, 117, 119, 120, 121, 122, 123, 124, 125, 128, 129, 130, 131, 137, 149, 154, 192, 194, 207, 216
Special Powers legislation 72, 73, 92, 96, 119
Stack, Austin 236
Staunton, John 154
Stewarts Corner 105
St John Gogarty, Dr O. 35
St Johnston 137, 148
Strabane 58, 64, 86, 90, 94, 105, 116, 118
Stranorlar 61, 70, 93, 98, 103, 152, 159, 167, 175, 178, 188, 222
Sumner, Lord 133
Swanzy, DI 100
Sweeney, Bernard 43, 59, 92
Sweeney, Jack 168, 169
Sweeney, Joseph 21, 22, 25, 26, 28, 29, 45, 47, 49, 53, 68, 74, 91, 92, 98, 106, 107, 108, 109, 110, 111, 116, 120, 122, 146, 147, 157, 158, 195, 196, 216, 227, 228, 231
Sweeney, Willie 168, 169
Swilly, Lough 49, 109, 164, 213

T

Teachtaí Dála (TDs) 21, 45, 48, 51, 52, 53, 55, 63, 91, 212, 214, 218, 219, 235, 236
Templedouglas 169
Termon 166, 186, 204, 214
Third Dáil 114, 143
Thompson, Alfred 66, 67
Timmins, Hugh J. 43, 59
Timmoney, Seamus 59
Tipperary 21, 85, 169, 236, 237
Tirconaill 50, 53, 89, 185, 223
Toner, Joe 194
Travers, John 67, 124
Treacy, Seán 21
Treaty 16, 17, 36, 41, 42, 45, 46, 47, 48, 49, 50, 51, 52, 53, 54, 55, 56, 61, 62, 63, 68, 70, 71, 73, 75, 76, 86, 94, 95, 100, 114, 115, 132, 133, 134, 135, 136, 139, 141, 143, 146, 179, 240, 241, 244
Trentagh 160
Truce 27, 33, 34, 37, 38, 45, 55, 58, 69, 77, 85, 91, 92, 94, 95, 121, 139, 145, 154, 240

Tullaghan 99
Tullymore 58
Tully, Patrick 43, 59
Twohig, Richard 212
Tyrone 18, 23, 32, 36, 38, 42, 43, 60, 63, 68, 75, 92, 93, 94, 96, 98, 99, 103, 105, 113, 115, 116, 117, 119, 120, 127, 128, 137, 160, 208, 241

U

Ulster Volunteer Force (UVF) 17
Unionists 21, 42, 60, 61, 62, 63, 64, 65, 67, 70, 72, 81, 87, 90, 91, 100, 109, 114, 115, 119, 120, 122, 128, 129, 135, 143, 166, 167, 198, 216, 217, 241, 244

W

Walsh, James 71
Walton Prison 33, 34
Wandsworth Prison 142
Ward, Fr 105
Ward, Frank 211, 212, 222, 235
Ward, James 204
Ward, P. J. 21, 49, 52, 53, 91, 218
War of Independence 15, 16, 20, 22, 27, 32, 54, 69, 75, 77, 81, 96, 144, 240, 242
Waterfoot 123, 124, 125, 126, 128
Waterford 109
Wattlesbridge 43
Westport 154
Wexford 36
Wilkin's Hotel 157, 179
Willis, William 64, 65
Wilson, Field Marshal Henry 18, 128, 139, 140, 141, 142, 144, 242, 243
Wyatt, Colonel 126

Z

Zammit, Charles 153

Also available from Mercier Press

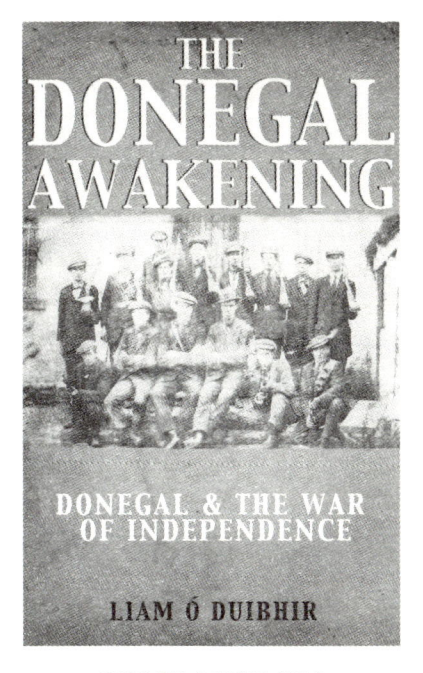

THE DONEGAL AWAKENING

DONEGAL & THE WAR OF INDEPENDENCE

LIAM Ó DUIBHIR

ISBN 978-1-85635-632-9

Liam Ó Duibhir charts the struggle for Irish independence in Donegal, both militarily and politically, from before the events of Easter 1916 until the Truce in 1921.

Long perceived as one of the quietest counties during the War of Independence, Donegal's reputation belies the intriguing story of how republican sentiment grew in the county. From the first mention of Sinn Féin, through the threat of conscription during the Great War and the success of the 1918 elections, up to the Truce, *The Donegal Awakening* charts the rise of the new political leaders in Donegal and how they built their own system of justice and local government.

www.mercierpress.ie

MERCIER PRESS
IRISH PUBLISHER - IRISH STORY

We hope you enjoyed this book.

Since 1944, Mercier Press has published books that have been critically important to Irish life and culture. Books that dealt with subjects that informed readers about Irish scholars, Irish writers, Irish history and Ireland's rich heritage.

We believe in the importance of providing accessible histories and cultural books for all readers and all who are interested in Irish cultural life.

Our website is the best place to find out more information about Mercier, our books, authors, news and the best deals on a wide variety of books. Mercier tracks the best prices for our books online and we seek to offer the best value to our customers, offering free delivery within Ireland.

Sign up on our website or complete and return the form below to receive updates and special offers.

www.mercierpress.ie
www.facebook.com/mercier.press
www.twitter.com/irishpublisher

Name:
Email:
Address:

Mercier Press, Unit 3b, Oak House, Bessboro Rd, Blackrock, Cork, Ireland